THE CINEMA OF SCANDINAVIA

First published in Great Britain in 2005 by
Wallflower Press
4th Floor, 26 Shacklewell Lane, London E8 2EZ
www.wallflowerpress.co.uk

ISBN 1-904764-22-3 (paperback)
ISBN 1-904764-23-1 (hardback)

Printed by Antony Rowe Ltd., Chippenham, Wiltshire

THE CINEMA OF
SCANDINAVIA

EDITED BY

TYTTI SOILA

 **WALLFLOWER PRESS** LONDON & NEW YORK

24 FRAMES is a major new series focusing on national and regional cinemas from around the world. Rather than offering a 'best of' selection, the feature films and documentaries selected in each volume serve to highlight the specific elements of that territory's cinema, elucidating the historical and industrial context of production, the key genres and modes of representation, and foregrounding the work of the most important directors and their exemplary films. In taking an explicitly text-centred approach, the titles in this list offer 24 diverse entry-points into each national and regional cinema, and thus contribute to the appreciation of the rich traditions of global cinema.

Series Editors: Yoram Allon & Ian Haydn Smith

OTHER TITLES IN THE **24 FRAMES** SERIES:

THE CINEMA OF LATIN AMERICA *edited by Alberto Elena and Marina Díaz López*

THE CINEMA OF THE LOW COUNTRIES *edited by Ernest Mathijs*

THE CINEMA OF ITALY *edited by Giorgio Bertellini*

THE CINEMA OF JAPAN AND KOREA *edited by Justin Bowyer*

THE CINEMA OF CENTRAL EUROPE *edited by Peter Hames*

THE CINEMA OF SPAIN AND PORTUGAL *edited by Alberto Mira*

THE CINEMA OF BRITAIN AND IRELAND *edited by Brian McFarlane*

FORTHCOMING TITLES:

THE CINEMA OF FRANCE *edited by Phil Powrie*

THE CINEMA OF CANADA *edited by Jerry White*

THE CINEMA OF THE BALKANS *edited by Dina Iordanova*

THE CINEMA OF AUSTRALIA AND NEW ZEALAND *edited by Geoff Mayer and Keith Beattie*

THE CINEMA OF RUSSIA AND THE FORMER SOVIET UNION *edited by Birgit Beumers*

THE CINEMA OF NORTH AFRICA AND THE MIDDLE EAST *edited by Gönül Donmez-Colin*

THE CINEMA OF INDIA *edited by Lalitha Gopalan*

CONTENTS

NOTES ON CONTRIBUTORS

BO FLORIN is Associate Professor in the Department of Cinema Studies, Stockholm University. His PhD dissertation, *Den nationella stilen* (*The National Style*, 1997), dealt with the 'golden age' of Swedish silent cinema (1917–23). He has also published several articles on Victor Sjöström and Mauritz Stiller.

KARL HANSSON is a PhD candidate at the Department of Cinema Studies, Stockholm University. His research focuses on the concept of the figural in film, video and new media. He has published several articles, including works on Chris Marker's CD-ROM *Immemory* and the use of slow-motion in the films of Wong Kar-Wai.

NIELS HENRIK HARTVIGSON is a PhD candidate at the Institute for Film and Media Science at the University of Copenhagen. His research focuses on Danish film comedies, 1930–39, and he has published related articles on child stardom of the 1930s and music in early Danish sound films.

JAN HOLMBERG is Executive Editor of *Face to Face*, the website devoted to the works of Ingmar Bergman at the Swedish Film Institute. He holds a PhD in Cinema Studies from Stockholm University which focused on the cinematic close-up in historical and theoretical perspective.

GUNNAR IVERSEN is Professor of Film Studies at the Department of Art and Media Studies at the Norwegian University of Science and Technology, Trondheim, Norway, where he teaches European, North American and Asian film history. He has co-authored and co-edited several books, including *Nærbilder* (1997), *Nordic National Cinemas* (1998), *Virkelighetsbilder: nors dokumentarfilm gjennom hundre år* (2001), *Blikkfang – fjernsyn, form og estetikk* (2003) and *Estetiske Teknologier 1700–2000* (2003).

MALENA JANSON is a PhD candidate at the Department of Cinema Studies, Stockholm University. Her dissertation focuses upon aesthetics and audience reception of Swedish children's film. She is also active as film and television critic at *Svenska Dagbladet*.

ANU KOIVUNEN is a Research Fellow at the Christina Institute for Women's Studies, University of Helsinki. She has written extensively on the history of Finnish cinema, including a monograph on wartime women's cinema, *Isänmaan moninaiset äidinkasvot* (1995), and is the author of *Performative Histories, Foundational Fictions: Gender and Sexuality in Niskavuori Films* (2003). Anu is currently researching the history of Finnish television drama.

MAARET KOSKINEN is Associate Professor at the Department of Cinema Studies, Stockholm University. She is the author of numerous articles and essays in national and international film journals, and is film critic for the national daily *Dagens Nyheter*. Maaret is co-editor of *Swedish Film Today* (1996) and author of two recent books, one on the intricate relations between Ingmar Bergman's films and his work in the theatre (*Ingmar Bergman: Allting föreställer, ingenting är. Filmen och teatern – en tvärestetisk studie/Everything Represents, Nothing is: Ingmar Bergman and Interartiality*, 2001), and a second on Bergman as author, based on the unpublished materials in his private archive (*I början var ordet. Ingmar Bergman och hans tidiga författarskap/In the Beginning Was the Word: Ingmar Bergman and His Early Writings*, 2002).

HANNA LAAKSO is a PhD candidate in Humanities at at the University of Montreal. Her research focuses on acting styles in cinema, specifically within the Danish Dogme films.

KIMMO LAINE is a Principal Lecturer in the Department of Media at the Helsinki Polytechnic. He received a PhD in Cinema and Television Studies at the University of Turku with a dissertation on the construction of Finnish national cinema in the 1930s. He has recently co-edited a book on the Finnish film director Valentin Vaala (2004).

PETER LINDHOLM is a PhD candidate at the Department of Cinema Studies, Stockholm University. His research explores relations of gender, ethnicity and sexuality in early Swedish television, with a special focus on the representations of jazz musicians.

TROND LUNDEMO is Associate Professor at the Department of Cinema Studies at Stockholm University. He was Visiting Professor at Seijo University, Tokyo, in 2002 and 2004. Trond has mainly worked and published on the philosophy of technology in cinema and new media, and is currently engaged in research on the films and philosophy of Jean Epstein.

JAN OLSSON is a Professor of Cinema Studies at Stockholm University. As a Visiting Professor he has been teaching regularly at various universities in Europe and the US, most often at the University of Southern California, Los Angeles. He has published numerous essays and a handful of books, most recently two anthologies: *Allegories of Communication* (with John Fullerton, 2005) and *Television After TV* (with Lynn Spigel, forthcoming). Jan is currently undertaking research on pre-classical film culture in Los Angeles.

PER OLOV QVIST is an independent scholar and has written extensively on Swedish film history, most notably on Swedish cinema from the 1930s to the 1950s. He is co-author of the *Guide to the Cinema of Sweden and Finland* (2000), and co-editor of *The Swedish Actor's Encyclopaedia* (2002).

HANNU SALMI is Professor of Cultural History at the University of Turku in Finland. A historian of film and popular culture, he has also published on the history of music in Finland and Germany. His books include *Elokuva ja historia* (*Film and History*, 1993) and *Imagined Germany. Richard Wagner's National Utopia* (1999). His latest book, *Kadonnut perintö* (*The Lost Heritage*, 2002) explores the emergence of fiction film in Finland in 1907–16. Hannu has also contributed to the anthologies *Hollywood's Indian: The Portrayal of Native Americans in Film* (1998) and *The Columbia Companion to American History on Film* (2004).

HENRIK SCHRÖDER is a PhD candidate in the Department of Cinema Studies at the University of Stockholm. His research focuses on the representation of the so-called 'Third World' in television news. He is also is involved in a research project exploring Swedish Nature and Wildlife film. Henrik appears regularly on radio as a television critic, and has assisted Swedish State Television's media critical programme *Mediamagasinet*.

JUKKA SIHVONEN is Professor of Film Studies in the Department of Media Studies, University of Turku, Finland. His various research interests extend from the history of Finnish children's films to more theoretical problems of audio-visual technology. He is currently researching the organic and machinic in David Cronenberg's films.

KATHRINE SKRETTING is a Professor in Cinema Studies at the Norwegian University of Science and Technology, Trondheim, Norway. She is the co-author of *Kinoens mörke fjersynets lys* (1994) and *History of the Moving Image: Reports from the Norwegian Project* (1994).

TYTTI SOILA is Associate Professor of Cinema Studies at Stockholm University. She has undertaken extensive research and publications on Scandinavian film history and feminist film theory, including *Nordic National Cinemas* (1998) and *Att synliggöra det dolda* (2004) on Swedish film directors. She is currently a Researcher in Gender Studies at the Swedish Research Council.

JOHN SUNDHOLM is Senior Lecturer in Film Studies at the Division for Culture and Communication at Karlstad University, Sweden, and Reader in Cultural Analysis at Åbo Akademi University, Finland. Among his latest publications is an edited book on experimental cinema, *Gunvor Nelson and the Avant-Garde* (2003).

ASTRID SÖDERBERGH WIDDING is Professor of Cinema Studies at Stockholm University. She has many published books and articles on Nordic cinemas, art cinema and visual culture, including *Blick och blindhet* (1997) and *Stumfilm i brytningstid* (1998).

BJORN SORENSSEN is Professor of Film and Media Studies at the Norwegian University of Science and Technology, Trondheim, Norway. In addition to several articles on documentary, film history and new media in international film and media journals, he has published books in Norwegian on film and television, most recently *Å fange virkeligheten* (*Catching Reality*, 2001), a book on international documentary history and theory.

LOUISE WALLENBERG is Lecturer in Cinema Studies at Stockholm University. She has published articles on queer studies and gender issues, and her dissertation thesis, *Upsetting the Male*, is forthcoming as a monograph.

ACKNOWLEDGEMENTS

We wish to extend our cordial thanks to the Finnish Film Archive, the Norwegian Film Institute and the Swedish Film Institute as well as Roy Andersson for permissions to use photographs from films in this volume. Also thanks to the Swedish Research Council for financial support in the preparation of this volume.

PREFACE

The time when the five countries in the northernmost part of Europe – Sweden, Norway, Denmark, Finland and Iceland – were one disappeared with the Vikings. Since then they have been in fierce competition with each other, eager to stake their own independence. But just like squabbling siblings, the five co-exist and collaborate closely, in the film industry and beyond. Though foreigners often have a hard time distinguishing one from the other, the national differences are bigger than they appear. Most importantly, they are not all 'Scandies'. Scandinavia most accurately refers only to Sweden, Denmark and Norway, the countries with the most closely-knit languages and cultures. And they possess hugely differing populations (Iceland has 300,000, while Sweden has nine million) and tastes, conditions and state support for film varies greatly across the region.

As this book will explain in great detail, cinema has always been close to the hearts of the Nordic people, even if the popularity of homemade product has varied drastically over the years. But now is actually the best time to look back at the film history of the region as a whole, because recent years have proven the most fruitful since the earliest years of the medium. It is not just local audiences who have rekindled their interest in their national cinema, international ones have also opened their arms and eyes to Scandinavian cinema like never before.

In the last decade a new generation of filmmakers from across the region has emerged from the shadows of Ingmar Bergman and Erik Balling and is producing audience-friendly films with the kind of elan that also appeals to international buyers and festival directors. The key to this rebranding of Nordic filmmaking as fresh and exciting was Denmark's no-frills Dogme collective, which was fathered by Lars von Trier and Thomas Vinterberg back in 1995. The movement has been critised for being at best a commercial gimmick, and at worst the inspiration for a deluge of badly-made, Dogme-lite films from around the world. But looking back today, the importance of Dogme on independent filmmaking cannot be over-estimated. Fortuitously emerging just as digital technology became a viable option for filmmakers, the success of the Dogme films sanctioned low-budget filmmaking. Although there was nothing in the rules that said they had to, the Dogme directors tended to use highly versatile digital video cameras that had the fortunate by-product of keeping budgets well and truly down. This had a hugely democratising impact on the Nordic film industry as newcomers were finally able to get their low-budget projects financed. Traditionally, the region's film funds favoured established names for the bigger budget films. Dogme's other legacy has been to fundamentally change the perception of Nordic filmmaking in the eyes of foreign audiences. Up until the mid-1990s the relatively few international successes came from a small but significant group of filmmakers that included Ingmar Bergman, Aki Kaurismäki, Fridrik Thor Fridriksson and Bille August. Rightly or wrongly, the Nordic industry was freeze-framed in the international consciousness as the home of weighty portentous opuses. By contrast, the Dogme films were seen as fresh and exciting.

Dogme's master stroke has been to refocus the international spotlight not just on the band of young and innovative directors tackling the rules, but also the raft of new talents inspired by them. Without Thomas Vinterberg's *Festen* (*The Celebration*, 1998) there would have been no Norwegian *Når netterne blir lange* (*Cabin Fever*, Mona J. Hoel, 2000) or Icelandic *The Sea* (Baltasar Kormakur, 2002). For Dogme's reflected glory reaches far beyond Denmark. The low-budget digital approach it led quickly gave voice to new filmmakers in Sweden such as Josef Fares (*Jalla! Jalla!*, 2000), Reza Bagher (*Vingar av Glas/Wings of Glass*, 2000) and Geir Hansteen Jørgensen (*Det nya landet/The New Country*), 2000). In Iceland, Robert Douglas (*Islenski draumurinn/Icelandic Dream*, 2000) and Mikael Torfason (*Gemser/Made in Iceland*, 2002) had a similar approach. It took a little longer to seep into Norway and Finland but recent years have seen the emergence of a young group of Norwegian filmmakers, who have brought a new energy and crowd-pleasing skills to digital low-budget films such as Morten Tyldum's Buddy in 2003. In Finland, neither Markku Polonen's *Emmauksen tiellä* (*On the Road to Emmaus*, 2001) nor Esa Illi's *Broidit* (*The Brothers*, 2003) convinced local audiences Dogme was the future, but Hannu Tuomainen's *Matkalippu Mombasaan* (*One-Way Ticket to Mombasa*, 2002) was a surprise hit both at home and abroad.

However, one thing which has not changed and never will change is the fact that each country is too small to support privately-financed national film industries, so government funding remains the key to film financing throughout the region. Yet the time when producers could greenlight projects based on the nod from a film commissioner alone are long gone. In the last decade, the financing puzzles have become increasingly complicated as the national film funding bodies have undergone major changes. While some are on the right path, others are still struggling to find their footing. The upheaval coincides with the unprecedented success of local films at the national box offices which has encouraged distributors to invest in films at an earlier stage than ever before and co-productions have also taken on a new form. In the past ten years, the five countries have become regular partners as the level of localised state support has fallen. As well as bringing the industries closer, actors and crews from across the region now all regularly work on the other's films. However, this closer collaboration between the countries has yet to influence audience interest across the Nordic borders. Each country retains its own idiosyncrasies and it is virtually impossible to lump them altogether. What works in one territory does not guarantee success in another and few local films cross borders unless riding a much bigger international wave. You could say a Dane is as likely, or rather unlikely, to go see a Swedish film at the cinema as a German one. While the big pan-Nordic distributors know how to use the differences in the markets to their films' advantage, it is hard to predict how local films will travel inside the region. A rule of thumb has been that while no Finnish films travel and very few Icelandic or Norwegian do either, Swedish films tend do well in Norway, while the Danish films that are successful abroad, such as *Italiensk for begyndere* (*Italian For Beginners*, Lone Scherfig, 2000) or Festen, also work in the rest of the region. Generally, Norwegian audiences are the most receptive to art-house films from anywhere in the world, while Danish cinema-goers are the least.

The bottom line is that the countries in Scandinavia are as tightly-knit and totally different from each other as many other countries in continental Europe. They nevertheless share a common rich cinema history which can only expand ones understanding of not only the countries themselves, but their people and most essentially their films. There is much to be discovered; happy reading.

Jacob Neiiendam
Copenhagen
May 2005

INTRODUCTION

This book introduces a number of films produced in what are generally called the Scandinavian countries, together with the expression 'Nordic Countries', a collective label for five nations: Finland, Denmark, Iceland, Norway and Sweden. Considering geographical proximity, these countries certainly share many common features, but numerous differences also exist. For example, one could say that they share a common language, but this is only partly true as, although many people in Finland are native Swedish-speakers, the Finnish language itself is in no way related to other Scandinavian languages. Likewise, the indigenous population, the Sami, live in all parts of Scandinavia, but their native speech, their traditional customs and way of life, differ from those of the rest of the population.

The notion of one common Scandinavian history is also certainly questionable. Norway and Iceland, as well as parts of Sweden, have belonged to the kingdom of Denmark, and Finland and Norway have belonged to the kingdom of Sweden. The cultural exchange has been constant, but so too have the wars between some of these countries.

Yet some notion of unity amongst Scandinavian countries is possible to distinguish in the cultural arena. At the same time, however, it is important to realise that the notion of Scandivanian cinema, no matter how familiar it may be for film enthusiasts throughout the world, is a synthetic one. For every cultural/political/economic tie possible to find between these countries, a handful of exceptions is bound to appear. Still, the focus of this collection is a technological medium which is based on deception of the eye. Let us therefore remember the visual experiment of Adalbert Ames Jr: a box depincting random lines dangling in a space; when seen from a certain angle the random lines make an image of a chair, i.e. they create a meaningful unity. The unity that this book presents is thus a temporary one, albeit with *some* reality.

One central purpose of this collection is to show how cinema has been influenced by art, literature and theatre over the last century. Political events also affected the character of both the production and reception of cinema – even if the impact was not the same in every country. Thus, the First World War resulted in a decline for the prospering Danish film industry and decimated Finland's cinematic output altogether, whereas Sweden benefited greatly from it, producing a remarkable body of work.

In each of the Scandinavian countries governments have always actively overseen the operation of the film industry; initially in terms of censorship and then through various tax systems and numerous state-funded projects. This may have its roots in the ideological atmosphere of the late nineteenth century, when large groups became influenced by popular movements (labour, temperance and reformatory religious groups, amongst others) all dedicated to changing and moulding people's character and living conditions. Such an atmosphere, together with strong and centralised government, stipulated that for the common good, people should be protected, educated and cultivated and that the responsibility for such an effort should be shouldered by public authorities. Disputes preceding the establishment of censorship authorities during the 1910s were only the first in a series of debates concerning the allegedly corrupt impact the medium was held to have on people.

In Scandinavian countries the number of major production companies has varied from one to four – yet that does not mean that others did not exist. During periods of fair wind – especially in the 1930s and 1940s – many production companies did see the light of day, but only to vanish after a handful of productions. The basic problem for these minor enterprises has been their insufficient access to the distribution and exhibition of film. In Sweden, for instance, the major production companies controlled most of the country's exhibition facilities. In Norway, though, the situation has been quite the contrary: Norsk Film A/S was established in 1932 and owned by municipal cinemas. In 1971 the Norwegian government became a major owner and investor of the company which has dominated the country's film production from the outset.

In Denmark the oldest and perhaps most significant of the companies, Nordisk Films Compagni (Nordic Film Company), was already established in 1906, initially becoming the second largest production company in Europe. During the 1930s two other major producers established themselves: Palladium and ASA. Towards the end of the 1940s another company named Saga made its way among the dominating production establishments in the country. In Finland the market was long mastered by two major companies: Suomi-Filmi, established in the 1920s, and Suomen Filmiteollisuus in the early 1930s: the latter perished in the 1960s whereas Suomi-Filmi still functions as a distribution company.

In Sweden Svenska Bio, the producer of legendary Victor Sjöström and Mauritz Stiller films during the 1920s, changed its name to Svensk Filmindustri and is still going strong.

Together with two companies, Europa-Film and Sandrews, it dominated the screens all over the country. Of the latter two, Sandrews still sporadically produces films. It is noteworthy that the oldest companies also have survived longest, perhaps thanks to their accumulated know-how and capital invested in different divisions in the field. Thus Europa-Film was able to survive another twenty years after closing down its film production, thanks to sound recording studios it owned.

The deep economic crisis in the late 1950s and early 1960s, during which harsh taxation was imposed on each country's production, affected their cinema – both politically and in terms of production – in a similar manner. Large companies suffered great deficits as audiences were more attracted to other new entertainments. The small companies went bankrupt unless they specialised in work at the 'periphery' of the film industry, such as the production and distribution of commercials, industrial films and pornography. Against all the odds, however, small independent companies, often owned by film directors themselves, appeared, due to the stimulating effect of the film institutes. Denmark, for instance, counted around forty production companies in existence during 1965–72, although three-quarters of them produced under three films during the period.

The objectives for film institutes dating from the 1960s prescribed production of 'culturally valuable film' but have gradually been changed. Basically, two tendencies may be distinguished. On the one hand, the division between the 'art film' and mainstream popular cinema has become distinct. Thus, for example, the tendency towards production of well-made 'heritage-films' became significant during the 1980s. Ib Bondebjerg stresses, too, that the public support system was 'definitely identified as a national culture issue' where films were meant to uphold and express specific national identity and culture. On the other hand, however, an intense tendency towards Nordic co-operation and thereafter towards internationalisation may be discovered towards the end of the 1980s. It may simply have begun as an economic issue, as production costs soared and it became practically impossible to produce a full-length feature film within one Scandinavian country alone. Fundraising in several Nordic countries has become a rule, and then not only are different film institutes involved but national television companies as well. Nordisk Film och TV Fond (The Nordic Film and Televison Fund) was established in 1990, and is today based in Norway overseeing a budget of 67 million Norwegian Crone.

The aim of the fund is to promote Nordic audio-visual productions, yet without presenting any Pan-Nordic thematic requirements, and it has been said that the fund has been crucial for the production of, among other things, Icelandic cinema. Iceland has traditionally been more oriented towards the Anglo-Saxon countries and has avoided the protectionist tendencies typical for the other Nordic countries. Until the Icelandic Cultural Fund in 1972 began supporting film creation there hardly existed any feature-film production in the country. A national film fund was established six years later, which saw immediate results. Young film directors educated abroad returned home and two film premieres took place in 1979: *Land og Synir* (*Land*, directed by Ágúst Gudmundsson) and *Odal fedranna* (*Father's Estate*, Hrafn Gunnlaugsson). Henceforth, Icelandic directors have favoured themes from the country's rich treasure of ancient sagas and mediaeval history as well as adaptations of national literature, such as the Nobel Prize laureate Halldor Kiljan Laxness's novels.

The international success of Norwegian film in recent years, instead, seems rather to be based on the production of genre film such as thrillers *à la* Hollywood in line with the path-breaking *Orion's belte* (*Orion's Belt*, Ola Solyom, 1985) or, notably, *Veiviseren* (aka *Ofelas*, *Path Finder*, Nils Gaup, 1987). The latter film was the first film ever to be shot in the indigenous Sami language and was based on a mediaeval Sami saga.

Another tendency towards internationalisation during the last decade of the twentieth century was the radical film producers abiding outside the mainstream production companies. The Dogme group in Denmark and the Finnish independent producers and directors like Aki and Mika Kaurismäki and Pirjo Honkasalo may be included in such a group as well as film-makers contributing to the recent boom of Icelandic film. Such inclinations have given rise to the question whether it is possible to speak about national cinemas or Nordic cinemas at all. In any case, observers seem to be unanimous about the fact that a shift towards internationalisation on a wider basis has taken place from the 1990s onwards.

The idea behind the selection of films presented in this volume has been '*seminal but off*' in the sense that the aim is to present a number of films beyond the list of canonised feature films that the cultural institutes, as well as literature abroad, usually present as 'interesting' or 'culturally valuable' or, even worse, 'typical for' Scandinavia. At the same time the ambition has been that the presentations still would say something central and important about the history of film production in the region. Consequently, this collection is able to present an exciting survey of Nordic cinema that offers an overview of films from each decade since 1905. It also highlights a variety of genres where the different films, from different countries, 'speak' to each other illuminating differences and similarities between them. Thus, for instance, this anthology introduces Scandinavian films that are not necessarily critically considered 'artistic' or 'culturally valuable, yet they are highly representative of certain periods – such as the folksy comedies and popular melodramas of the 1930s and 1940s. In addition, the present book contains two accurate analyses on Scandinavian pornographic film – an issue most familiar to foreign audiences at least by hearsay, but products that contributed to the survival of several small companies during times of crisis. By the same token, the book presents analyses on commercials: short films that most people see but that are seldom discussed and reflected upon.

It has been impossible not to exclude films made by certain world-famous film directors, but this time they, too, are dealt with from an off-angle: Maaret Koskinen discusses a soap commercial directed by Ingmar Bergman, and Jan Olsson writes about a 'failure' of Carl Theodor Dreyer. Similarly, it has been important not to exclude two of the tremendously popular films dealing with national traumas during the Second Word War in Finland and Norway.

The first entry of this anthology is Trond Lundemo's chapter on one of the first documentary films in Norway, *Kong Haakon VII ankommer Christiania* (*The Arrival of King Haakon VII in Christiania*, directed by Hugo Hermansen) from 1905. In Norway, the film represents the founding of the nation-state, establishing the relationship between the symbol – the King – and his cheering subjects – the crowd. These elements also form the actual subject of the film and the cinema is here presented as the technological apparatus which supports and promotes the idea of a unified nation.

The discussion of such cinematic mechanisms is especially relevant in Anu Koivunen's analysis of the *Heimat* syndrome in the Finnish 1950s film *Niskavuoren Heta* (*Heta Niskavuori*, Edvin Laine, 1952), as well as providing a basis for Gunnar Iversen's chapter on *Kampen om tungtvattnet* (*Operation Swallow*, Titus Vibe-Müller, 1948) and Jukka Sihvonens' chapter on *Tuntematon sotilas* (*The Unknown Soldier*, Edvin Laine, 1955), but it also finds an echo in Karl Hansson's analysis on the Danish art film *The Wake* (Michael Kvium/Christian Lemmerz) from 2001.

One of the first Finnish feature films, *Sylvi* (Teuvo Puro/Teppo Raikas, 1911–13), was a joint venture of three enthusiasts. Hannu Salmi's chapter illustrates the agonies of a film scholar when the film is missing – a typical fate for early cinema, when the medium was not considered a cultural product of substantial value. Salmi's analysis also shows how many films found, and still find, their topics in (scandalous) reality as he contextualises the film in terms of the society at that time.

Sweden dominated the international film market during the Great War, laying the ground for what has been called the 'golden age' of Swedish cinema. From 1919 until the introduction of sound film the Swedish film production reached artistic peaks with films such as *Terje Vigen* (1916), *Sången om den eldröda blomman* (*The Song of the Scarlet Flower*, 1919), *Körkarlen* (*Phantom Carriage*, 1921), *Erotikon* (1920) and many others directed by Mauritz Stiller and Victor Sjöström.

Instead of writing yet another analysis on such celebrated films, Bo Florin reflects upon a film from the beginning of the period; *Dunungen* (*Downie*, 1919) directed by Ivan Hedqvist, an actor who also plays one of the main characters in the film. Apart from showing how the expressive devices in cinema had developed from the days of *Sylvi*, this discussion also demonstrates how closely these are tied to the contemporary themes in painting and the use of signifying conventions – more exactly, a painted portrait and windows in *Downie*.

Kimmo Laine's chapter on the slapstick comedy *Kun isällä on hammassärky* (*When Father Has Toothache*, 1922), directed by Erkki Karu, counterproves the common belief that Finns only produced rural melodramas during the early days of cinema. The comedy is set in contemporary bourgeois milieu and Laine's analysis contextualises the film within Finnish theatre traditions influenced by the Artistic Theatre of Moscow and the director and theorist Konstantin Stanislavsky. An echo from this period may be found in Hanna Laakso's chapter on the acting style of one of the main characters in Lars von Trier's Dogme film *Idioterne* (*The Idiots*, 1998). She relates the ideals of Stanislavsky to the ideas presented by Scandinavian playwrights such as Henrik Ibsen and August Strindberg, showing how artistic influences have circulated throughout the Nordic countries.

Naturally, Laakso's analysis also offers an example of a film expressing the new artistic austerity and the increasing internationalisation of Scandinavian cinema. Another example of such tendencies is John Sundholm's study of Aki Kaurismäki's film *Juha* from 1999. Kaurismäki's film is a fourth re-make based on the novel of Juhani Aho, one of the most celebrated Finnish authors. The film is set in an undefinable past, black-and-white, utilises excessive acting style – and is silent. Thus, *Juha* constantly exhibits references to its fictitious and historical/political past, but in his analysis Sundholm also focuses on the construction of masculinity in the film from psychoanalytic point of view.

A common strategy for all Scandinavian production companies struggling with the economic problems caused by the Depression and the high investment costs of sound recording equipment was to exploit public favourites such as revues and folksy comedies. Niels Henrik Hartvigson's chapter presents a Fyrtornet and Bakvognen ('Long and Short') film *Med fuld musik* (*With Pipes and Drums*, 1933). The comic duo and their 'melancholy madness' had become familiar for international audiences, too, in films by Lau Lauridsen who had directed popular comedies in Denmark since 1914.

Such a repertoire was met with disdain by critics and culturally-oriented audiences, especially in countries such as Denmark and Sweden, which both had a recent glorious past to revere. Here, the demand was for films with artistic stature or political and social engagement. An example of the Scandanavian film industry's attempts to win over the cultural élite was the Swedish film *En kvinnas ansikte* (*A Woman's Face*, 1938) directed by Gustaf Molander, a director who started his career as a scriptwriter for Mauritz Stiller and who carried on working well into the mid-1960s. Tytti Soila presents a feminist reading of the film based on the concept employed by Bo Florin: an interpretation of visual signifiers embedded in the screen image. *A Woman's Face* was one of the two Swedish films adapted by Hollywood, the other being *Intermezzo* (1936), also a Molander film, starring Ingrid Bergman. The American version of *A Woman's Face* (1941) was directed by George Cukor and starred Joan Crawford.

Jan Olsson's chapter not only gives an interesting insight into the co-operation between Nordic countries with visiting directors, actors and crew, it also presents an analysis over misunderstandings and intrigues around the production and reception of Dreyer's *Två människor* (*Two People*, 1945). In addition, Olsson also accounts for the political play in the international film market, where the contacts with and membership in the German-controlled International Film Chamber actually became compromising for all Scandinavian companies towards the end of the Second World War.

Anu Koivunen's analysis of *Heta Niskavuori*, a film based on a cycle of popular plays by the author Hella Wuolijoki and one of the last works which may be seen as a product of the studio era in Finland, discusses the popular appeal of the film, which was by no means founded on easy stereotypes, but on the film's emphasis on assiduous ambivalence.

Gunnar Iversen's chapter analyses the historical background of *Operation Swallow*, comparing it with the later American version *The Heroes of Telemark* (Anthony Mann, 1965). In dialogue with the opening chapter of this volume, Iversen reflects upon the fact that the film – and the entire genre – has contributed to the imagination of Norwegian national memory, developing it into a 'heritage event' where 'the past has been turned into an entertainment experience'.

In his analysis Iversen also discusses the 'mixed docudrama form' of this film, which is also one of the topics examined by Jukka Sihvonen who reflects upon the significance of the documentary material that permeates *The Unknown Soldier*. Sihvonen also lays bare the story's roots embedded in the Finnish literature of the end of the nineteenth century, stressing the stereotypes of Finnishness and Finnish masculinity created by and with literature by 'national writers'.

Arne Sucksdorff's film *Det stora äventyret* (*The Great Adventure*, 1953) has always been perceived as a documentary. However, in Henrik Schröder's analysis the film is seen to follow the pattern of classical drama, where animals 'play themselves' in highly arranged scenes. Schröder also demonstrates the fashion by which the moral values of the filmmaker orchestrate the conflict between man and nature.

The Great Adventure represents those experimental investments in new genres common to the 1950s. Another example is the ballet film *Eldfågeln* (*The Fire-Bird*, Hasse Ekman, 1952), a Swedish-Italian co-production and a combination of artistic genres. Apart from analysing the film itself, the chapter by Astrid Söderbergh Widding sheds light on the period in Scandinavian cinema when producers hoped for a new international breakthrough as a solution for the problems caused by the hardening market.

During the 1960s, the radicalisation and politicisation of the cultural sectors in Scandinavian countries was a fact that had its affect on the films produced. Realistic, low-key stories and working-class descriptions had been a valued constituent of the Norwegian and even Danish cinema repertoire, and now such topics became dominant in all Nordic countries. Apart from the debates preceding the aforementioned changes in the countries' film politics, one of the most notable public debates of the period concerned film censorship for adults. In Finland, Jörn Donner stretched the constrains of the allegedly forbidden by his much discussed films *Sixtynine* (1969) and *Naisenkuvia* (*Portraits of Women*, 1970). The central argument for the dispute against censorship in Sweden was that 'art films' – such as Ingmar Bergman's *Tystnaden* (*The Silence*, 1963) and Vilgot Sjöman's *491* (1964) – should not be violated by the censors' scissors. As a result, censorship was abolished in 1969 in Denmark – the first country in the world to take such a step – and furnished with liberal objectives in the rest of Scandinavia.

Eva – den utstötta (*Swedish and Underage*, Torgny Wickman, 1969) was a film that made an effort of combining social criticism with erotic elements. In their analysis, Per Olov Qvist and Tytti Soila show how morally confused a product from this period could become: it gives legitimacy to paedophilia by depicting a molested child as a confident piece of nature for whom sex is 'natural' because 'she's always done it'. According to Qvist and Soila the production of pornographic films became a lucrative survival strategy for a handful of small film companies: some of their films reached over one million spectators in the home country alone. Consequently, an ample number of erotic films were produced in Scandinavia for export, too, and in some circles 'Swedish' and 'Danish' came to equal 'pornographic'.

Basically, porn movies of the period came in two modes: either as explicit argumentative films concerning sexual freedom and a woman's right to her own body (as with *Jeg – en kvinde* [Mac Ahlberg, Denmark, 1965] or *Kärlekens språk* [*Language of Love*, Torgny Wickman, Sweden 1969]) or in the form of frivolous, erotic comedies. As an example of the latter subgenre, Louise Wallenberg accounts for one of the most popular Danish porn movies, namely *Mazurka på sengekanten* (*Bedroom Mazurka*, John Hilbard, 1970) and the first in the long-running series of 'Mazurka' ('Bedroom') films. Such series belong to the sub-genre of 'happy porn' – '*blød porno*' in Danish – and as Wallenberg shows, they are a direct heir of the kind of folk comedies that Niels Henrik Hartvigson discusses in his presentation of *With Pipes and Drums*. Emblematic for the genre was, besides its inexhaustible emphasis on the comic and the farcical, Ole Sølstoft, the libidinous stallion who appeared in the majority of films in the series.

Pornographic films were certainly not the only ones to employ the serial form, which of course is a part of Scandinavian (and other) film history since the days of Fyrtornet and Bakvognen: exploiting a success has always been worth repeating. One of the most popular film series in Scandinavia – about thirty films in all – has been the Danish *Olsen-banden* (*The Olsen Gang*) series from the late 1960s, first directed by Knut Bohwim. The Gang consists of three individualistic small-time criminals hoping for the ultimate catch. The scripts were successfully recycled by Norwegian producers, and later by Swedes who called the gang *Jönssonligan*. The series have lately continued by depicting the childhood of the gang members, but if critics treated the films about the grown Olsen Gang with some tolerance, such exploitation of children's film genre has been criticised as being exactly that.

Children's film has traditionally been one of the most flourishing genres in all Scandinavian countries. Malena Jansson's chapter accounts for the strong discourses that promote a child's point of view in *Elvis! Elvis!* (Kay Pollack, 1977). The film is based on a popular novel written by Maria Gripe, who also contributed to the script of the film. *Elvis! Elvis!* deals with problematic issues such as loneliness, alienation and failure, thus deviating from the mainstream happy-go-lucky-films. Characteristic for this and many other Scandinavian children's films is that they address adults, sometimes even more than children.

One of the reasons for the excellent array of children's film in Scandinavia is the fact that film institutes have consistently earmarked funds to stimulate production of film for youngsters. Also, on occasion, film institutes have employed advisors and producers especially for this task.

One such producer was Lisbet Gabrielsson at the Swedish Film Institute. During the 1980s, she was responsible for the short, documentary and children's film, and as such she produced *Ebba the Movie* (Johan Donner, 1982). This film is about a punk rock band from the suburbs of Stockholm, and Peter Lindholm's chapter on the film recounts the strong appeal it had for its young audiences. It also focuses on the construction of masculinity in this documentary, giving an echo to the gender discussions presented by Koivunen, Sihvonen and Soila. Moreover, his chapter provides an example of the popular culture media mix: music promotes the cinema and vice versa, and both promote other fringe products. In this collection this aspect is most notably reflected in the analysis of *With Pipes and Drums* and *The Fire-Bird*, as well as in the discussion of the Norwegian world success, the documentary film *Heftig og begeistret* (*Cool and Crazy*, Knut Erik Jensen, 2000).

Cool and Crazy is a story of the members of a male choir resident in northern Norway. Bjørn Sørenssen's chapter contributes to the scrutiny of masculinity in the aforementioned chapters in this volume. It also resonates with the analysis of *Operation Swallow* while it shows that the memory of Nazi occupation and the political consequences of the Second World War are still in effect in certain areas, and the demarcation line between the military superpowers of the USA and Russia are part of the quiet everyday life in Finmark.

Many feature films as well as documentaries discussed in this book could be studied from within an *auteur* perspective, as products of one artist's efforts. However, in most cases such an angle has been toned down for the benefit of other aspects, such as the study of the films' ideological and cultural roots, different contexts of production and reception, and so on. An *auteur* perspective has, however, been one of the most vital ones in film studies in spite of the sometimes heavy criticism it has faced. In this collection, it is put to use in affiliation with the most anonymous of all the film genres, namely that of a commercial.

Maaret Koskinen's analysis of *Tvålen Bris* (*Bris the Soap*, 1951) displays a most intriguing performance with cinematic devices and meta-effects created by Ingmar Bergman. In his hands a series of soap commercials has become a veritable showcase of visual contraptions, radical cinematic experiments and tricks by means of animation, pixillation, advanced superimpositions, and so on – all squeezed into seventy seconds.

The case of Roy Andersson's becoming one of the most popular *auteur*s of commercials in Sweden is similar to the situation of Bergman thirty years earlier. In 1970 Anderson directed a much-awarded film *En kärlekshistoria* (*A Swedish Love Story*) but after the problematic production process of his second film *Giliap* (1975), he was not able to find funding for any other of his feature-film projects until the 1990s. Instead, he started directing commercials in his own style, and one of them, *Kan vi bry oss om varandra?* (*Can we bother about each other?*) from 1988 is here analysed by Jan Holmberg. Far from the abundant play with cinematic devices of Bergman, Andersson has cultivated his archaic style to the extreme and in doing so, manages to criticise the society and things he seems to promote in his commercials.

An ardent defender of the *auteur* and the film directors' right to final cut has been Pirjo Honkasalo, one of the few Finnish women film directors and the director of *Melancholian 3 Huonetta* (*The 3 Rooms of Melancholia*, 2004). The film is a documentary of the current situation in the Russo-Chechnyan war and a portrait of the children who suffer as a result. In her imagery, faithful to her principle just to observe, to wait and show without any explanations, Honkasalo juxtaposes the realistic situation of the children with influences from Russian religious painting and film directors such as Andrei Tarkovsky. Thus her film – analysed in this volume by Anu Koivunen and Tytti Soila – becomes not only a comment upon the war films here discussed by Sihvonen and Iversen, but also upon Pan-European artistic currents.

In her analysis of another commercial, the Norwegian *Lotto* advertisement *Taxi* (2001), Kathrine Skretting also discusses the ideological atmosphre that has surrounded gambling and lottery systems in Norway – and the rest of Scandinavia as well. Today different lotteries have become one of the major pastimes for people all over the world – but the hard-working puritan Northerners initially considered it a waste. Skretting's discussion combines with the discourses about the censorship and ideologies considered elsewhere in this book, but to the extent that her analysis regards the strategies of information distibution utilised by commercials, they may be applied to the two other commercials as well. It may even give an explanation to why commercials have become 'chic'.

One of the most recent films discussed in this book is *The Wake* (Michael Kvium/Christian Lemmerz, 2000) presented by Karl Hansson – a film that, quite contrary to the commercials, is long enough with its 462 minutes. As Hansson demonstrates, this film – or art-work – finally seems to dissolve the generic bounds and constraints that have been characteristic for the other films presented in this book. Yet tendencies for such transgressive elements are present in most of the films if one takes close enough a look. In a sense *The Wake* in fact ties together all features common to the cinema of the region: it is based on a well-known, canonic novel, namely James Joyce's *Finnegans Wake*; it displays elements from genre films, such as pornography, documentary and others; it was produced with support from the Danish Film Institute as a part of the national project of promoting visual art. But it also exceeds all the features displayed in this book and dwells on the borderline between the film and video, between cinema and other visual art. *The Wake* thus both collects and dissolves the features presented here, creating a kind of closure for the entire discourse of this book.

Tytti Soila

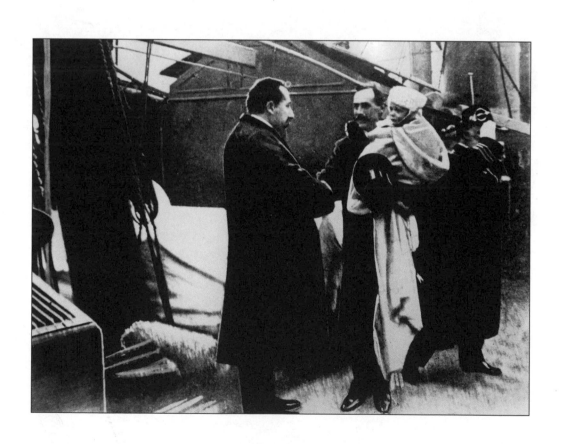

KONG HAAKON VII ANKOMMER CHRISTIANIA

01

THE ARRIVAL OF KING HAAKON VII IN CHRISTIANIA

HUGO HERMANSEN, NORWAY, 1905

The first Norwegian film images are of the King. In this case, the advent of cinema coincides exactly with the arrival of the futire King, Haakon VII, on Norwegian soil and the formation of the nation-state. These were not the very first Norwegian film images in a chronological sense, but they are the very first regarding the constitution of a projected national image. Earlier films have presented images from Norway, or even images by Norwegian producers and distributors. The German Skladanowsky Brothers had held film projections in Norway as early as 6 April 1896, and cameramen had captured national events before the arrival of the King on 25 November 1905.

These shots of the King could, for many good reasons, be considered the first national film images because they project an image of a nation and an ethnic group. From this moment on Norway became an independent state, had a king as a national icon and entered the League of Nations. This cinematographic passage into independence is certainly uncomplicated for Norway compared to subsequent questions of national cinemas in postcolonial contexts. Cinema was a young, untainted medium, and Norway was part of the rich, Western world.

The images of the King draw upon the past, as the end of government by proxy from neighbouring countries. Only by invoking the past is it possible to project a future. After being under Danish rule for centuries, Norway had been the weaker part of a union with Sweden since 1814. With the demise of the Union, Norway was a 'new' nation under national fervour. The first images of King Haakon promised a future as a nation, but they also poignantly prefigure the dominant subject and image of Norwegian cinema, at least in its classical period. The struggle for Norwegian independence, this time from Nazi occupation, was such a recurrent topic in the country's cinema that it constituted a line of continuity which has its beginning in the images of the arrival of the future king in 1905.

These early images have parallels with the first 'national' shots following the end of the Nazi occupation of Norway in May 1945. Again the King-to-be arrives in Norway by sea, this time from England, and this time it is Crown Prince Olav. Olav had spent the occupation years in England, where he had also played a role in the resistance movement during the war. As the formal Commander-in-chief of the country's military forces, he returned to Norway only a couple of days after the Nazi capitulation. Olav was the child on Haakon's arm upon his arrival in 1905; his own arrival forty years later was no less important as an image of a national event as it settled the symbolic promise of the first image. These documentary shots, in their turn, introduced one of the most important elements of Norwegian cinema: the occupation film.

Arguably, cinema has been the most powerful tool for forming an image of nationhood in the twentieth century. The ultimate example of cinema's projection of an image of the national past could arguably be *The Birth of a Nation* (D. W. Griffith, 1915). This film also marked the beginning of the world dominance of the American Film Industry as French dominance ended with the shots that rang out from Sarajevo. The emblematic title of the film demonstrates how the American Civil War is projected as the beginning of the United States, as confirmed in *Gone With the Wind* (Victor Fleming, 1939), *The Searchers* (John Ford, 1956) and a number of other Civil War pictures.

For Norway, the days of international power lay too far back in time – almost a thousand years – for them to be practical as images of the national past. People in the modern age would not have identified with 'the nation' in terms of the Viking era. The resistance to the Nazi occupation is undoubtedly the privileged Norwegian national image of the past in terms of cinema. The post-war production dealing with the Second World War, either as its main topic or as a background for other events, made up a large percentage the total feature-film output over the next few decades. But at the turn of the century, there is no such image available. Thus national film history begins with shots of the new King upon independence from the Union with Sweden in 1905.

A king has always been an iconic image of national identity. Before cinema, the most important means of dissemination of the image of the king's head was on coins. Currency has been, and still is, one of the most powerful symbols of national identity, and the wide European conversion to the Euro is telling for the new role of the nation-state. The framing of early film images was different from the framing of coins. Coins have close-ups of the king's head, whereas cinema framed the King in a long shot. When you think of it, the film image of the king is actually less of his features and body than of his subjects. The inaugural national event of the King's arrival depends as much, or more, on the crowd greeting him as on the document of his physical presence.

Another obvious reason for the difference in framing of the King's body is the size of the projected image compared to that of the coin. The mechanical and indexical properties of cinema would make the close-up of the King too intimate and perhaps too vulgar (as the close-up was often deemed in cinema's early years) to make of him an image of a collective future. On the coin, however, the image is made by an artist's hand, and thus already an interpretation abstracted from distinct physical features.

The coinciding events of the advent of cinema and the birth of a nation in Norway are, in other words, all but a coincidence. They are deeply intertwined, and, as with many cases in the early twentieth century, each other's preconditions. However, not every national cinema looks the same, and the immense success of some countries in projecting a national cinema – such as the US – is contrasted by the neglected image of the nation of other states. The most striking counter-example in the twentieth century is the Soviet Union. After its influential early years, leading up to the development of film montage in the 1920s – a style based for the first time on a true philosophy of cinema – the Soviet Union's projection of the Revolution is soon substituted by other, far more distant historical images, designed and circumscribed to the extent that only eight films were made in 1953, Stalin's last year in power.

The early years of Soviet cinema often followed the principles of Griffith's 'birth' of American cinema; it depicted, portrayed and framed the crowd. As Sergei Eisenstein later observed, Griffith's films were like 'a race between the rich and the poor'. Similarly, the film images of the constitutional event of the arrival of the King in Norway were not just of the King, but also of the crowds gathering to see him. Because cinema projects a common, national image of the past, the crowd is essential to its workings. Thus, images of the crowds figure more prominently than the shots of Haakon VII. Steady, slow pans reveal the enormous crowds present, showing that 'the whole nation' is behind its king.

In many shots, the crowds even block the view of the King, as the image is shot amongst them, representing the average subject's view – albeit partial – of the celebrated event. The crowds thus function, physically and symbolically, as framings of the royal cortege. Waving hands, flags and hats form elaborate compositions of movement, revealing the carefully chosen camera positions that correspond to the movement of the crowds.

Cinema has always been good at celebrating itself, and films have often documented illustrious visitors to the cinema. This is the case in Norway, and among the other early images of the King is his visit to the cinema. This allows the film industry to secure the respectability of the new medium; after a visit of the King, no man could feel too superior to the popular entertainment. But these images also allowed the film industry to testify to the popularity of the new medium, as the images bear witness to the crowd flowing in and out of the cinema.

Adding to the complexity of the situation were other cameras, present at the event and appearing in the image. This is of course coherent with the logic of the cinema of attractions, where the exposition of cinema alongside other new techniques is 'the content' of the medium itself. In another early film depicting Haakon VII's crowning journey of 1906, his arrival by ship to Trondheim frames the many cameramen present to document the event. As in *The Arrival of King Haakon VII*, masses in movement are the focus of the projected film images. Projection is key to the argument about the connection between cinema and nation, since it brings together the historical and technical dimensions of the cinematic apparatus.

The newsreels are structured according to a narrative logic, perhaps common to all inaugural events, of a before and after in relation to the privileged moment; in the current case, Haakon's first steps on land. This structure of the event is emphasised by a reframing of the shot in the journey from the boat onto land, as the camera thus follows the crucial movement of the passage onto national territory.

The King's coronation tour through Norway was depicted as a series of arrivals and departures. The images form a travelogue of trains, ships and automobiles, framed by greeting people. Further, the shots such as those of the train with the King arriving at the station of Ringebu draw from the famous film by the Lumière Brothers, and are intercut with views from within the train. They are again designed to display the crowds, rather than the King. These camera positions used the crowd as a spatial delimitation as established in the construction of space in other visual media such as photography and painting.

The newsreels of the celebration of the liberation of Norway from German forces in 1945 continue with centring the crowd in the film. They include occasional shots from a high angle, which further de-personalises people into a general image of a nation. As the 'avant-garde' aesthetics of the 1910s and the 1920s – both in cinema and still photography – amply demonstrated, there is always an abstraction operating in the high-angle perspective. The high-angle pans from the day of liberation convey an image of a collective, national boundary, drawing a line of demarcation between occupants and the nation.

These images resonate with yet another popular genre, in early Norwegian cinema just as in the rest of the world; that of the travelogue. In newsreels and fiction films, the Norwegian landscape played a major role, and these are probably the views that most often come to mind as the truly national images of Norwegian cinema. The images of Haakon's crowning journey form a catalogue of places visited by the King. Around 1910, emblematic aerial shots also appeared in Norwegian newsreels. Shots of and from the appropriately named 'Norge' (Norway) airship offered new perspectives of the national territory. The view from above offers an overview, geographically, metaphorically and intellectually. This renders an image of the national landscape as a cartographical abstraction, inscribing the territory's borders and boundaries in the image. These spatial constructions produced a cinema ranging from Georges Méliès to contemporary science fiction, from early newsreels to the live-image transmission from outer space of the 1960s. From above, you can see land transform into water, the farmland between mountains and woods giving way to cities. You can see a crowd from above and that one nation borders on to the next. These images charted the national territory, and were apt for the nation-building project of cinema. They are deeply inscribed in the project of cinema as well as in that of the national state.

The films from the crowning journey of 1906 became the first major hits of the newly-established cinema houses. The crowds greeting Haakon on his journey made up much of this attraction, casting the images as a national event. This in turn drew the crowds to return to the cinemas. Every Norwegian King swears his oath in the Nidaros Cathedral of the old capital of Trondheim. Cinemas thus covered this ongoing event, rather than documenting it as a single occasion. Just as exhibition practices in early cinema presented a series of films as an integrated part of the technological attraction of going to the cinema, the crowning journey constituted a serial at the cinemas, disciplining the crowds to return to the cinemas again and again. It would, however, be wrong to think of this mode of programming as a 'flow', to borrow Raymond Williams' televisual term, since the images from the crowning journey attracted huge audiences due to the specific content advertised.

The crowd, in the image as well as in the cinemas, was made possible by the projecting capability of the Cinématographe. The technique offered sufficient light to screen complex images shot without additional lighting. The projected images of the Lumières had the physical space for the crowd, and brought across an image of the group, of the population, of the nation. In technological terms, this is a decisive difference from other competing techniques. Thomas Edison's Kinetoscope, for instance, never allowed for the projection of the image, and the films were seen individually at the illuminated film frame through a magnifying glass.

The claw mechanism of the Lumières' Cinématographe allowed for projection, and an image large enough for cinema to be projected in the public sphere, and for this reason even more suited for the social projects of the twentieth century. (Even if – as Jean-Luc Godard and

Harun Farocki have argued – it would have been even more apt for the nineteenth century, when public life took place fully in the 'open'.) With projection, cinema acquired the taste for gatherings, fairs, parades and processions; the basic conditions for projecting the image of a nation.

As we have seen, when the King arrived in Christiania (Oslo), the images were not only of His Majesty, but of the crowds gathering to see him. These were the images that secured the common ground for the future of the nation. The celebration of Kings and statesmen, just as with visits of cinema's own royalty, like Douglas Fairbanks' and Mary Pickford's visit to Oslo in 1926, is formed in the cinema as a document of the crowd, of getting together, of belonging. There seems to be a parallel between the social operation of the cinema and its *dispositif* in this respect.

Just as parades and processions were huge attractions in early cinema, the filmstrip proceeds by passing before the gate of the projector, repeating the movement before the shutter of the camera. This reversal between shooting and projection – the Cinématographe could do both in the same box – is based in the intermittence of movement in the apparatus. The claw mechanism holds still the frame for projection, and this is the element lacking for projection of the Kinetoscope image (even if Edison later created a Projecting Kinetoscope based on the Lumières' design). There is in this sense a movement of the photograms in the apparatus that echoes the procession of people. The procession of the filmstrip is parallel to the storage of the individual before the crowd in the projection of the national image. In Christiania, King Haakon's procession is always before the people, thus securing the unity between the King and his subjects, and between cinema technology and its subject.

Through its predisposition for describing the crowd and attracting an audience, the *dispositif* of cinema is crucial in the forming of a nation. This process depends on the storage capacities of cinema, investing it with uniquely powerful mnemotechnical properties. These are the technological conditions of the projection of the image of the nation: by screening an image – no matter how illusory – of a common past, cinema projects an unifying 'project' for the future, which is exactly what makes up a nation. The repeated images of King Haakon VII among his subjects becomes, then, a prophecy and confirmation as the images of King Olav arriving are projected on the screens forty years later.

This projected image does not mean that everyone identifies with it. On the contrary, the inevitable discrepancies between this general image and the individual's image of the self (depending on class, ethnicity, gender, and so on) is the condition for the process of individuation. Each person negotiates his or her relation to this image, thus securing a position partly in opposition to, partly converging with, this image. This space for negotiating one's role in relation to this image secures that the individual understands his or her position in relation to the common image of the ethnic unity making up a nation.

Cinema forms the recollection of events we have never witnessed. It thus constitutes a memory which is disconnected from first-hand experience, and which often portrays events outside of our life span, or ones that have not even taken place. It does so because it is a temporal object. The phenomenologist Edmond Husserl's example of a temporal object is the melody, but each performance of music involves interpretation and variations. With the invention of the cinema and the phonograph, exact repetitions of temporal events become possible for the first time in human history.

This fact marks a decisive rupture in the experience of temporal continuity. With films and records time can be fragmented, repeated, run backwards, looped and movement can be frozen, with evident consequences for our faculty of memory. Husserl's two categories of memory – perception of an event that is always after the fact, and the wilful or automatic recollection of past events – are still based in the present tense of the experiencing subject. With the cinema and the phonograph, inscription and repetition becomes automatic, and is made independent of the present tense of subjective experience.

This is the tertiary memory of time-based media. The technical storage of temporal events is not subsidiary to the others. On the contrary, technological memory is really the primary one, as the technical apparatus constitutes the historical changes and ruptures in mankind's memory and idea of time and space. The technological *dispositif* forms how we perceive and remember, and for this reason the tertiary memory set the angle, framing and lighting of the other two forms of memory. This is, for instance, indicated by our taste for technological metaphors for the workings of the mind, today predominantly exemplified by computer metaphors. This is also the reason why it is theoretically insufficient to separate mental images from 'object-images'; cinema as the most powerful tertiary memory constitutes a recollection that becomes both personal and shared, and forms the perception and memory of our everyday experience.

By commemorating past events, films thus become virtual monuments. The monument has its origin in the grave, by its function to demarcate what is sacred and meaningful from what is mute and insignificant. It is a property of the temporal storage of the media that cinema as well as the gramophone has been connected to death. Edison envisioned the phonograph as a means to capture and store 'the last words of great men', and the first projections of the

Cinematograph convinced some viewers that death was no longer final. The impression was that we would go on moving and acting on the screen long after our biological deaths. It is only logical that the moving image was soon used as a mortuary mask for people who had passed away. Or at least to document the funeral procession. The newsreel from the funeral of the national poet Bjørnstjerne Bjørnson in 1910 is one of the most important films in early Norwegian cinema. By highlighting the crowds of people paying their last respects to the Nobel Prize winner, the film brings together the attraction of the crowds' procession with the tertiary memory of the medium.

The funeral for Bjørnson foregrounds the notion of cinema as a tomb, since the medium's monumental dimensions are always related to the grave. But the success of the film must also be seen in relation to the fact that the audience, when visiting the cinema, went to see a document of a past event. The funeral had of course already been described and commented upon in the press and on the radio. This means that the audience was aware that the 'live-ness' that early cinema so often proposed was really illusory, and it adds to the mnemotechnical dimensions of cinema to know that these images are of a past event.

The time-gap between the event and its screening is perhaps most profiled when the delay is made minimal, as in the case of *The Arrival of King Haakon VII*. A Christiania cameraman developed the images shot aboard the Royal ship 'Heimdal' and exhibited them to a cinema audience that same evening. By making the time delay between shooting and projection minimal, the storage capacity and the monumental aspects of cinema are highlighted. The screening of the arrival of the future King foregrounds the fact that 'this is history!' The minimal time-gap between event and projection produces a preconception of the historical importance of the event. The viewer might or might not have been there at the original event, but he or she was present at the first exhibition of this representation of a historical event.

At one of the King's many visits to the exhibitor Hugo Hermansen's cinema in Stortingsgata in Oslo, shots of his arrival were developed during the exhibition, and became the closing attraction of the event. The look at oneself in this cinematographic hindsight was probably uncanny to a viewer who had only known temporal storage media for a few years, and for this reason still expected time to evolve continuously from a present point in time. This is also certainly at the core of the many discourses on cinema as a medium of artificial life, of the 'doppelgänger', of reflections and phantoms.

Seeing oneself in moving images, or even hearing oneself in sound recordings, lends the representation the appearance of it being someone else. Or better; to be another. The high resolution of the audio-visual image of cinema invests it with a present tense. The impossibility to be at several places at the same time transforms the film image into a ghostly, inhuman form of life. This is the impulse described in the famous account of the 1896 Cinematograph screening in St Petersburg accounted for by Maxim Gorky: 'It is the movement of shadows. Curses and ghosts, evil spirits that have cast whole cities into eternal sleep come to mind … This is not life but the shadow of life and this is not movement but the shadow of movement.'

Together with its mnemotechnical powers, this is perhaps another reason why cinema has been considered so apt for documenting funeral processions. Is it today the end of the nation-state that is documented in cinema's move from the film projection's collective reception to other forms of exhibition?

Trond Lundemo

SYLVI

TEUVO PURO/TEPPO RAIKAS, FINLAND, 1913

The actress Aino Manner – whose appearances on screen have all disappeared along with the early Finnish silent features – spent long periods of time in a mental institution. Her life story seems to be bound with the moral turmoil that characterised the atmosphere of the late nineteenth and early twentieth centuries. She was not only haunted by religious austerity and sexual nightmares, but she even heard 'voices'. Those were not only voices of male authorities such as Tolstoy, Blavatsky and Saint Paul, but she was also mysteriously addressed by the famous Finnish female playwright, Minna Canth, the author of several dramas that dealt with the role of women in contemporary Finnish society.

While spending her time in hospital, Manner happened to read the memoirs of Eino Leino, one of the most celebrated poets of the time. She was shocked by the story of a crime of passion that had taken place in the birth-town of the author. The Latin teacher at the local public school – Mr Sainio – had been poisoned to death by his young wife who had had an affair with a student of her husband. Manner later described her reading of the case:

> I once read the autobiography of Eino Leino, *The Picture Book of My Life* (*Elämäni kuvakirja*). The poet tells about a crime, the famous Sainio murder that had occurred in his school town, Hämeenlinna. Being unaware of what really affected me, the text suddenly and brutally terrified me. The whole incident, as if by magic, came curiously close to me. This was perhaps because I had once played the title role of Minna Canth's *Sylvi* which is said to be an image of Mrs Sainio … I slammed the book closed and threw myself on the bed. How horrible it was when I neither could keep my eyes shut nor open. They blinked restlessly and my breath was blocked so that I was about to suffocate. Then I started to pant hard and – fell asleep.

No doubt, Aino Manner was paralysed by the memory of the Sainio case, which had occurred in 1892. The murder was widely reported in the press, both at home and abroad. Young Mrs Sainio was known for her beauty; Mr Sainio for his impeccable, dreary and dry character. He was a Latinist who preferred sitting in the attic writing his dissertation and who openly neglected his wife. One day, Mr Sainio was found dead, with a frightening grimace on his face. Already the next day, Mrs Sainio was seen in the town dressed in black and wearing a mourning veil. Suspiciously enough, the young wife had asked the doctor to write a large amount of strychnine only a couple of days earlier, to kill the dog as she had explained. Under these circumstances, an autopsy was delivered and the worst suspicions proved to be true: Mr Sainio had been poisoned either by his own hand or by somebody other's. The widow argued that her husband had suffered of a headache and probably had taken the poison by accident. A trial followed, during which Mrs Sainio was hounded by the prosecution. Although it was clearly proven that she was guilty, the audience was stunned by the cruelty of the justice meted out to her.

The destiny of Mrs Sainio moved her female contemporaries in particular, and Minna Canth used the case as raw material for her play *Sylvi*. No wonder Aino Manner was so confused while re-living the drama. She was not to play the role in the future film, but instead had acted on stage and identified with the main character and an image of Mrs Sainio. In Canth's drama, the focal point is on the conventional idea of a marriage in which a woman has only limited possibilities to make decisions concerning her own life. In *Sylvi*, the husband, named Aksel Vahl, is originally a caretaker who has married his adopted child. And Sylvi, who saw upon her husband more like a father, falls in love with her childhood friend Viktor. The lover, however, is engaged to be married to a girl called Katrin and cannot make up his mind. Finally, Sylvi's situation becomes so oppressed she is driven to give poison to Aksel – strychnine, in fact, as in Sainio's case. At the same time, Viktor has already decided not to continue his relationship with Sylvi. The story ends, then, in catastrophe: Sylvi collapses and is sent to prison.

After the sensational publicity of the trial, the Sainio case found an afterlife on stage. The Canthian play became a success and continued to arouse debates while being staged throughout the country. In addition, it should be remembered that, at the turn of the century, theatrical activities were extremely popular both in the countryside and in the cities in Finland. Amateur theatre was a major social activity, supported and encouraged by the temperance movement as well as by the workers' associations. Those stages favoured light pieces, musical dramas and comedies but they also gave room for plays with a social emphasis, such as *Sylvi*.

When actors Teuvo Puro and Teppo Raikas, together with cinematographer Frans Engström, joined forces in order to start the production of Finnish full-length feature films in the summer of 1911, it was immediately clear that they would turn to Minna Canth's melodramas. Before 1911, only two fiction films had been produced in Finland. Puro, Raikas and Engström had already met in 1907 when a photo and film company, Atelier Apollo, produced Finland's first fiction film. The idea for the first production did not, however, stem from the team itself. It was the result of Apollo and their announcement of an open competition for ideas that could be transformed into films.

The public showed great enthusiasm, with the company receiving over six hundred suggestions. The winning manuscript became *Salaviinan polttajat* (*The Moonshiners*), a film that dealt with the theme of illegal alcohol production at the same time that the Finnish senate was establishing a prohibition law. Finland was an autonomous province under Russian rule until 1917, and Czar Nicholas II refused to give his assent to the legislation. It is, too, difficult to draw any definite conclusions on how *The Moonshiners* dealt with its theme as no fiction film produced before 1920 has been preserved in Finland.

After *The Moonshiners* the owners of Atelier Apollo probably doubted the commercial possibilities of fictitious production. Meanwhile, another company, Maat ja kansat, produced a short farce called *Vasikan häntä* (*The Calf Tail*, 1908), but this did not encourage any further creativity within feature-film production. The turning point came in 1911 when, after the silence of four years, Puro, Raikas and Engström used their own savings to plan the filming of three works. Compared to *The Moonshiners*, the new dramas were envisioned to be considerably longer than the earlier endeavours. This mirrors the fact that films in the international market had gradually become longer.

In Denmark, Urban Gad and Asta Nielsen had completed their *Afgrunden* (*The Abyss*) in September 1910 and, in Sweden, Gustaf Linden had managed the production of *Regina von Emmeritz och Konung Gustaf II Adolf*, an 800-metre-long historical photoplay which had its premiere in November 1910. It is most likely that Puro, Raikas and Engström had recognised this change in the character of film production, simply because the same shift occurred on the screens of Helsinki. *Afgrunden* premiered in Finland in January 1911.

There are no sources describing how the trio finally chose the works to be filmed. They decided, however, on two plays by Canth: *Anna-Liisa* and *Sylvi*, and, additionally, to make an adaptation of a Swedish novel. The latter was, according to Teuvo Puro's reminiscences, Axel Jäderin's *Brottsjöar*. This is uncertain, though, because nothing that we know today about the filming seems to have any link to the themes and locations of this novel.

Canth's dramas were appropriate for the filmmakers for several reasons. First, in their capacity as professional actors, Puro and Raikas were already familiar with them. Second, both plays foregrounded a female character, just as Gad's melodramas had done in Denmark.

Furthermore, *Sylvi* and *Anna-Liisa* were well-known by Finnish audiences who would have had no difficulty in following the plot. Both dramas also possessed a socially-critical undercurrent, which the producers knew would arouse general interest. *Anna-Liisa* dealt with the problem of premarital relationships and showed a desperate mother unable to bear the shame of having a baby out of wedlock. In addition to this general social dimension, *Sylvi* referred to an infamous and relatively recent crime of passion. In the case of *Sylvi*, there would be an audience eager to see a cinematic recreation of the crime.

The shooting of *Sylvi* took place in the summer of 1911, with every scene taking place indoors. As there were no studios in Finland before 1915, filming had to take place on sets constructed by the designer Carl Fager on the roof of a hotel called Fennia, which offered plenty of sunlight. Other circumstances, however, were less favourable. The weather tended to be windy during the shoot. Houseplants, curtains and clothing moved with the breeze, and the chimney of the hotel occasionally blew billows of smoke onto the set. Aili Rosvall, who played the role of Sylvi, recalled later that the actors, blackened by soot, had to constantly interrupt their performances to clean their faces.

In spite these problems, shooting was completed on time, just before autumn. At that point, however, the filmmakers had run out of money and were unable to send the negatives to be developed. By then, Atelier Apollo already owned a film laboratory, but perhaps Engström considered that it would be safer to send the negatives abroad as the material amounted to the equivalent of three full-length features. The trio had to wait until the following year before they were able to raise enough money to send the material to Copenhagen.

When the film boxes were returned, *Anna-Liisa* and *Brottsjöar* were completely destroyed. The material had been overexposed, either before it was sent to Denmark or by someone opening the boxes by accident in the laboratory. Only *Sylvi* was in such a condition that it could be salvaged. Some parts of the footage were slightly darkened but not beyond repair. However, Engström, Raikas and Puro once again found themselves out of funds. Finally Engström, who in his capacity as cinematographer owned the material, sold all of it to a certain Hjalmar V. Pohjanheimo, the owner of several movie theatres in Finland and a film producer just planning to start a business of his own. With the help of Pohjanheimo, *Sylvi* finally had its premiere in Viborg on 24 February 1913.

In advertisements, posters and handouts *Sylvi* was characterised as 'an hour-long art film' and as 'a tragedy in three acts'. Since 1911, film censorship had been exercised in Finland by the Helsinki police department, and when *Sylvi* was approved on 18 February 1913, the film was measured to be 890 metres long. This means that, if screened with the speed of 16 frames per second, it was about 48 minutes long. After its premiere, *Sylvi* was shown in Turku, Helsinki and at least eleven other cities before the end of the year. The press paid little attention to this new, longer work. This was not unusual as film journalism and criticism were yet to be established in Finland.

It is likely, however, that *Sylvi* aroused the interest of the movie-going audience. The advertisement of the Lyyra Theatre on the 16 March 1913 maintained that 'considering the inquiries from the wide audiences' the theatre had decided to show Minna Canth's *Sylvi* 'which had become enormously popular among the audiences of the Capital, and had been shown for a full house for the entire week'. Comments on film were, then, rare in the press of the time, but the newspaper *Sosialidemokraatti* wrote on its popularity: 'The film has been shown in Helsinki for weeks, and it is still screened always for full houses. The newspapers of the capital have given praising statements, such as: "The film is the first successful effort in this area in Finland. The performance has been a complete success. The photoplay has aroused well-deserved attention among the cinematic audience of the city", etc.' Most of these comments had actually been lifted from the advertisements of the movie theatre itself and not from newspaper articles. There seems, however, to be plenty of evidence that *Sylvi*, being recognised as the first Finnish full-length film, was regarded as an exceptional case, and that it also appealed to those unused to attending cinemas.

Despite this success, *Sylvi* disappeared a year after its release. There is no record of it in the newspaper advertisements over the next decade. The Finnish fiction-film production experienced its first real upheaval in the years 1913–14 when, in sum, fifteen fiction films were produced. In the forthcoming years, the situation changed dramatically, due to the impact of the First World War and the tightening stranglehold of Russian rule. The promising beginning soon vanished and there was a cessation in production in 1917–18: the establishment of the independent Finnish republic in 1917, and the outbreak of the Civil War next year offered no possibilities for filmmaking. During these years, *Sylvi* disappeared completely. Film narration had been developed further in the major production countries of the period, and the theatre-owners obviously saw no point in trying to screen the pioneering work of the bygone years.

The Pohjanheimo family probably owned the one copy of the film, which was stored at their estate until the breakdown of their business in the 1920s. Finally, in December 1933, a junk store holder from Helsinki contacted the film company of Heikki Aho and Björn Soldan. Mysteriously, a reel of footage had ended up in his possession. He used to buy nitrate celluloid film in order to sell it to youngsters who, at the time, had a hobby of burning pieces of film in the sun with a magnifying glass.

The quality of the film had proved to be so bad the boys refused to buy it. The storekeeper thought that perhaps some filmmaker would want to use the material, as it had no value for him anymore. When Aho and Soldan took a closer look at the reel, they soon became convinced that the negative material originated from *Sylvi*. They could not date the material exactly, but they certainly had heard about the production that had been made almost two decades earlier.

Aho and Soldan got in touch with Engström and agreed on the rights to use the material in a short film. Engström helped to compile the necessary intertitles. It became clear that the reel found was not a coherent part of the film. It consisted of fragments or separate shots and included no text. It is difficult to estimate how long the discovered footage actually was, but today there are two reels of material at the Finnish Film Archive. One is the short film (210 metres) produced by Aho and Soldan, the other a 345-metre long reel with several shots in succession. The latter reel probably consists of the left-over material from the short film. The 210 metres of the short film include the intertitles written in the beginning of 1934. In sum, there is around 500 metres of material from *Sylvi* that has been preserved to the present day. There are, however, overlapping shots within the material. Some shots were taken three or four times. At its premiere, *Sylvi* was almost 900 metres long, which means that approximately one half of it could be reconstructed.

Though this was bad news for film archivists and historians, it may still be stated that the source material for the film is ample. The film is, as far as can be known today, the only one from this period, of which any footage has been preserved. None of the fiction films made in Finland prior to 1920 have been saved. Seen from this point of view, the discovery at the junk store was of essential importance giving at least one vague possibility to try to analyse the aesthetics of early Finnish fiction film.

Based on the material found, Aho and Soldan completed a short film that premiered in January 1934. Intertitles were added, which was in keeping with Canth's play. Strangely, the producers did not consult Teuvo Puro, who originally had written the script. As the cinematographer Engström owned the copyright, he was the only one of the three to supervise the resurrection of the film. Since 1934, this short film has been used in discussions of the original.

The fact is, however, that there still exists no evidence that the material discovered really was used in the copy shown in 1913. The material was found in negative form and might as well be footage that was rejected during the editing process. The junk store material included scenes where the weather was especially windy and the chimney of Fennia turned the view completely grey. Engström was so experienced in his profession that it hardly is possible to think that he would have accepted such flawed shots in his film. The fact that the rediscovered 345-metre material reveals that some shots had been taken several times, supports this assertion. Furthermore, it seems that Aho and Soldan wanted to amuse their audience by showing humorous takes, as there would have been better choices in terms of pictorial quality. This resulted in an implication that early Finnish cinema was somewhat childish and aesthetically inferior to its international rivals.

Despite these reservations, the *Sylvi* material still offers the only opportunity to ponder the stylistic principles of early Finnish fiction film and is therefore of great significance. In addition to the fact that the remains might stem from out-takes, it is still worth remembering that *Sylvi* represented initial steps in the field in Finland.

At first glance, *Sylvi*'s visual appearance brings to mind the international production of the earlier decade. The perspective of the camera is clearly identified with the position of the spectator: the events are shown from a distance so that the whole stage can be controlled by the viewer's eye. This was also typical of the melodramas of the 1910s, especially of the German *Autorenfilm* which were usually based on the texts of famous writers. *Autorenfilm* were clearly theatrical by nature. Their style was somewhat inflexible and characterised by slow cutting rate, tableau-like framing and theatrical stage acting. As Barry Salt has stated, shot-lengths were usually extensive in the German film of the period. In Max Mack's *Zweimal gelebt* (1912), for example, the average shot-length is 27 seconds (at 16 frames per second). At the same time such American films as George L. Tucker's *Traffic in Souls* (1913) and D. W. Griffith's *Birth of a Nation* (1915) used only 7-second long shots. Because material in Finland was so scarce, it is difficult to draw definite conclusions on how *Sylvi* relates to these figures. If the average shot length of the 345-metre material is counted, the result is as high as 56 seconds. The longest take that has been preserved is 194 seconds which, however, does not reveal much of the actual feature copy. Shots were cut and combined and, of course, seasoned by intertitles. The shot-length in the final film must have been shorter, but it remains apparent that Finnish silents, following the German example, used fairly long shots.

Another interesting point is *Sylvi*'s use of close-ups. Teuvo Puro recalled that he, as director, would have liked to use close-ups and bring the actors nearer to the spectators. Puro had probably already seen close-ups in international films. According to Salt, the change of framing and the moving of camera closer to its object had become more common after 1905. But, as

Puro has argued, Engström refused absolutely to use such novelties: 'Engström insisted that, in interior scenes, three walls should be visible at the same time. This caused much debate among us when the directors sometimes wanted to use only a corner. I don't mean that we would have known too much on close-ups either, but we understood that this would have been a way to make people look bigger. As Engström was keeping his machine in one place only, they seemed to disappear completely especially in the background.' According to an anecdote told by the film critic Hans Kutter, the audiences at early film screenings in Finland were sometimes suspicious of the shift of camera positions. The audience could even demand their money back if actors were not shown from top to toe: 'Feet, feet … Where are the feet? We have not paid our tickets in order to see invalids.'

Carl Fager, the set designer, claimed that the question of close-up had become an issue when filming the death scene of Aksel Vahl. Puro – who played the role – asked Engström to take a close-up of Aksel's struggle. This clarifies the earlier comment by Puro, too, because the bed where Aksel finally was to be convulsing was set 'in the background' of the stage. For sure, Puro did not mean the use of extreme close-up either, but he would have moved the camera a bit closer to the bed in order for the audience to be able to share more of its compassion with Aksel's destiny.

At the same time, we know that Aili Rosvall was strongly inspired by Asta Nielsen's and Betty Nansen's acting. She was especially impressed by Nielsen's way of using her face as the means of her mime. As Rosvall interpreted, Nielsen did not use her mouth but had moved her expression upwards, to eyes and forehead. This was something that Rosvall also wanted to apply in her interpretation of Sylvi. In the end, the use of such subtle means is not only a matter of acting. Urban Gad employed close-ups to stress the little expressions and gestures of Nielsen. In the footage of *Sylvi,* however, the camera stays in its remote position and does not support Rosvall's acting. It seems also that Puro thought of using close-up to accentuate the suffering of Aksel in the first place, not the tragic destiny of Sylvi.

Puro's aesthetic intentions were not realised, as we know, because Engström firmly followed his own principles. Or, to be more precise, this is how Puro and others have remembered Engström's role. It is of course possible that Puro later wanted to emphasise his position as the director who not only took care of the actors, but who also wanted to participate in the film's cinematographic appearance. One cannot, however, avoid the thought that Puro had identified with Aksel's character not only as an actor but also as director. His interpretation of Canth's play seems to have underlined the male perspective more than the original theatre piece.

As we remember, the actress Aino Manner felt confused after reading about the Sainio case in a book. Had she seen *Sylvi* as a film, she would probably have not undergone such a strong emotional experience, as the focal point in it was shifted from the female character Sylvi to her husband Aksel. Few shots have been preserved from the final sequence of the film, showing Sylvi in front of the court. In this scene, Sylvi seems cold and distant as if the idea was that she no longer is a character to be identified with. In Canth's play, however, Sylvi remains desperate and deals with her emotions until the curtain falls.

As a genre film *Sylvi* followed international examples by centralising a female character but, simultaneously, it expressed something that became typical of the Finnish silent cinema. Minna Canth was the only female writer whose works were adapted onto the screen before 1920. The final result, shown in 1913, did not perhaps carry Canth's social criticism, nor did women's position become an issue in other films of the era. But Sylvi's was a passionate crime story, known by the public, and gave an afterlife to the disturbing real-life murder case.

Hannu Salmi

REFERENCES

Kutter, H. (1957) 'Murhaavan kaunis', in *Uutisaitta*, 5.

Puro, T. (1942) 'Muistelmia kotimaisen elokuvan alkutaipaleelta', *Uusi Suomi*, Sunnuntailiite, 24 May.

Salt, B. (1996) 'Early German Film: The Stylistics in Comparative Context', in T. Elsaesser and M. Wedel (eds) *A Second Life: German Cinema – First Decades*. Amsterdam: Amsterdam University Press.

DUNUNGEN DOWNIE

IVAN HEDQVIST, SWEDEN, 1919

Before December 1919, only Victor Sjöström and Mauritz Stiller were directors of Selma Lagerlöf adaptations. On 1 December at Röda Kvarn in Stockholm, actor Ivan Hedqvist's first film as director, *Dunungen* (*Downie*), premiered. The film, with Julius Jaenzon as cinematographer, was the fourth in the series of Lagerlöf adaptations. In Sweden, it was hailed by a unanimous group of critics. *Downie* also became one of the biggest export successes during the 'golden age' of Swedish cinema, 1917–23. French critics, in particular, were astonishingly positive in their praise.

The son of the mayor, Mauritz (Ragnar Widestedt) falls in love with the baker's daughter, Anne-Marie (Renée Björling), nick-named Downie. The young ones become engaged – to the horror of the mayor and his wife. The father, however, promises to give his blessing if Mauritz (who intends to go to his rich uncle Teodor at Bohult – played by Hedqvist himself – to ask for a farm of his own) promises to sell Teodor a couple of worthless share emissions.

The uncle turns out to be somewhat nervous, but as Anne-Marie takes the opportunity to discover the glories of country life, she even gets to know Teodor. Mauritz on the other hand engages in other interests, not least his old girlfriend. The matters are brought to a head during a ball for the newly engaged, where Mauritz completely ignores Anne-Marie, while the uncle, displaying his infatuation with her, becomes increasingly drunk.

In the morning, when the young couple is about to leave, the uncle wanders around aimlessly in his park. After a talk to his mother, he decides to offer Mauritz a position as administrator of her farm, under the condition that he gets married. When he explains his plans over breakfast, Mauritz tries to sell the worthless share emissions to his uncle. This turns out to be too much for Anne-Marie, who reveals everything to Teodor. Mauritz becomes furious and threatens her. She then seeks refuge and solace in the arms of her uncle, where she is obviously going to stay. Mauritz leaves in anger, accusing her of being a fortune-hunter.

In the *Svensk Filmografi* (*Swedish Filmography*), Selma Lagerlöf's short story, *Downie*, is mentioned as literary source to the film. An additional commentary mentions that the short story was dramatised by Lagerlöf herself twenty years after the first edition in 1894, and that the play was brought to the stage, at Stockholm's Royal Dramatic Theatre in 1914 with Hedqvist in the role as uncle Teodor. The same cast was reprised for the film. In a preface to the drama, Lagerlöf also noted that the piece had already been dramatised in a French version by a certain M. Edouard Schneider.

What strikes the spectator, however, is that the film much less resembles the short story than the drama. This is clearly indicated by a comparison between the three versions. Unlike the short story and the drama, where the number of chapters and the acts respectively are limited to four, the film contains five reels (in the credits as well as on the posters, however, the number of reels is said to be six). Reels two to five in the film basically correspond to act one to four in the drama, where only the last act corresponds to the fourth chapter of the short story.

Most interesting, however, is the number of specifically cinematic additions made in the film compared to both literary sources: variations on the literary text and its dramatisation for the stage, created out of the specific premises of the new medium. Among these additions, the first one holds the major part of the first reel of the film, which tells the story of Anne-Marie's and Mauritz's first meeting and the path leading up to their engagement. The central point with this part is obviously to present the characters in the drama to the spectator (however, most of them turn out to disappear completely by in the second reel).

The presentation of the second male lead, Uncle Teodor, is only made in the beginning of the second reel. This introduces a narrative suspense particular to the film, which also casts a backward glance to classical dramas. The presentation of him is first introduced by an intertitle: 'Proprietor Teodor', which is followed by an image of the uncle from behind. It is only after a few seconds that he slowly turns around towards the camera.

The first reel of the film begins with a long intertitle, which looks back on the life of Downie, and traces her back to her home place: 'Ah Downie, ah silken flower! You were certainly not a fortune-hunter only; you were also a fortune-giver, otherwise there would be nothing left of your happy peace in the house where you lived. To this day the garden is shaded by big beeches. And when I come there, I feel that there is festival in the air, and it seems as if the birds and flowers still sing their beautiful songs of you.'

This text is a condensed version of the last part of the short story. Through its general view, it is placed outside the diegetic time of the story. Therefore, it is just as easily integrated into the beginning, as the end of the film. The narrative presence of Lagerlöf the author in this quotation is not followed up later in the film. In the short story on the other hand, the 'I' has spoken already in the introduction to the first chapter, remaining as an abstract narrative instance throughout the text. In the film, another fact turns out to be confusing, namely that the inter-title is followed by an introductory shot of Downie blowing a dandelion in an iris-open.

The first reel also contains an interesting semi-subjective image, to borrow from Jean Mitry. It appears when Downie's father the baker is on his way home from the restaurant after becoming much more drunk than was his intention. The camera is placed in front of him, and he staggers towards it – at the same time, the whole image staggers with him. This is a scene absent from both the drama and the short story. The visit to the restaurant does not have any real function in the story but the addition was made most likely in order to exploit the visual extravagances caused by intoxication.

In the short story, 'it' – falling in love – captures Anne-Marie during the second chapter. The chapter starts with a rhetorical question: 'How has "it" come? That which she dares not call by name? "It" has come like the dew to the grass, like the colour to the rose, like the sweetness to the berry, imperceptibly and gently without announcing itself beforehand.' Then follows the observation that it was not at any particular time, that 'it' came. Then, suddenly, during the night of the ball, 'it' manifested itself: 'Then "it" came over her while he stroked her hair. It came stealing, it came creeping, it came rushing, as when elves pass through dark woods.'

The drama moves this secret development to another scene in the third act during the night of the ball, where Anne-Marie confides herself to Jenny, uncle Teodor's small dog whom she has been asked to take care of. She does so in the film as well. Yet in the screen version the change in Anne-Marie's feelings is instead depicted gradually and more indirectly – mediated as it is through an image: an oval portrait of the uncle, which becomes the object of varying kinds of attention from Anne-Marie.

The oval portrait appears for the first time in the second reel of the film, when the newly engaged have just arrived in Bohult. As soon as Anne-Marie has settled herself in her room, she finds the portrait on the wall and says to Frida the maid: 'Would you believe that he is so terrible!' The phrase is followed by a cut-in on the girl and the portrait. This close-up marks the end of the scene. The second time occurs a bit later in the same reel, when Anne-Marie is busy unpacking. Now, she takes down the portrait from the wall and looks at it. Its oval is shown in extreme close-up, covering the screen.

A cut from the close-up of the portrait to Anne-Marie shows her talking to it playfully and teasingly. Mauritz and uncle Teodor talking in the garden then catch her attention and she puts the portrait down. What she says to the portrait is never revealed. However, in the garden, it turns out that Teodor tells Mauritz off. Furious, Anne-Marie turns to the portrait a third time, telling it off as she turns it. This act also appeared in the stage directions of the drama, but there she addressed the uncle directly, even if at a safe distance. As with the drama, in the film she shakes her fist at the uncle, via the portrait. When trying to put the portrait back on the wall, she is too violent and the peg falls down. She then puts the portrait into a drawer in the dressing table below, turns the key, takes it out and throws it on the floor, as if she wanted to disarm the angry uncle once and for all.

The portrait appears for a fourth time in the third reel, when Anne-Marie retires to her room after having made a tour around the estate with the uncle, and having been treated in a patronising way by her fiancé. Now she looks up towards the place where the portrait should be, and then opens the drawer and takes it out. She looks at it and kisses it, only to turn away from the portrait with a quick, embarrassed glance. Then, she puts it back on the wall again.

The portrait reappears one last time in the end of the third reel, as the uncle in a fit of rage has chased Anne-Marie, and she comes into her room, weeping. This is shown through the mirror on her dressing table. She walks into the frame, her back at the camera, and sits down in front of the mirror. Again, she looks up at the portrait and takes it down from the wall. A cut to mid-shot from the side shows her intensely gazing at the portrait. She lifts her head with her eyes closed, and then again with a sigh looks at the portrait.

In an article on mirrors and portraits in early Russian cinema, Yuri Tsivian writes that objects tend to inhere different meanings depending on the medium within which they are used; they can never remain neutral and unchanging: 'The correct way to put it should be: what we are studying are theatre mirrors, literary mirrors, cinematic mirrors.' The same is true of the portraits. Tsivian notes that they may also have a meta-function, using an example where the portrait of a person from the past is juxtaposed with his mirror image in the present.

The portrait in *Downie* is indeed a cinematic portrait. Not only are the passages in the short story or the drama that explicitly refer to 'it' – her loving feeling – condensed into these five encounters with the portrait. Several narrated parts in the short story depicting the change of focus in Anne-Marie's feelings are gradually motivated by the dialogues with the portrait. All the scattered parts of the written text are brought together and compressed into a series of looks and facial gestures. The cinematic mode of expression, then, is much more efficient in its economy than the literary description.

The portrait also introduces a meta-level in the story. Partly, this happens through the different ways of approaching the portrait that Anne-Marie demonstrates, but partly also through the juxtaposition of the framed mirror image of Anne-Marie and the framed portrait of the uncle. Such an image holds a key position in the series of images that gradually establishes visual connections between the two of them. In its juxtaposition of two different frames, this particular figure also functions in a more obvious way as a meta-cinematic expression.

The scene where Anne-Marie makes the tour of the estate is particularly elaborated in the film when compared to the drama; the limits of the stage allow for no other solution, so it is only briefly indicated in the play. The short story in its turn contains a longer passage which starts with the girl in high spirits at the beginning of the walk and then concentrates on describing the surroundings. The emphasis is on her qualities as a potential housewife, aroused by the discovery of all the marvellous possibilities at Bohult.

Beside the possibility of enlarged space in cinema, the tour of the estate is used to underline the many graces of country life. This emphasis on nature and country life was also one of the general concepts of the 'golden age' in Swedish cinema. Nature and the general depiction of scenery had, not unexpectedly, been mentioned in several reviews as a valuable cinematic addition to the play. The importance ascribed to nature, however, is also justified by a passage in the short story: 'Then she was overcome with pleasure at the beautiful place and that nature was so wonderfully near … People thought she was a city girl. But she had become a country lass as soon as she put her foot on the sandy path. She felt instantly that she belonged to the country.'

Without being more explicit, this little passage still functions as a divide, further developed in the cinematic narration. On one hand, there are the unspoiled and healthy people who belong to country life and on the other hand the city people, impersonated by Mauritz. He remains totally occupied by himself or by questions of stock trading, and his ambitions for country life are only inspired by his own possible gains, whereas he lacks practical competence.

Once again, nature functions as ethical divide. In the film, this is not only revealed thematically, but also through its visual form. Anne-Marie's enthusiasm concerning cows and sheep is pictured through her gestures and facial expressions as quite exuberant. She may be a bit scared of the geese, but soon finds relief in the arms of the uncle, and as soon as they both are brought together within the same image frame, he becomes her guide into country life.

The image of Mauritz is presented in contrast to that of Anne-Marie. He has gone hunting to escape his uncle's rage, but does not seem particularly persistent: the camera depicts him asleep whisking away disturbing flies. However, he wakes up as he hears two young ladies on the road, one of which turns out to be his former fiancée. He jumps to his feet and finds new outlet for his talents as a hunter.

The contrast between urban and rural reaches its peak as Mauritz and his two companions walk back to the estate where they meet Teodor who is driving a loaded hay-cart. Anne-Marie hides in the hay behind him, but peeks out. The two young ladies exchange significant looks and Mauritz, embarrassed, apologises for his fiancée's lack of manners. He then leaves screen-right with the two ladies, while Anne-Marie and Teodor remain together on-screen…

Later, Anne-Marie sits by herself in the garden daydreaming, which gives rise to the only subjective memory image in the film. It is the image of her in the arms of the uncle, which on each side is surrounded by a fade out with a following fade in. She is surprised by Mauritz and thus hurries to kiss him goodnight. This incident provides the basis for the next scene, which shows the change in Anne-Marie's attitude as described in the scene with the portrait.

The fact that 'it' in the film thus takes place earlier than in the short story or the drama, namely in addition to her rural escapades (instead of during the night of the ball) also actively contributes to giving nature its central role in the cinematic narration. A third motive – apart from the significance of nature and the above-analysed function of the portrait, central to the narrative in *Downie* is the window motive. It becomes clear, namely, that the window scenes on five occasions each represent key moments in the development of the story.

In an essay entitled 'Romantikkens ikonografi i Norden', Per Jonas Nordhagen attempts to explore the existence of Romantic visual motives in Nordic art of the nineteenth century. He notes that the concept of 'Romantic iconography' is rather new in art history. Lorentz Eitner used it in an article from 1955, 'The Open Window and the Storm-Tossed Boat: An Essay on the Iconography of Romanticism'. Eitner's analysis shows that the motive of the open window is frequent in both French and German art – particularly in the circles around Caspar David Friedrich in Dresden – where a person looks from inside dark rooms through open windows at the landscape outside.

At the same time, the open window was frequently used as poetic metaphor in poetry of the period. Eitner analyses the window as symbol of the human longing for infinity, with the window frame as an element both opening up and closing in. He also underlines Friedrich's great importance for Nordic art history. In a study by J. A. Schmoll gen. Eisenwerth, the prevalence of the motive is further underlined. He groups the window images into seven categories, which Hans Lund has summarised:

1 Persons in a window seen from the outside

2 Interiors with a person seen from behind, looking out on a landscape

3 Interiors with a person seen from the side, looking out on a landscape

4 Interiors with a person with the window at his back

5 Self-portraits at the studio window

6 Interiors with a person working at a window

7 Window images without any persons present

This kind of background is worth keeping in mind when considering *Downie*, where the window motive plays a central role on five occasions. On the first one the scene is filmed from the outside. Anne-Marie is seen through the window, staying in her room in her parents' house, playing with a kitten. Mauritz then arrives on one of his first visits. On the second occasion, however, the perspective changes: Anne-Marie is listening at her window in the evening, and overhears a conversation between her father and Mauritz, who asks for her hand.

The third time she is also eavesdropping, but now at uncle Teodor's place, to the conversation between him and Mauritz. The fourth time, it is instead Anne-Marie who is outside the window, talking to uncle Teodor who is inside with his dog. This scene parallels and inverts the first scene with Mauritz outside Anne-Marie's window. On the fifth and last occasion, Anne-Marie sits alone in her room at the uncle's place, sad that she will soon have to leave. She leans forward, sitting in front of a window at the left of the image. The composition and the static pose of the girl makes the image very similar in its composition to interior painting.

The windows in these scenes do not open towards any wide landscape. Nor do they contain any simple metaphors concerning the longing for infinity or the fear of being locked in. But they do function in the same way as the weather-driven boat in *Terje Vigen* (1917) as a case in point showing how Romantic iconography is integrated and diversified within the 'golden age' of Swedish silent cinema. It is the window in its function as threshold between two positions or two conditions which is particularly emphasised. The window makes possible an opening towards something new, but at the same time risks to confine people within given circumstances. The outcome is never evident. There are always two sides of a window.

The visual adjoinment of Teodor and Anne-Marie logically reaches its peak in the last reel. It happens on three occasions with increasing intensity. In the morning when Mauritz's and Anne-Marie's departure is planned to take place, the uncle wanders around in the garden, and an intertitle states that he has done so all night long. He drops into a garden chair. There is down flying in the air. He fiddles about with a wad of down and drops down on the table with his head bowed. There is a cut to an interior, showing Anne-Marie in profile at the window (the last interior discussed above). She, too, sits with her head bent down over her arm, which rests on the window frame.

After an interlude where first Teodor and then Anne-Marie talk to his mother, the main protagonists gather for breakfast. Teodor is situated in the background with Mauritz opposite, his back to the camera. Anne-Marie is seated to the right and the mother to the left, so that an angle of ninety degrees is created between each character. After a cut-in to a mid-shot on Anne-Marie, there is a cut to the uncle who pulls himself together and begins to talk. An intertitle shows that he has planned to offer his nephew a farm. The intertitle is followed by a cut to *plan américain* on Teodor and Anne-Marie, who now in order to be contained within the same frame are seated much closer to one another.

Mauritz comes dashing into the frame from the right and throws himself upon the uncle in delight. After another intertitle, 'You are much too kind to us, Uncle', there is a short cut back to the three, still in *plan américain* but now with Mauritz placed at the centre of the image and Anne-Marie talking, turned towards the uncle. The previous line is thus ascribed to her. This is one of the few occasions where the film returns to a more primitive praxis concerning intertitles by showing them before the corresponding shot on the person talking, which in this particular case easily leads the spectator to believe that the line should be ascribed to Mauritz.

After a cut to mid-shot on the uncle, looking to the right in Anne-Marie's direction, there is another cut to mid-shot on Anne-Marie, staring straight in front of her. After the establishing shot, the scene is thus symmetrically composed: mid-shot Anne-Marie diagonally from the right – frontal mid-shot Teodor – frontal *plan américain* Anne-Marie, Teodor, Mauritz – frontal mid-shot Teodor – mid-shot Anne-Marie diagonally from the right. The symmetry is strengthened by the fact that both mid-shots on Anne-Marie are filmed from exactly the same angle. This, however, also introduces a clear distance in the cut between the two last images.

The first cut-in on Anne-Marie and the following on Teodor brings the spectator step by step into the image compared to the position in the establishing shot. The corresponding images in the end of the sequence functions as visual counterpart. This is partly because the uncle turns to his right towards Anne-Marie and the camera then is placed on her other side. Partly, it is also because in the cut to Anne-Marie there is a change of perspective in relation to the earlier frontal shorts, which creates a kind of twist away from the uncle's position. Teodor's generosity towards his nephew seems to separate him forever from the nephew's fiancée, and the ending of the drama cannot yet be anticipated.

After breakfast, the two gentlemen go into the uncle's study in order to carry out their business. First, they stop in frontal *plan américain*. Mauritz then moves to the left, shot in profile. To the left in the background the closed door through which they entered earlier in the same shot is visible. It is opened, which leads to a cut on action to Anne-Marie in mid-shot, entering the room with the looks of the Fate. Another cut back to the previous composition shows her walking up towards the two men, putting herself between them. Intertitle: 'Don't buy these shares, Uncle!' Back to the previous composition, Mauritz takes a step towards Anne-Marie and then retires again. New intertitle: 'Do you think that Uncle could be fooled by someone like me?' Back to the same composition, where Anne-Marie now turns towards the uncle and clarifies herself, while Mauritz pulls her arm: 'Uncle, these shares are not worth the paper they're written on, and never will be. They all know it back home.'

A last cut back to the same composition shows Mauritz pulling Anne-Marie out of frame to the left. After a cut to the left they are both shown in profile in mid-shot. Mauritz: 'Anne-Marie! You're making me out a rogue!' A new cut-in to the same composition shows the two standing up against each other in conflict. Her quick response: 'What else are you?' is followed by a short cut on Mauritz who raises his arm as if he wanted to strike, followed by a new intertitle: 'Uncle! He wants to hit me!'

A new cut back to the uncle with the camera in an angle left of the previous position shows Anne-Marie dashing into the frame, throwing herself in Teodor's arms. The next cut, back to Mauritz, shows him alone in mid-shot, followed by an intertitle: 'Forgive me, Anne-Marie! Uncle knows you are only a child. Now, come here and kiss me.' A new cut to a long shot on the uncle and Anne-Marie includes two intertitles: 'Downie, should I let him get you?' and 'Mauritz, you surprise me. Love makes you weak. How can you continue to be engaged to a girl who has called you a rogue?' He stretches his arms, and Anne-Marie looses her grip on him. This leads to a cut to *plan américain* on the three of them, still from a position slightly to the left, though Anne-Marie remains on the uncle's side. But she takes a few steps in Mauritz' direction, insistently staring at him. While in the middle of the frame, however, she stops, puts her hands to her face and – with a sudden cut, she is back in the arms of the uncle, now with the camera approximately from Mauritz' position.

A reverse shot to Mauritz, showing him alone in mid-shot, with the intertitle 'Come, Anne-Marie!' is followed by a cut back to previous shot in *plan américain*. Uncle starts to talk, gesturing: 'Go home alone, Mauritz! This young lady is my guest, and I don't intend to allow you to abuse her any longer. Take your ill-gotten gains and go.' Within the same shot, Mauritz responds: 'I am decieved. My fiancée has been stolen. I congratulate you on this business deal, Anne-Marie.' He then dashes to the door, still within the same frame. In the moment that he opens the door, there is a cut-in to mid-shot, where he looks back and cries out: 'Fortune-Hunter!'

The image of Mauritz on his way out follows for a short instant after the intertitle, which is followed by a cut to the other two in mid-shot from a new angle, closer to the door, about ninety degrees from the initial establishing shot. The uncle turns towards the door, as if he wanted to chase Mauritz, but Anne-Marie stops him: 'Oh Uncle Teodor! Mauritz is always right. A fortune-hunter is just what I am!' After this intertitle, there is a cut back to the same framing, where the uncle first pushes Anne-Marie back but soon spreads his arms to embrace her: 'No, you are no fortune-hunter. You give! You give!' Then, the couple unites in a final kiss, closed by an iris-in.

The whole last scene of the film is thus composed, both visually and thematically, as a tug-of-war between Anne-Marie's two rivals. In particular, the dialogue between the two men in the intertitles motivates such an interpretation. However, the scene could also be described in less passive terms as concerns Anne-Marie, as her own choice between her loyalty to her words and the voice of her heart. Mauritz's purpose with the whole affair is first of all to get the uncle to buy the shares, then to save his pride and finally to get the resisting girl to join him.

The uncle on his side also fights a battle between the voices of reason and of love. This battle is created both through *mise-en-scène* and montage. Both through cutting in on Mauritz – and on one occasion, the uncle – and through the cut-ins in *plan américain* showing all three persons, Anne-Marie's balancing between the two men is demonstrated. The whole scene thus functions as a balance, with certain overweight to one side from the beginning, which then all of a sudden tips over.

This scene demonstrates a smoothly functioning classical narration, an invisible style, which directs the spectator's attention towards the story while at the same time structuring it and focusing on its most central aspects. Straight cuts dominate with few exceptions (three iris-out and two iris-in, marking the end of reels, and two fade out and fade in shots surrounding the flashback). *Mise-en-scène* and montage are all the more varied: shot/reverse-shot, centered images, cut-in shots on central characters, cut on action, symmetrical compositions. A few exceptions from Hollywood norms related to the intertitles have already been noted. Besides, there are also three clear cuts through the 180-degrees line. Like in many other Swedish films from the period, these cuts are used at nodal points in the narration – in this case foreboding the turning point in the film.

With its obvious roots both in literature and theatre – to which Ivan Hedqvist remains faithful in the slightest detail – *Downie* is, then, above all *cinema* from beginning to end. This is not only due to the images of nature or the larger space of action, which was noted already by the critics of the time, but as we have seen, above all because the whole story is narrated cinematically.

Bo Florin

REFERENCES

Eitner, L. (1955) 'The Open Window and the Storm-Tossed Boat: An Essay on the Iconography of Romanticism', *Art Bulletin*, 37, 281–90.

Nordhagen, P. J. (1992) 'Romantikkens ikonografi i Norden', in J. Weibull and P. J. Nordhagen (eds) *Natur och nationalitet*. Höganäs: Förlags AB Wiken.

Schmoll gen. Eisenwerth, J. A. (1970) 'Fensterbilder. Motivketten in der Europäischen Malerei', in L. Grote (ed.) *Beiträge zur Motivkunde des 19. Jahrhunderts*. München: Prestel-Verlag.

Svensk Filmografi Part 1 (1986) Uppsala: Almqvist & Wiksell.

Tsivian, Y. (1992) 'Portraits, Mirrors, Death: On Some Decadent Clichés in Early Russian Films', *Iris*, 14–15, 78.

KUN ISÄLLÄ ON HAMMASSÄRKY WHEN FATHER HAS TOOTHACHE

ERKKI KARU, FINLAND, 1923

Kun isällä on hammassärky (*When Father Has Toothache*) was shot in the winter of 1922, during the first highly creative period of its production company Suomi-Filmi. It was first screened in Pori, a smallish west-coast town in April 1922, but the 'official' Helsinki-opening took place a year-and-a-half later, after the release of three prestigous films by Suomi-Filmi in 1923. The first of these was *Koskenlaskijan morsian* (*The Logroller's Bride*), also directed by the president of the company Erkki Karu. The film was quite consciously modelled after Mauritz Stiller's *Sången om den eldröda blomman* (*The Song of the Scarlet Flower*, 1919) and *Johan* (1921), both of which had gained remarkable critical and popular success in Finland. The second feature was *Rautakylän vanha parooni* (*The Old Baron of Rautakylä*), a historical drama directed by Carl Fager, the set designer of Finnish National Theatre and one of the founding members of Suomi-Filmi. The third film, *Nummisuutarit* (*The Village Shoemakers*), also directed by Karu, was a rustic comedy based on the most famous play (1864) by the 'national author' Aleksis Kivi.

Since Suomi-Filmi openly declared that its main object was to produce films of high profile and national subject, a two-reel comedy like *When Father Has Toothache* might have looked like an oddity at the time. Correspondingly, according to the *Suomen Kansallisfilmografia* (*Finnish National Filmography*) the film was primarily a vehicle of experimentation for Erkki Karu. A short comedy such as this allowed the use of several tricks that would have been more difficult to integrate into a full-length drama.

However, *When Father Has Toothache* was more than a curiosity. It was also a part of a series of short comedies directed by Karu during the 1920s. He had made his directorial debut with two comedies shot in the summer of 1919 and released in 1920 by Suomen Biografi, a distributor and owner of a nationwide theatre chain that merged with Suomi-Filmi a decade later. Both of these films, *Ylioppilas Pöllövaaran kihlaus* (*Student Pöllövaara's Betrothal*), a one-reeler, and *Sotagulashi Kaiun häiritty kesäloma* (*War Profiteer Kaiku's Disrupted Summer Vacation*), a two-reeler, were in all likelihood strongly slapstick-influenced. Today, unfortunately both exist only in fragments.

Runoilija muuttaa (*The Poet Moves*, 1927), a two-reeler loosely based on Margaret Mayo's play *Baby Mine* (1910), was even announced to begin a series of short comedies by Suomi-Filmi. Although this series never actually continued, the plan indicates that Suomi-Filmi had an interest both in the short fiction format and in the urban comedy genre.

As a short comedy with a remarkable amount of physical acting and a tendency to foreground cinematic expression *When Father Has Toothache* does belong at the margins of Finnish film history. It seems most likely, though, that this 'marginality' has been constructed after the fact, mainly by critics who up to very recently have been eager to place the essential nature of Finnish cinema in realistic aesthetics, rural landscapes, verbal humour and restrained acting – that is, in films like the above-mentioned *The Logroller's Bride* and *The Village Shoemakers*.

When Father Has Toothache opens with Father, a considerably wealthy businessman, playing cards with his friends in a private restaurant room. Between games he phones his secretary, who assures that the staff are doing fine without the manager. In fact she is fixing her make-up while on the phone. Suddenly the card game is interrupted because one of Father's associates is suffering from a toothache. 'In a bad mood for a tiny bit of bone', complains father disappointedly and leaves for home.

While preparing dinner Mother also starts suffering from a toothache. Father once again mocks, 'In a bad mood for a tiny bit of bone.' Mother goes to a dentist and immediately feels better. Father takes a nap, only to wake up with a horrible toothache. After rolling on the couch, jumping on the floor and biting his own knee he suddenly gets an idea: he opens his safe, gets out a huge bottle of liqueur and almost downs it in one. For a short moment he feels better, but soon the pain comes back. 'In a bad mood for a tiny bit of bone', says his son who recommends a dentist. Afraid of all doctors, Father starts to hallucinate. He sees a devil-shaped dentist who uses a giant hammer for anaesthesia and an equally giant chisel and tongs for dentistry.

When Father starts speaking of his last will, Mother calls the dentist and asks her to pay a visit dressed up as a nurse. Upon her arrival, the dentist/nurse hides her tongs from Father, suddenly pulling out the aching tooth. After his miraculous recovery Father dances with joy and, suddenly becoming serious, solemnly declares to his son, 'Son, there's no need to be in a bad mood for a tiny bit of bone.'

The relationship between narrative and gags in the film is somewhat ambiguous. Some of the gags (Father jumping on the floor or emptying the huge bottle) can be seen as self-enclosed narratives, while at the same time they have a function in the overall narrative. The jumping expresses the growing pain in Father's tooth; drinking is an attempt to solve his problem, as well as an explanation for the hallucination that follows. There are, however, also several gags that have no connection whatsoever to the development of narrative. For example, on her way to the dentist Mother sees her son fighting with another kid on the street and separates them, but as soon as she turns her back, the boys are fighting again. And again, while the dentist is on the phone, a male patient of hers decides not to wait for the cure ('No need to pull teeth when there's medicine'): he drinks the alcohol meant for disinfection and leaves without saying a word.

These examples represent comic events that, certainly, take place along the narrative but provide no information necessary for understanding the story. Then again, in spite of such loose ends, the overall structure of the film is tight, which is reflected in the systematically repeated use of the phrase 'in a bad mood for a tiny bit of bone'. The phrase is first uttered by Father who is mocking his friend and his wife for not coping with pain. Second, it is used by the narrator who ironically refers to Father; third, by the son making fun of his father, and fourth, by Father again, this time, however, being mocked at by the implied author.

Thus, *When Father Has Toothache* features elements of well-made comedy as well as those of slapstick. It has a tense narrative structure, and it provides the spectator with sufficient knowledge to comprehend the cause/effect relations between events. It does, however, also display elements of excess. In addition to the above-mentioned narratively independent gags, it is possible to find several cinematic tricks that have a fairly arbitrary relation to the narrative. First, when Father leaves the restaurant there is a close-up shot of his galoshes, which he presumably forgets to put on. Suddenly, images of his wife and his mate pop up as double exposures in the galoshes, an image not marked as a point-of-view shot. Second, when Father is suffering from toothache, we see him not only jumping wildly and standing on his head, but actually climbing up the wall in a trick shot echoing the 'cinema of attractions' era. Third, we see Father almost emptying a bottle of about ten litres literally at one draught. Fourth, Father's hallucination of the devil practising dentistry is not clearly marked as taking place in a separate space. It begins as a typical 'vision scene': we see a double exposure of the horrified Father hallucinating on the left and of the devil fixing Father's teeth on the right. However, when the devil hits him on the head with a hammer, there is a 'match cut' to a straight shot of Father falling off the couch, implying that the hallucination actually affected Father's physical being.

All of these tricks take place in scenes that are quite clearly integrated in the narrative. Yet, even if these scenes do serve narrative purposes, the tricks as such stretch the limits of plausibility in an otherwise verisimilar and recognisable narrative environment. Only the fourth example, the hallucination, is at least partly marked as Father's subjective experience, whereas the others represent tricks for trick's sake – they are absurd little details meant for our eyes only. None of the tricks, then, is necessary to the comprehension of the narrative, which becomes clear when we take a look at the original script for *When Father Has Toothache*.

The script does include a close-up of the galoshes and a remark that Father forgets to put them on (shot 11 in the script), but no indication of a trick. The script does state that Father is trying to climb up the wall in his pain, but 'doesn't succeed' (shot 21). Also according to the script, Father does keep alcohol in his safe, but not in one huge bottle but several small ones (shot 25). Further, the script does indicate that Father really thinks he sees the devil by his side (shot 31), but he falls of the couch out of fear, not because of continuity between the hallucination and what is actually happening to his body.

Such differences between the script and the finished film suggest that on one level *When Father Has Toothache* indeed served as a means of experimentation for Suomi-Filmi. The film follows the script rather closely – considering that it is not an actual shooting script. But whereas the comic situations in the script are based primarily on transgressions of socio-cultural expectations (the head of the household being laughed at by women, children and servants; massive amounts of alcohol being drunk despite the prohibition prevailing at the time, and so on), the final film puts more emphasis on aesthetic transgressions that are not necessary for narrative comprehension.

This, however, does not mean that these experimentations, more or less invented through improvisations while shooting the film, should be seen as something entirely exceptional in Finnish cinema. Not only did the short comedy format have some permanence, and not only did these kinds of cinematic tricks come up in comedies of later decades, but at times mainstream narrative films also involved a certain amount of formal experimentation. In *The Village Shoemakers*, for example, there is a famous scene shot from a tree-top, where the camera rotates wildly around its axis. To be sure, this device is narratively motivated: the protagonist Esko is drunk for the first time in his life and thinks he is a bird. However, the mere fact that this scene is frequently singled out in Finnish film histories (popular as well as academic) indicates that while being integrated in the narrative the device also served as, and was conceived as, an independent *tour de force*.

In spite of its tense structure – and in a sense also because of that – *When Father Has Toothache* comes closer to 'low' farce than to a legitimate comedy like *The Village Shoemakers* with its coherent and developing characters. It is estimated that in addition to the hundered or so permanent stages there were approximately four thousand amateur theatres in Finland during the interwar years. Hundreds of plays were published for the use of these amateur stages. Most of such plays, whether aimed at bourgeois stages, workers' stages or both, were either short comedies, melodramas or morality plays, none of them longer than one or two acts. A typical evening's entertainment consisted namely of a variety of short performances. A manual for amateur theatres from 1930 recommended a composition of drama, comedy (staged after the drama), dance, magic tricks, comic orchestra, and so on. Another manual from 1932 indicated growing suspicion about the variety form, especially if it involved a full drama whose acts were separated from each other by dance, lectures, and such things. In order to show respect to the inner structure of the play and to intensify the audience's experience, amateur theatres were encouraged to keep to short, one- or two-act plays. Such pieces of theatre – very much like *When Father Has Toothache* – valued the unity of time, place and action but paid less attention to character psychology.

With regard to acting, *When Father Has Toothache* relates more closely to amateur stages than professional theatre. Both contemporary witnesses and theatre histories have characterised the 1910s and 1920s as a period of transition in Finnish acting styles. Playwright Arvi Kivimaa – later the head of Finnish National Theatre – wrote in 1932 that this transition had involved a gradual and sometimes hardly noticeable move from the grandiose and mannierist style of the first generation of actors at the Theatre to an intensive style that was more intimate and economical in expression.

In 1923 playwright Lauri Haarla – an advocate of expressionist theatre at the time – complained that the National Theatre was burdened with an unbalanced mixture of three different generations of actors: the first generation that was historically important and professionally admirable but that had remained stuck in the by-gone tradition; the in-between generation who benefited neither from the virtues of the old school nor the new one; and the young generation of creative and innovative actors. The main problem, according to Haarla, was in matching these different 'schools' with each other. However talented the individual actors in each group, creating ensemble acting seemed like an impossible task.

The transition was partly due to the growing influence of Stanislavskian realism in Finland. The major spokesman of the new theatre philosophy was Eino Kalima, who had become impressed by the Moscow Art Theatre while studying in Russia between 1904–8. 'They don't act here any more, they live', he summarised his experience. After being appointed as the artistic manager of the National Theatre in 1917 he began to apply Stanislavskian methods systematically – although not necessarily under that name, as anything coming from Russia was a potential subject of controversy after Finland gained independence in 1917.

The transition to Stanislavskian-influenced realism – from externality to internality, from staginess to intimacy, from theatre-reality to psychology – was anything but absolute. Rather, realist tendencies were constantly rivalled by theatricalist, stylised and, at least to a certain point, anti-illusionist movements, especially expressionism, which gained remarkable success in the 1920s. This rivalry, however, concerned mainly professional stages: the emphasis in the manuals for amateur stages was on realist, 'invisible acting', on 'living the role', and against grandiloquence and mimic exaggeration. One could, of course, assume that the real circumstances on amateur stages did not always fulfil the ideals implied in the manuals – why else bother to warn against undesirable practices?

However, if amateur performers did indeed show signs of stylisation and visibly self-conscious acting, the background was more complicated than that. Without doubt, it had something to do with modernist anti-illusionist movements. It also related to the influential grand acting style of the 'first generation' National Theatre performers. However, in addition to these there did exist a third and more immediate background: that of popular showmanship. If amateur plays were often part of a variety show, it is plausible to assume that amateur acting bore some resemblance to performance in the other variety acts like dance, lecture or magic tricks. At least the contact between performers and audience members was more intimate than in professional theatre, which relied on a certain distance, both literal and figurative, between stage and auditorium. Even much later, long after turning professional, the most popular performers on workers' stages might be accused of hunting for loose applause – that is, breaking the theatre illusion in order to get in direct contact with the audience.

Ideals of acting, of course, differed somewhat according to genre. Comedies traditionally included moments of direct contact with the audience, remarks and glances aside, and so on – although some of the manuals recommended revising old plays in order to minimise these 'unnatural' features. However, Finnish actors, whether amateur or professional, whether performing in drama or comedy, were expected to show temperance. Kivimaa echoed common sentiments among those commentating on theatre when he wrote in the early 1930s that Finnish theatre was poor in top comedians but rich in humourists. Kivimaa's analysis was both descriptive and prescriptive, since it was based on a firm belief that different national characteristics gave rise to different kinds of acting. Compared with the profound (if pathetic) German, the sophisticated (if superficial) French and the emotional (if socially unstable) Russian actors,

Kivimaa saw Finnish stages, by now, filled with externally spare but internally vigorous and trustworthy performers. Thus, restrained acting should be the forte of Finnish stages. An ideal actor was to go through an effective physical training, but not in order to use his or her body in an overdramatic manner, but rather to be able to control it perfectly.

How does this ideal correspond with acting in *When Father Has Toothache*? Not very well, if we consider the main protagonist, Father, played by Aku Käyhkö. Käyhkö was an artistic manager of several remarkable theatres in the 1920s and 1930s, as well as a renowned stage actor of dramatic roles. He celebrated his twentieth anniversary on stage as the leading character in August Strindberg's *The Thunderstorm* and his thirtieth anniversary in Henrik Ibsen's *The Master Builder*. But he was also capable and willing to play minor comic parts and, what is more important, he had in the beginning of his acting career studied modern dance in Moscow and was still in the 1920s involved in dance education.

Käyhkö's performance in *When Father Has Toothache* is, indeed, often closer to dancing than dramatic acting in a traditional sense. Even more accurately, to quote James Agee's classic essay on early comedy, he combines 'several of the more difficult accomplishments of the acrobat, the dancer, the clown and the mime'. His very gestures and facial expressions are as exaggerated as the size of the devil's dentistical tools and the bottle in the safe. When Father gets an idea, he raises his arm with one finger pointed in the air, and when he wakes up in toothache, he puts his hands on his cheeks and furiously shakes his head. And finally, when he is in full pain, his gestures and movements go well beyond conventional expression: he starts to dance, jump up and down, bounce his head on the bed, roll on the floor, climb up the wall and finally, frightened of the devil, he rushes under the bed. Thus, Käyhkö's performance is quite antithetical to the Stanislavskian ideals of internalised, invisible acting, and this exaggeration is further emphasised, since the other performances, especially that of Naimi Kari as Mother, are relatively temperate.

While such bipolarity – a radical mixture of different acting styles – is by no means exceptional in comedian comedy in general, it can be seen as typical of Finnish films of all genres in the 1920s – and to a certain extent also beyond that period. In *The Logroller's Bride*, for example, a combination of what Roberta Pearson calls histrionic and verisimilar performance codes is highly visible. Thus for instance, as Konrad Tallroth as a father who has lost his son expresses his pain subtly, mainly by pointing his eyes downwards, Jaakko Korhonen in a similar situation – finding his son in danger – tears his hair, jumps up in the air and puffs his chest towards men who are undecided whether to help or not.

Critics of later periods, irritated by the coexistence of different performance styles in films, have sought an explanation either in the theatrical background of many actors and directors – in the use of amateur and professional actors side by side – or in the sheer incompetence of film directors. Moreover, since verisimilar acting has generally been preferred to more stylised kinds of performance, the fact that *When Father Has Toothache* has a relatively recognised status in Finnish film history seems somewhat peculiar. This status, as suggested earlier, is based on an understanding of the film as an exception rather than as a part of a tradition.

Writing in 1936 Roland af Hällström characterised the positive qualities of Erkki Karu's films as simplicity, clarity, vernacularity and carefulness – qualities that found best expression in stories of the countryside and the seashore. However, continued af Hällström, great men tend to have their little weaknesses, and Karu's was having a certain penchant for the cultural circles of Helsinki. This would occasionally lead him to show bad judgement in trying to mingle with subjects of excessive 'literary' or 'aesthetic' quality. Karu's misjudgement, according to af Hällström, culminated in *Suvinen satu* (*Summery Fairytale*, 1925), a 'continental style' drawing-room comedy that took place in salons, mansions and ballrooms.

Af Hällström's tendency to dismiss most efforts of Finnish cinema to deal with urban or 'continental' subjects has been echoed by countless commentators ever since. Yet while it is true, as Tytti Soila notes in her account of Finnish film history, that in the 1920s Suomi-Filmi's founders invested 'in the old well-known popular rural melodramas they had played during their tours around the country', they also invested in other kinds of films, and much for the same reason: beside the fact that Finnish screens were filled with European and American sophisticated comedies and urban melodramas, drawing-room stories had proved every bit as popular on stage as rural melodramas. Sven Hildén, for example, the leading man in *Summery Fairytale*, was an extremely popular stage actor who specialised in operettas and salon plays.

Thus, *When Father Has Toothache* need not be seen quite as exceptional as commentators since af Hällström have claimed. As a short comedy it had both predecessors and followers; as a comedian comedy it was succeeded by, for example, the *Lapatossu* films in the 1930s and 1940s, the *Pekka Puupää* films in the 1950s and the *Uuno Turhapuro* series that was launched in the early 1970s. As a trick film that foregrounds non-realistic cinematic experimentation it was connected not only to the comedian comedy tradition but also to certain films closer to classical narration like *The Village Shoemakers*; as a mixture of realist and stylised acting it might have been an extreme case, but by no means was it an exception; finally, with its urban setting *When Father Has Toothache* came much closer to the mainstream of Finnish cinema than several generations of commentators have been willing to admit.

A typical view has it that it was not until the 1960s that cityscape became a 'natural' setting of Finnish films. Before the New Wave era, it is claimed, cities (mainly Helsinki) served primarily as a false front for depicting the social life of the (in reality practically non-existent) upper classes in comedies, or as a depraved point of comparison in melodramas aimed at celebrating the traditional non-urban ways of life. True, a handful of melodramas built around the opposition of country and city were made, especially in the 1940s and 1950s. However, for every such melodrama there is a comedy, a romance or a social problem film that takes place in a city or a town and that does not tie the urban setting to any particular value system. In the 1910s urban themes clearly dominated Finnish production, and during the following decades countless films depicted modern city life – not to mention those that took place in the country but that were laden with modern commodities and mentalities. For some reason these films just do not seem to count in film histories.

Sometimes this is due to critical evaluation. Antti Alanen, for example, does admit that statistically, 'if non-fiction shorts are included, urban milieux dominated Finnish cinema from the earliest days'. The most enduring films, however, were, according to Alanen, stories of countryside and sea, while urban silents were 'poor cousins to the international models they copied'. Often the matter is more complicated than this. Film critics, historians and sociologists alike have tended to associate films with twentieth-century anti-urbanist tendencies. On the one hand, films are used for evidence of the thinness and novelty of urban identities in Finland; on the other, appropriate films are selected and interpreted according to the belief that the core of Finnish mentality lies in traditional rural life. Thus, we are in a vicious circle.

The problem with this view is not only that it relies on uncritical reinforcement of mythologies of national character, nor that it turns a blind eye to films that are in discord with the view maintained. It is also based on a limited conception of film as historical evidence. Without doubt, certain films made in the studio era, between the early 1920s and the early 1960s, were apparent manifestos of antiurbanism, while certain other films were manifestos of the opposite tendency. Most films, however, were neither, at least not in an obvious way. The point is that as long as we tend to interpret films as mirroring apparently pre-existing mentalities, we fail to see the active if sometimes contradictory role they are capable of taking in both current and on-going problems. To be sure, urbanism and internationalism were topical problems in 1920s Finland. Consequently it is all the more important to see *When Father Has Toothache* with its unproblematic relation to international film trends, cinematic experimentation, theatricalist acting and popular theatre forms, not as an exception but rather as a part of several intertwining traditions.

Kimmo Laine

REFERENCES

Agee, J. (1979) 'Comedy's Greatest Era', in G. Mast and M. Cohen (eds) *Film Theory and Criticism: Introductory Readings*, second edition. New York and Oxford: Oxford University Press.

Alanen, A. (1999) 'Born Under the Sign of the Scarlet Flower: Pantheism in Finnish Silent Cinema', in J. Fullerton and J. Olsson (eds) *Nordic Explorations: Film Before 1930*. Sydney: John Libbey & Aura.

Haarla, L (1923–24) 'Näyttelijäkunta ja Kansallisteatteri', *Näyttämö*, 16.

Hällström, R. af (1936) *Filmi – aikamme kuva. Filmin historia, olemusta ja tehtävia*. Jyväskylä and Helsinki: Gummerus.

Kalima, E. (1962) *Sattumaa ja johdatusta. Muistelmia*. Porvoo and Helsinki: Werner Söderström OY.

Kivimaa, A. (1937) *Teatterivaeltaja. Kirjoista, kirjailijoista ja näyttämön taiteesta*. Porvoo and Helsinki: Werner Söderström OY.

Soila, T., A. Söderbergh Widding and G. Iversen (1998) *Nordic National Cinemas*. London and New York: Routledge.

Suomen kansallisfilmografia (1996) K. Uusitalo, S. Toiviainen, J. Junttila, R. Kautto, M. Kejonen, L. Tykkyläinen, K. Vase, M. Marttila. Helsinki: Edita and SEA.

MED FULD MUSIK WITH PIPES AND DRUMS

LAU LAURITZEN, DENMARK, 1933

Sound film effectively meant the loss of international sales for the Danish film industry, and the economy had to rely on around three and a half million Danes in 1930, the year of the first sound film. The best way to secure an audience was to produce comedies, but the comic matrices required a significant redefinition. Sound in its very form *and* different strategies of utilising it in connection with pictures and visual effects became the *alpha omega* of the first years after the transition. Partly because of the Danish dialogue, the films moved in the direction of folk comedy, which saw the comic impulse deriving primarily from *nationally* determined characters, often older or more rural. The introduction of musical stars and strategies from popular revue along with the factors mentioned above changed the sound, look and sensibility of Danish comedy. What evolved was the musical comedy, the dominant film genre in 1930s Denmark.

Radical contemporaries and later critics have dismissed the musical comedies of the 1930s as pure escapism, making it practically unacceptable for generations of film students to acknowledge anything else but depression and its negation in the entertainment of that decade. Few works from this period are tolerated – usually for their use of a natural scenery and anthropological interest – such as *Lajla* (1937) by George Schnéevoigt – or for experimental style and supposedly radical views, such as the revered documentary *Danmark* (1935) by Poul Henningsen.

The critics wanted the medium to be a barometer for social and cultural change in depression-laden Denmark. In fact, we may argue that they got what they were asking for. The only problem was that the musical comedy had a strange way of delivering this. Comedies set up mirrors to the world, but while they magnify certain things for us, they can camouflage and distort. From twisted mirror images an analyst may extract wisdom, demonstrate alternative modes of address or uncover subversive radicalism. However, when holding it back up to the mirror, the film may seem nothing but silliness, and seemingly rendering the findings null and void.

Director Lau Lauritzen was not especially concerned with film style, which was often noted, when Fyrtårnet and Bivognen's films were compared to the snappier flicks of Laurel and Hardy, Keaton, Lloyd and Chaplin. The sophistication of *Med fuld musik* (*With Pipes and Drums*, 1933) in terms of both style and its comic strategies should at least be partly credited to Alice O'Fredericks, collaborating with Lauritzen since 1927, and his son Lau Lauritzen Jnr who joined in 1930. O'Fredericks and Lau Jnr went on to make some of the most popular comedies of the decade such as *Kidnapped* (1935) and *Snushanerne* (1936).

With Pipes and Drums is a wonderful example of a musical comedy replete with common stereotypes. It had savvy and sophistication, partly because it was borne out of circumstances where filmmakers were forced to think creatively and come up with new ways to exploit comedy's potential. However, more than simply a sign of its time, the film is a fine example of how comedy could be both extremely intricate and yet quite simple.

The artist colony Seventh Heaven in the centre of Copenhagen and a music publisher's villa in the posh suburbs are the main locations of *With Pipes and Drums*. During the film, the two milieus meet, clash, and merge romantically, professionally, socially and above all, musically. The lyrical high point of *With Pipes and Drums* is the rendition of the sentimental 'The Wishing Song' performed by the inhabitants of Seventh Heaven. It is a spontaneous group effort, where the inhabitants are allowed a couple of lines each about the joys and hardships of bohemian life. During the chorus, which states, 'If you only wait, happiness will come around', the group sings directly to the camera. The direct mode of address, supported by the spontaneous nature of the song, overtly addresses the spectator with its intimacy.

This sudden intimacy, however, has surely not been experienced as a breach of contract with the audience. There are many similar instances in Danish comedies of the 1930s. It is more a matter of understanding the films as a goldmine of stylistic approaches and modes of address. The films are quantitatively dominated by a classical film style that is characterised by a discrete mode of address and an unobtrusive style, but several scenes and segments throw discretion to the wind. The audience that demanded films such as *With Pipes and Drums* was prepared to change viewing positions often during a film. 'The Wishing Song' invites the film audience to assimilate a position, known from revue, where manifest audience response and participation is essential to the performance. It is not implausible that the melodious choruses have welcomed community singing.

The film's formidable odd couple consists of the tall, melancholy Fyrtårnet and short, uncouth yet well-meaning Bivognen, played by Carl Schenstrøm and Harald Madsen, respectively. Lauritzen had created and developed this hugely successful couple, first seen in *De keder sig paa landet* (1919). The two friends Fyrtårnet and Bivognen had the ability to simultaneously incarnate a striking vision of human nature and of being plainly ridiculous. Their films sparkled with a melancholy madness that derived from the confrontation of the two fictional milieus.

By 1933 the star couple had an impressive career behind them, which would continue into the 1940s. Drawing on their international successes they made films around Europe during the 1930s and 1940s (going by names such as Pat und Patachon, Long and Short, and Helan and Halvan). However, in *With Pipes and Drums* Bivognen is played by popular comedian Hans W. Petersen, due to Harald Madsen's illness, which makes some connoisseurs disregard the film. The two play bohemian tramps who involve themselves in plots that put them in frequently destructive contact with their surroundings. As they are never conscious of consequences and planning; it is as much to the surprise of them as it is to the spectator when they finally make a career move from bohemians to businessmen.

Seventh Heaven, situated in the attic of an apartment building in a working-class neighbourhood, is home to an array of artists, bohemians and outcasts. Among these are Fyrtårnet and Bivognen, who are earning a living by cooking for the colony. Other prominent inhabitants are the jovial and rotund sculptor (Christian Møllback), the equally hefty and jovial authoress (Olga Svendsen) and the eccentric, hearing-impaired poet (Christian Arhoff).

The whole crowd is lovable and charming: the characters are easily recognised as stereotypes with a broad comic delineation, partly due to an emphasis on outer appearance – size, poise, costume and acting style. The dwelling upon recognisable characters in a predictable, if exotic, milieu lends the description of Seventh Heaven a sense of hominess.

The second important location in the film is, as mentioned, that of the music publisher's home. He resides in an upper-class villa, the social antithesis to Seventh Heaven. His household is comprised of an eligible son who collects birdcages, seemingly without any good reason, two teenage children obsessed with jazz, a butler and a musical cook (played by Victor Cornelius, the film's composer).

Both worlds are inhabited by groups of characters that live in a family way, but differ completely from a normal conception of family. Obviously, there are no blood relations in Seventh Heaven, but the inhabitants assemble to eat, enjoy themselves, and console and protect each other. The publisher's family is characterised by a surprising power structure, seeing the father treated as a plaything by his children, or the cook mingling with his employers.

Over the first 25 minutes, the film paints a portrait of Seventh Heaven's bohemian paradise and the screwball upper-class home, with little story emerging from the material. Situations with a narrative potential such as the accidental dropping of objects on the downstairs neighbour of Fyrtårnet and Bivognen, their coffee-making extravaganza, or the scat performance by the cook and the children, never evolve to anything but isolated incidents or sketches. Nor are any of the characters presented as bearers of any salient conflict. Therefore the parallel between the family groups and their worlds must be said to constitute a major structural cue, which is emphasised musically throughout the film. One may well argue that this parallel strategy is a discrete method of organisation, since it is determined by milieu rather than character. Hence, the emotional potential only gradually becomes evident and its full potential is not realised until the very end of the film.

Several theorists have worked with the notion of *duality* as the structuring principle of the musical comedy. These works, including Rick Altman's highly influential *The American Film Musical*, agree that the prime denominator and the point of departure for such a structure is the man and woman that constitute the romantic couple. *With Pipes and Drums* is hereby seen alongside a majority of Danish musical comedies from the 1930s that have often been termed romantic comedies due to a mandatory presence of such lovers who form unions across class barriers.

An important reason of this misconception – for it certainly is a misconception – is the fact that character traits are confused with an overall narrative structure. Identifying lovers such as the young couple in *With Pipes and Drums* implies identifying a certain behavioural/ narrative potential embedded within them, the single most important being an inherent need for a romantic partner. Neither the potential nor the fulfilment of it should necessarily be confused with a predominant structuring principle or even a dominant element in these films. The limited screen time combined with the stereotypicality and predictability of the young lovers gives the audience a clear sense that they are not the main focus of the film. This is not to say that Aase, the shop-girl from Seventh Heaven and Poul, the birdcage-collecting publisher's son, cannot be enjoyed for their charm, vulnerability and coming together in the pet store 25 minutes into the film, when they declare their affection for each other singing 'For one alone my heart is beating'.

The romantic union in the pet store is a predictable one. They are fated to be together, but it lies within character and is not necessarily of overarching importance to the film's structure. The love-making of Aase and Poul is more akin to a motive, one instance of class merging that will be repeated and varied throughout the film.

The juxtaposed milieus – the artist colony and the bourgeois home – are mirrored musically, setting the scene for the eventual reconciliation between the two. When it happens, a series of elements turns out to motivate and support the dual focus of the settings: the physical parallelism between large and skinny characters in the households; the acceptance of the lovers' song by both worlds; the musicality and nature of that musicality of the respective households; and the inclusive familiarity of both of them.

The scat number performed by the publisher's cook and children and 'The Wishing Song' serve to demonstrate parallelism in terms of the respective musicality of the households. They are very different numbers, but both are clearly group efforts with spontaneity and inventiveness playing a major role. The title number 'Her er vi med fuld musik' ('Here we come with pipes and drums') manifestly demonstrates music's potential as a barrier breaker.

Fyrtårnet and Bivognen compose and perform the number for the inhabitants of Seventh Heaven. Later, when the newly betrothed Aase tentatively presents her not-so-well-off friends to the publisher, they all make a musical entrance. The song impresses the publisher, who finally invites Fyrtårnet and Bivognen into his house and makes a deal with them in order to buy their song. In the last scene the odd couple attend the Royal Guard's marching band, as they did in the film's opening scene with the exception that now they are sat, all dressed up, in a fancy car enjoying the guards' rendition of their composition.

The meagre love plot between Aase and Poul is supported by a number of musical refrains. Firstly, the love song, 'For one alone my heart is beating', is performed by the lovers in the pet store where Aase works. Later, a fragment of the song is heard during the musical soirée in Seventh Heaven, where its loveliness is commented upon. Also, during the party scene in the publisher's home, the song is played by the cook.

That fact that the song is heard twice after its original performance, and in both Aase's and Poul's homes, signals an acceptance of the union by all, which lends it an ambience of security and predictability. Importantly, it also demonstrates the affinity of the two social groups.

Soonafter, however, it is revealed that Aase has a shadowy past. The spectator's perception of her as the nicest of the pretty girls in Seventh Heaven is undermined. The sudden presence of a baby unwanted by the orphanage, a coarse and threatening boxer and a shady magician who wants the baby for his magic tricks, obviously delineates a serious predicament, both in terms of the innocent child's well-being and Aase's ability to fulfil her potential for romance with Poul.

The film restricts the viewers' information, finding out less than those involved in the drama. It turns out that the child belonged to Aase's deceased sister. For close to 40 minutes it seems plausible that the child is in fact hers, born out of wedlock, and that the boxer is the father and, hence, her estranged lover. The complication of a hitherto accepted, positive stereotype and the withheld information about her is used to generate interest and emotional investment in Aase's character.

With Pipes and Drums includes a host of character types, whose behavioural patterns are more oriented towards localised action. This goes for the teenage brother/sister couple, the cook, the butler and the inhabitants of Seventh Heaven. Outstanding in this respect is the celebrated odd couple of Fyrtårnet and Bivognen. They were the film's most important attraction and beyond any doubt the main focus for the film's audience.

However, if we make the plot our starting point for analysis of their film we will be hard-pressed to demonstrate the significance of Fyrtårnet and Bivognen, since on the whole it seems that they are simply not important to it. In various synopses of their films, Fyrtårnet and Bivognen are described as unsuccessful helpers of a central character, who is entangled in some kind of intrigue or problem. This is certainly the case in *With Pipes and Drums*, where their every dealing with the villains – trying to protect Aase, the child and themselves – is unsuccessful and ultimately of no consequence to the plot. In terms of narration their actions amount to little more than playful obstruction or distraction. The same goes for some of the other notable comical characters, the Fyrtårnet and Bivognen regular Olga Svendsen and newcomer Christian Arhoff, whose dynamic presences dominate scenes but whose implication in the narrative is of minimal importance.

The character-centred plot involving Aase and the baby certainly has a dramatic, exciting and moving potential. However, the potential is more often than not sidetracked as Fyrtårnet and Bivognen take centre-stage and render her story a backdrop, which primarily functions to complement and highlight Fyrtårnet and Bivognen's comedy of incompetence. Especially close to climactic scenes such as the assault on the baby-snatching magician or the confrontation at the police station, their actions most clearly represent a potential disruption of the story.

Being ridiculous in a very sweet way the odd couple often entangles the spectator emotionally to the point of distorting the investing of feelings connected to the plot. A typical and glorious example is the scene where Aase, Fyrtårnet and Bivognen are delivering animals to the publisher's home and Aase is spontaneously invited to a youth party. The teenage daughter promises to lend Aase a dress and pleads with her: 'If you don't come, we'll be thirteen at the table.' Aase reluctantly agrees. Then with all the shy charm he can mount, Fyrtårnet tries: 'If you don't want to be fourteen around the table, I'd love to come', responds Bivognen, 'and I'd gladly join if you don't want to be fifteen', both inventive yet unsuccessful follow-ups.

These last exchanges last only a few seconds, but successfully shift the emotional focus. From our being excited about the lovebirds meeting, the film asks us to laugh at Fyrtårnet and Bivognen's misconstrued logic regarding the nature of unlucky numbers and feel a twitch of pain at their being turned down when they try so hard.

Also, the film style that contextualises the physical behaviour of Fyrtårnet and Bivognen represent a threat to the film's coherence. The animal delivery that follows indulges in the mayhem caused by escaping pets and Fyrtårnet and Bivognen's unsuccessful attempt to catch them. This nearly ruins the dinner party and effectively complicates the lovers' union. The chase and its effects on the dinner party are tied to each other by means of cross-cutting.

Interestingly, however, the segment is made up of two different representational modes. The upset dinner party is represented by a realistic speed and not accompanied by music. However, the chaotic animal chase accelerates into fast motion, emphasised by the acceleration of the music. In an earlier scene, too, Fyrtårnet and Bivognen's unorthodox coffee-making reaches lyrical dimensions when subjected to a variation of film speed and underscored by noticeable music and obvious sound effects. These examples demonstrate how the film uses the interaction of different modes to create suppleness.

Moreover, the scenes show how the film is inclined to play with Fyrtårnet and Bivognen's potential for stylisation. Heather Laing's thoughts on how musical performers become powerful when they connect with the non-diegetic level in the film seems very applicable here. Notable, especially in the coffee-making scene, is a sense of the powerful characters who are in control of every aspect of the performance, underlined by the brief acknowledgement of the audience by Bivognen. This makes us regard Fyrtårnet and Bivognen close or equal to the organising system of the text. The other scene is completely different. Trying in vain to catch the animals, the two are not at all in control diegetically speaking, which makes their physical behaviour a helpless predicament rather than a dominant prank.

It becomes evident that Fyrtårnet and Bivognen are successfully competing for the spectator's attention at the expense of other characters, plot lines or principles of structure. They sometimes mirror the actions of the 'straight' characters, achieving the same success and happiness, but in weird and unpredictable ways. Their mere presence in a context may function as the sweetest sabotage, seeing the audience emotionally distracted and torn away from stories, morals and principles of structure. Without the security of an emotional and rational focus, the spectator is offered several arbitrary motives to give us a sense of recognition and structure throughout the film.

The use of motives gives the audience discrete markers of a determining principle in the film based on a limited number of recognisable elements. When a motive is connected to an overarching structure it is symbolic or indexical of that structure, such as the different stylistic elements or the musical parallelism that cue us to recognise the milieu duality. These motives, however, are constantly threatened by the film's comic strategies.

Arbitrary motives, on the other hand, represent a structuring principle in and of themselves. An example in this film is the bad hearing primarily connected to the poet, who constantly misinterprets what he hears, effectively jeopardising significant information that is relevant to a plot or structure.

The motive is also used separately from the poet, when Bivognen tries to communicate to Poul that Aase is not the mother of the baby. Standing outside his house yelling to him, Bivognen is unable to convey his message to Poul, who keeps replying: 'What?' Onlookers gather around, and after a while the whole crowd is yelling to Poul.

Niels Henrik Hartvigson

REFERENCES

Altman, R. (1987) *The American Film Musical*. Bloomington: Indiana University Press.

Laing, H. (2000) 'Emotion by numbers: Music, song and musical', in B. Marshall and R. Stilwell (eds) *Musicals: Hollywood and Beyond*. Exeter: Intellect Books.

EN KVINNAS ANSKITE A WOMAN'S FACE

GUSTAF MOLANDER, SWEDEN, 1938

When Gustaf Molander set forth with the production of *En kvinnas ansikte* (*A Woman's Face*, 1938) at Råsunda studios on the outskirts of Stockholm, he was determined for a success. The film was to be one of the serious attempts by Svensk Filmindustri – Sweden's largest film production company – to build a reputation as a producer of artistic 'quality films'. So Molander gathered his usual staff, including photographer Åke Dahlquist, scriptwriter Gösta Stevens and the well-known actors from the stable of the company: Eric Berglund, Anders Henriksson, Georg Rydeberg, Sigurd Wallén and Gösta Cederlund, Karin Kavli, Ingrid Bergman and Hilda Borgström.

Molander had started his career as a scriptwriter for Victor Sjöström and Mauritz Stiller and he was unquestionably the most successful and most productive of Svensk Filmindustri's directors during the 1930s and 1940s. He was a member of a theatre family – originally an actor himself – and his brother Olof was the head of the Royal Dramatic Theatre in Stockholm. This pervasive theatrical influence may have brought about a condensed melodramatic flavour in Molander's production: the mainstream style in theatres during this period was influenced by nineteenth-century French melodrama. As far as editing, *mise-en-scène* and narration were concerned, Hollywood set the standards for the well made film in Sweden as well. Not a surprise, then, that *A Woman's Face* would become one of the only two Swedish films which were to be re-made in Hollywood during the period – the other being *Intermezzo* (*Intermezzo – a Love Story*, 1936), also written and directed by Gustaf Molander and starring Ingrid Bergman.

Bergman wrote in her autobiography that she loved the role of Anna in *A Woman's Face*, and that she had to negotiate, beg and extort to get the part. The film company was hesitant about giving a role of a criminal woman with such a distorted face to a beautiful girl: the role of Anna deviated completely from the warm-hearted, healthy ingenues Bergman had played before. However, she promised to accept another part, as Eva in *En enda natt* (*Only One Night*, 1939) – a film she considered garbage – only if she was allowed to play Anna. So, the company finally relented.

The synopsis for *A Woman's Face* was taken from a 1932 French play, 'Il etait une fois' ('Once upon a time') written by Francois Croisset (alias Franz Wiener). The events in the original version take place in England and amongst the Scottish gentry, but in the Swedish (and the American) version, the story takes place in Stockholm and in the North of Sweden, providing the film with dramatic landscapes and thrilling sleigh-rides. The plot depicts a story of transformation. A group of gangsters manage to acquire a number of compromising love letters, written by a certain Vera Wegert (Karin Kavli), wife of a well-known surgeon. The leader of the gang, Anna Holm (Bergman) is provoked by Vera's beautiful looks and privileged position, when she contacts her in order to blackmail her. Anna herself has a scar that covers her left chin, embittering her life. She makes an appointment with Vera at the Wegert house to press her for more money. However, she is discovered by the doctor, who mistakes Anna for a burglar. In an attempt to escape she hurts her foot and, instead of calling the police, Wegert takes care of the injury. On detecting Anna's scarred face and desperate state of mind, he decides to perform plastic surgery on her.

Before visiting Vera, Anna and her gang has met with a certain Torsten Barring (Georg Rydeberg), a crooked nephew of an elderly mill owner, Consul Barring (Tore Svennberg), at the Forsa estate. Torsten is deep in debt, due to his extravagant life and wants someone at the estate to do away with the consul's five-year-old grandson, the sole heir of the Barring millions. Anna takes on finding a governess for the child, a woman ruthless enough to assist Torsten with whatever it might take to get rid of the child. When Anna's operation turns out to be successful, she takes the job as governess herself, concealing her real identity. However, a compulsory gesture that she has used to hide the scar with betrays her to Torsten.

At Forsa, where a certain engineer, Harald Berg (Gunnar Sjöberg), is a guest, Anna soon makes friends with everyone: Barring himself, his housekeeper Emma (Hilda Borgstrom) and the adorable little boy, Lars-Erik (Göran Bernhard). Harald starts courting Anna. The harmony is disturbed when Torsten, chased by his creditors, appears at Forsa. He lets Anna understand that he expects her to arrange an accident to kill the child. The next day, old Barring celebrates his birthday with a dinner and a sleigh ride, during which Lars-Erik is seated in Torsten's sleigh and Anna is allotted a place beside Harald. Torsten's horse is scared by fire and runs away. Anna, convinced of Torsten wanting to kill the child, urges Harald to follow the sleigh. In order to convince Harald she confesses to him the part she has played in Torsten's conspiracy.

Harald injures himself managing to save the boy, whereas Torsten gets drowned in a lake, along with his runaway horse. Harald is operated on, at Anna's recommendation, by Wegert. It is not just his body that has been injured, but also his confidence and love for Anna. She visits him in order to tell him that she has left her occupation at Forsa and to say farewell. Then, uncertain of her future, she confers with Wegert who offers her a trip to China, where his cousin's children need a nanny. As for himself, he is engaged with a Red Cross expedition after his now failed marriage. The film ends with the two aboard a ship on its way to the open sea.

The film begins by showing transgressions conducted by the two women. The initial scene reveals Vera's infidelity. Following this, we see Anna's offence against the law, through her criminal plans. In fact, Molander's film is itself a sort of a 'trespassing' against the prevalent order of mainstream cinema, in that it opens up a female discourse to dispute its dominant (patriarchal) discourse. However, rather than being a straightforward story about life and development of a headstrong woman, the film displays a struggle between the two discourses: one represented by the male gaze which nails Anna on the spot as its object, while the second(ary) discourse develops in two directions: on one hand, the narrative trajectory moves into Anna's past revealing her innermost motives, her (hi)story; on the other, the story depicts her personal, 'therapeutic' development. As the unveiling of the past occurs hand in hand with the film's forward movement, the latter is illustrated in a series of scenes where mirrors play a significant role.

In this film, then, the large and distorting scar on Anna's left cheek becomes a sign in which a number of meanings are condensed. It betrays the personal history of its carrier, or rather, it indicates that she has a story: that the woman is not just there to be looked at, as is the case in the mainstream films of the period. Conversely of course, the scar can be understood as a metaphor, as a burn mark of the patriarchal discourse that points out a female character it disapproves of. Anna's personality reinforces this ambivalence. She is intelligent, indifferent and calculating. She has an explicit wish to become rich; she has no family and she makes for a tough boss of her gang. In fact, on account of these characteristics she is competing with man.

The male gaze in *A Woman's Face* is depicted in an excellent and painstaking manner. Molander's notes in his script folder witness the fact that he planned the shooting carefully and ordered a considerable amount of takes. Shots of Anna are so arranged that throughout the scene the spectator is prevented from seeing her complete face. The image is either framed in a way that excludes the operated cheek, or it is composed so as to hide the scar by a lamp, mirror or Wegert's head. These images on trouble faced Anna are cross-cut with close-ups on the exploring eyes of Wegert himself. Next to the doctor's head is a lamp which he frequently directs towards his patient, a gesture that underlines the fact that he has the light – so necessary to looking – in his control, too. The sequence is entirely soundless except for a few clicks of metal instruments that stress the significance of the doctor's gaze as a means of (one-way) communication, as well as the increasing suspense of the situation.

The fundamental scenario of classical cinema is expressed here in a condensed and unambiguous way. Interestingly, this is one of the few things that the scriptwriters of the American version approved of when remodelling the story. The female character is a helpless object waiting for the execution of power performed by the male authority, and there is an obvious sensation of sadism in this scene. The clarity of it is underlined by the fact that, in spite of the intimate close-ups, the scene constantly maintains a certain distance between the doctor and his patient. Except for a few seconds when doctor Wegert with his forefinger turns Anna's face a bit, he never touches her. For instance, when he removes Anna's bandages, he uses a pair of tweezers instead of his hands. The man thus does not need his physical power to show his mastery over the woman, but all his power to control is concentrated in the gaze. In this scene, then, it is the male expert who controls not only the means of seeing but even distribution of knowledge to both Anna and the spectator. He is the only one able to see the result of the surgery and to give prognosis on the (healing) process. When he finally agrees to tell Anna that the surgery had been successful, the spectator has to take his word for it.

Throughout the first half of the film, the looks of Anna are the object of the spectator's desire to know and to see. Her personality is initially (re)presented only by her tough, determined voice and her shadow on the wall. The manuscript says that the shadow should be gigantic and grotesque, drawing on the archetype psychology of C. G. Jung where the shadow represents the negative sides of the human psyche. In such a context it is Anna's negative, evil principle that speaks and is represented in the introductory scene. Not long after this imaginary presentation, Anna contemplates her face in the mirror.

As if in order to protect him/herself against the evil that her *gestalt* seems to represent, the spectator – as well as Anna herself – assumes a position that is analogous to the one of Perseus. The terrifying Medusa, a woman whose appearance made everyone stiffen with horror, could only be mastered by Perseus if he used his shield as a mirror to look at her. Similarly, the spectator seems to be able to achieve control over this monumental representation of female strength and wrath only through the protective mirror. The mirror enables the act of seeing for the spectator, and for Anna of being seen and being acknowledged.

In this scene, Molander uses an interesting composition of the image. In a central shot the frame of the mirror divides the surface of the image on the silver screen into two halves. In the left half there stands the 'real' Anna, her hair and neck out of focus, blurred. In the right half there is the mirror image of her hideously deformed face. The disfigured looks of her in the mirror are a projection of Anna's conception of herself – but as she says, also the image that she thinks other people have of her. During her first encounter with Wegert she exclaims: 'I look detestable and guess I must be so too!' Yet the screen image consists of two halves where the spectator may see this awkward self-image juxtaposed with the 'real' Anna: out of focus, inarticulate and vague, merely suggesting that there are sides to Anna's personality that are hidden and undeveloped.

The next 'scene of reflection' that gives the mirror a heightened significance as a mediator of Anna's innermost feelings, occurs immediately before the bandage on her face will be removed. Vera Wegert meets Anna at the ward in an agitated mood expecting to make a deal concerning the compromising letters. Unexpectedly, Anna hands the letters out to Vera without asking for money. It is important to note that she does this before knowing of the outcome of the surgery, thus showing that the doctor's unselfish and compassionate act is about to change her cold, businesslike attitude in crime. There is a mirror on the wall in Anna's hospital room. When she is taken away in her wheelchair, the mirror is empty except that it reflects the similarly empty floor, both indicating that Anna still dwells in a moral void and that her sudden act of compassion may be an isolated one.

The mirror reflections follow Anna to Wegert's examination room where shining metallic surfaces reflect the characters, yet without revealing Anna's changed looks. As described above, Wegert examines the results of his work, turns his lamp off and states that the surgery has been successful. 'Oh, may I have a mirror!' Anna exclaims, and in an extreme close-up she looks at herself. Even at this moment the backside of the mirror hides the operated half of her face from the spectator's scrutiny. At this point only Anna is able to see her personal possibilities reflected in the mirror. The suspense created by the spectator's quest for knowledge – his/her desire to see – remains unchanged: Anna herself will stay as the subject of the story and the mediator of her past, her memories, feelings, behaviour and motivations.

At Forsa the little boy serves as a mirror in which Anna is able to locate her own incentives. Lars-Erik eagerly shows his toys asking whether Anna ever had such things when she was a child. She says no, adding that nobody ever cared to give her any. After a pause she continues with an affected voice that frightens the child·

Yes, you have it fine, Lars-Erik, you can get all you want – whatever you wish – you never need to be hungry, you only have kind people around you … nobody ever scolds you,

nobody says evil things, ugly words to you! You can be as capricious as you ever wish …
you've got everything, just point at your finger!

In Anna's retort there is an implicit reflection of her own childhood characterised by abuse and lack of love. Low-key lighting emphasises her feelings, hiding the ceiling and major part of the walls in a shadow as she approaches the child's bed. In a sense the boy may be seen as Anna's alter ego, and her approaching him as a psychological process. The problem/dilemma of Anna's transformation on the plot-level is: will she hurt this endearing child? On a more metaphoric level a question might be formulated: will she hurt the initial self-examination of her own mind, will she (fail to) face the child she once was?

As already mentioned, Anna and Lars-Erik make good friends as she – almost against her will – grows more and more protective of the child. Meanwhile, the creditors of Torsten Barring become more and more obtrusive and he arrives at Forsa in a desperate state. On his arrival, he confronts Anna and makes his cruel intentions clear to her: in case she thinks of abandoning their plan, he will reveal her real identity to the old Barring. In this scene, too, Molander uses a number of mirrors to reflect Anna's state of mind. She is not yet strong enough to tell Torsten of her change of heart, but the mirrors clearly anticipate her mood.

Initially, Torsten is visible in the mirror behind Anna, thus doubling his presence in the room. Anna stands in the foreground during their encounter, stepping back and forth. Finally the golden frames of the mirror enclose both of them, depicting their original mutual intentions. The image becomes, thus, saturated with significance as Anna towards the end of the scene takes a step forward, her image pacing out of the frames of the mirror. This anticipates her detachment from everything Torsten represents, as she breaks the 'frame' of their agreement. Anna runs out of the room blaming a headache and in the last cut of the scene the empty two mirrors on the wall paraphrase the earlier scene in her hospital room, indicating that Anna's attitude still is unarticulated, and that she still is lacking a conscious solution to her problem.

The next morning, Anna has her final settlement with Torsten. Now she suddenly gets back her hard voice and evil expression showing that her stay at Forsa has not totally transformed her into her opposite, but that it has just expanded her personality. Apart from her unequivocal declaration of independence – 'I'm not running your or anyone else's errands any more!' – she now shows that she still has her old strength and fearless posture unchanged. Neither is she afraid to be unmasked by her old gang but she is even prepared to take responsibility for her previous life. When she saves Lars-Erik during the sleigh-tour and confesses her part in the conspiracy, she even symbolically saves herself and her independence.

At the end of the film there is a scene where she completes her evolution by facing Harald. She has now understood the link between her childhood trauma and her later criminal behaviour. Anna tells about her alcoholist parents causing the fire, which destroyed her looks. She sits by Harald's bed in the hospital room. On the wall behind her there hangs a mirror reflecting the window with its light curtains, showing the way out, a solution. When she stands up to take farewell of Harald, her whole body is reflected in this mirror. Anna stands within the screen frames, 'real' and 'healed', her face clearly visible. This is an inversion of the first screen image of her: even this image is divided into two spaces with the only difference that the 'real' Anna now is clear in her contours. The image mediates the completed change: Anna still has her earlier strength and independence, but now without her physical handicap.

As already mentioned, the film was re-made in Hollywood a few years later, with Joan Crawford as Anna and George Cukor as the director of the film. In the American version the plot is structured as a trial, where Anna is prosecuted for the murder of Torsten Barring (Conrad Veidt). The film builds upon flashbacks as different witnesses, including Anna herself, tell their version of the story. Americans have changed the character list, too – Harald Berg, for instance, does not exist, and the surgeon who in this version is called Gustaf Segert (Melvyn Douglas) is both the doctor and later the lover of Anna. Vera Segert (Osa Massen) has a more conspicuous role in the American version. She is characterised as a deceitful little goose, in contrast to the distressed yet composed woman that Karin Kavli plays in the original film. Torsten Barring has a far more pivotal position in that his taking advantage of and manipulating Anna in the blackmail business is more active. The film also establishes a kind of love-dependency relationship between Torsten and Anna.

The patriarchal discourses in both films tend to describe Anna's criminality as a kind of flaw in her character and the scar is associated with her outsidership and criminality. As we have seen, in *A Woman's Face* Anna is characterised as quite an asocial but self-contented person with a spiteful attitude towards other people. In the Cukor version she is, instead, depicted as a sentimental, craving woman who because of her handicap has been prevented from experiencing what she is longing for, that is, love and attention. Thus, as the scar in Molander's version appears to be the reason and prime mover in all Anna's concerns, in the Cukor version it is only an obstacle for her desire to fill her traditionally-defined female role (as a desirable object).

In the Swedish version, Anna does not speak about love. She is coldly calculating in her business having complete control over the situation. Vera's anxiously spiteful phrases have no effect on Anna, who cynically underlines her matter-of-factness and business-like punctuality: 'Morally a bit in the periphery, perhaps, but still businessmen!' is how she characterises herself and her gang. Her relationship to her gang and to Torsten is strictly on a business basis. She shows friendly attentiveness to Harald, but little else. She expresses gratitude towards Wegert and even if the two walk side by side at the end of the film, implying that they have a future together, the idea remains a faint possibility.

In a way, Molander places Anna and Wegert in equal positions. When Anna expresses her fears concerning the future at the end of the film, Wegert – also needing to forget a past – says, 'Do as I do! Pack up the old things – again and again if necessary!' Thus Anna is urged to act as the male character and take a step into the unknown, not as the male character's (future) wife but as a fellow traveller that has broken with her past. The character of Anna thus deviates strongly from the concept of a female character in the mainstream cinema of the period.

In both versions the man/doctor removes the scar which gives him a key position in the narrative. He, however, disappears from the screen in Molander's version soon after his surgery, and Anna gets an opportunity to develop without his patronage. This is totally in contrast with the American version where Anna soon loses her (alleged) independence and comes under the scrutiny and influence of several men: first Torsten in a demonic relationship, then Gustaf Segert and finally the judge, the prosecutor and the attorney as well. In this version the bunch of male characters try figuring out the enigma of Anna, delivering their views to each other and to the spectator. Anna is exhibited in court, her story is told by witnesses and her situation is interpreted by professionals such as a doctor, a judge, a prosecutor and an attorney.

The American version conforms the (oppressive) strategy of the dominating discourse by doubling the woman's object position: partly by making her an object of a gaze, partly by depriving her of her own story and letting it be mediated by a few, mainly male, characters. In the Swedish version of the film Anna herself is trying to figure out who she is and mediates this to the spectator. A score of narrative devices in Molander's version – the *mise-en-scène*, props, lightning and camera-angles – aim at formatting the story as Anna's own. Consequently, the relationship between her and the spectator tends to establish itself without (a male) mediator.

Anna's development is in a sense facilitated by men in the Swedish version as well, but their function is as a catalyst, rather than interpreters of her behaviour and her motives. Torsten Barring suggests the job at Forsa and Allan Wegert accomplishes the change in her looks that makes her employable. Lars-Erik's childishly immediate warmth and Harald's rather awkward courting accompany the moral change in Anna's personality. Her relationship to all these characters is nevertheless essentially independent.

Moreover, the hierarchy constituted by the male characters in the Swedish version is disrupted and the centre of the narrative lacks an obvious male authority. This simply yields enough space to an independent female character development and this development contributes of course to the contours of the female subject positioning. Even Harald seems equally incapable for the role of a real lover: 'Harald Berg appears as a "pure-woollen" character who courts Anna with all that economised lack of fantasy which should be characteristic of a Swedish mill engineer. He arouses Anna's sympathy rather than her passion', as Rune Waldekranz, a contemporary critic, wrote in his review. This is a scenario that leaves an obvious void in the centre of the narrative and in this void it is possible to distinguish indications on several levels – interpersonal, visual and spatial – that allow contours of the female subject positioning to materialise, as they would in a palimpsest.

Tytti Soila

REFERENCES

Bergman, I. (1981) *Mitt liv*. Stockholm: Norstedts.

Waldekranz, R. (1986) *Filmens Historia, part 2*. Stockholm: Norstedts Förlag.

TVÅ MÄNNISKOR TWO PEOPLE

CARL THEODOR DREYER, DENMARK, 1945

Do we need to have a theory to account for artistic failures – or is it enough to look at obvious instances of artistic shortcomings and stick to the particulars in each case? Proverbially, Homer, too, suffered from occasional weak moments or lapses, so even – or perhaps only – the great ones can err in this respect. It seems, in fact, as if fiascoes and failures are only worth discussing in relation to masters and canonical figures. Without a high level of expectation based on an outstanding artistic track record, failures are deprived of their aura of sublimity.

Failure, or defalcation – a useful term since its monetary connotations can be translated into cultural/artistic capital – suggests an effort to achieve something out of the ordinary, a high-stake attempt against all odds, a challenge, a risky investment, which is far removed from Homer's alleged lack of attention to details once in awhile. Let me offer a preview of one illuminating reaction, penned by Carl Björkman and headlined 'Masterpiece or Pompous Trash', concerning the film in focus here, Carl Theodor Dreyer's *Två människor* (*Two People*) from 1945: 'One does *not* accept a film with intellectual ambitions that turns out to be totally intellectually insufficient. That is why *Two People* is and remains pompous trash.' The conclusion put forward by Björkman was not so much a first reaction, a review of the opening, but rather a rebuff of some fellow critics having, according to Björkman, more or less pronounced the film to be a masterpiece, which is to grossly overstate their evaluations. Irrespective of his fellow critics' appreciation, Björkman considered *Two People* to be nothing but bogus.

The storyline of *Two People* runs as follows: The biochemist, Arne Lundell, is accused of plagiarism when his colleague, Professor Sander, publishes a more or less identical work at the time Arne's dissertation on schizophrenia is made public. Shortly afterwards the Professor, who also happens to be the former lover of Arne's wife, Marianne, is found murdered. The entire story takes place in the couple's apartment, where they learn about the murder and the circumstances surrounding it. When evidence is mounting, Marianne eventually confesses that she is the murderess. The film ends with the couple's joint suicide.

On a day-to-day basis, film critics form posses – by chance or design – to steer audiences clear of mediocre or bland films. If artistic failures imply shortcomings operating on a magnitude removed from the run-of-the-mill flaws affecting the current film market, reviewing becomes of marginal interest for understanding artistic failures, and merely a historical point of departure for more complex processes of reception.

Thus, over time, critics' unequivocal dismay can be 'explained away', as in the case of the initial reception of Dreyer's *Gertrud* (1964), a film effectively killed-off by French critics. Recent scholarship, however, has valued the film highly as an attempt at laying bare filmic devices. *Gertrud* has thus become a film quoting style issues rather than using them in order to tell a story, as argued by David Bordwell.

Stylistical traits once described as weaknesses are thereby reframed as assets, as a series of devices perceived to operate in a different register than initially judged. Then again, some failures persistently remain just that; new readings and changing reception protocols only confirm and solidify the diagnosis. Concerning *Two People*, Bordwell thus opines, 'The film is indeed an embarrassment'.

Given that artistic failures seem to apply only to renowned filmmakers, they do not take on their full stature until the entire oeuvre is more or less closed, or at least forms part of a past phase in a body of work, and preferably one reinforced by a biographical legend of sorts. Authorship is crucial here, and some failures are surrounded by a discourse of disavowal making authorship a bone of contention or an elimination game between directors and producers.

Eric von Stroheim's *Greed* (1924) represents a somewhat different story since the film was shot and even edited in a version approved by the director. Von Stroheim's very long version was, however, pronounced an artistic failure and a commercial impossibility by the producers and was never released in that form. Critics and audiences were literally cut off from forming opinions on the merits von Stroheim's version. The recently restored version, mounted by Ric Smidlin, uses preserved still material from missing shots in the release version, and thereby manages to present an academic film account, mixing moving images and stills, of Stroheim's never released version.

The division of authorial responsibility for the version released by the studio is, however, far from clear-cut. Even in its reduced version the film was perceived as a masterpiece. Orson Welles' *The Magnificent Ambersons* (1942) also suffered from a radical hatchet job by the producers; what remains is described by one critic as a 'dazzling fragment.' The responsibility for the dazzle is presumably Welles'; the fragmentary nature of the work is the producer's contribution. As the examples show, producers' overruling of directors' versions do not by definition lead to total failures. Given the producers' control of the medium – or sometimes censors' final saying – directors often have reasons to act standoffish in relation to a released film, this goes for both von Stroheim and Welles.

Carl Theodor Dreyer experienced a complicated different predicament in relation to *Two People*, a film he directed and co-wrote from a Swiss play for the production company Svensk Filmindustri. Dreyer's point of departure for this film was much more radical in its approach and represented a grander artistic risk than *Greed* and *The Magnificent Ambersons*. Dreyer's ambitions were excessively minimalisitic. Eventually, he acted standoffish to the extreme by disavowing 'his' film due to overpowering producer intervention, and even claiming that the film did not exist; if it did at least not as his film.

'It was a film that was doomed from the start, completely', Dreyer concludes in an interview with Andrew Sarris. In another context, the editor for a volume from 1963 of reprinted essays by Dreyer, Erik Ulrichsen, informs the readers that there are no illustrations in *Om filmen* from *Two People* since 'Dreyer considered this to be the former Svensk Filmindustri CEO Anders Dymling's film rather than his own.' In the same volume, part of a talk Dreyer gave in Copenhagen the day before leaving for Sweden in early December 1943 is reprinted. There Dreyer again finds occasion to praise Victor Sjöström, which – as seen below – will prove significant in this context.

Two People, authorship aside, had a very limited release, being taken out of repertory in Stockholm after only five days. In the main, critics in the Stockholm press were not impressed, with the exception of a few appreciative voices. Overall, the initial reception is framed and informed by Dreyer's biographical legend. Irrespective of how the film's merits are valued, he is introduced with admiration and respect as an uncompromising film artist. Three Stockholm critics, however, stand out as champions for the film's qualities. Dreyer's self-imposed limitations on two actors in one room in a compressed timeframe defined the parameters for the experiment. Carlo Keil-Möller in *Morgontidningen* considered the disavowal of the filmic toolbox as a payoff generating morally compromised figures. The film medium's use of movement and shifting backgrounds as impetus for telling stories are replaced by a sparse approach that in Keil-Möller's view functioned well. Even the two actors, miscast according to Dreyer, are praised. Lill (Ellen Liliedahl) in *Svenska Dagbladet* detailed a similar trajectory, but expressed reservations concerning the male lead. Stig Almqvist in *Aftontidningen* explicitly addresses the pre-reception buzz anticipating an upcoming fiasco: 'To my mind, *Two People* is so far from being a fiasco that it must be placed among the most prominent Swedish films from this year, and in many respects it touches on the masterly.'

In disavowing the film, Dreyer argued that he had lacked control over three salient aspects of the production process: casting – which was the main problem for him; a removed and substituted key scene breaking up the spatial limitations chosen for the film was re-inserted by the producer; and the musical scoring of the closing scene was a catastrophe. The debate concerning the film and its production process surfaced several years after the release, in 1948, in the aftermath of a screening and discussion in a study group during which one participant proposed a new reading of the film's meaning.

The wife, Marianne, was not the killer, the interpreter claimed – instead it was Arne himself whom suffered from the affliction his dissertation researched: schizophrenia. Allegedly, he had killed his colleague who had stolen his work and published it under his own name. Arne was unaware of having carried out the murder in another schizophrenic incarnation. The title then alludes to the two people within Arne.

Dreyer commented upon this reading in his article from December 1948:

Unfortunately, I have to discourage [Sven-Olof Johansson] and his subtle interpretation; he is not right. The idea that in reality the husband, unaware of his act in a schizophrenic state, has murdered Professor Sander has not for a moment entered my mind.

This is an interesting mini-debate. Dreyer here seemed to regard himself as the final arbiter of the film's meaning. On the other hand this is a film he disavowed or was in the process of disavowing, which left the field open for critical interpretation.

Furthermore, Dreyer seems to have been under the mistaken impression that Dr Dymling, his producer, had participated in the course and publicly expressed opinions on the film, even attacking it. In the article, Dreyer summed up his misgivings concerning casting, the reinserted flashback showing Sander as a shadow on the wall, and the selection of music for the closing scene. Dymling retorted that the production process was one long suffering for everybody working with Dreyer. In a final installment, Dreyer claimed that Dymling was co-responsible for the film since he forced an unfortunate and unsuited cast on him.

Dreyer had arrived in Sweden on a double mission in late 1943. After many years away from active engagement with cinema, he once again had a chance to direct a feature film, this time in Denmark. However, the Danish reception of *Vredens dag* (*Day of Wrath*, 1943) was far from enthusiastic. After an appearance before a group of students in Copenhagen, Dreyer left for Sweden, hoping to find a distributor for his film.

His friend, Sven Nygren at Lux Film, encouraged the trip to Stockholm, but when Dreyer applied for a visa, he listed three references: Carl Anders Dymling, Victor Sjöström and Sven Nygren. Dymling was CEO at Svensk Filmindustri since 1942 and Sjöström headed the company's artistic affairs. More importantly, Sjöström was a director Dreyer admired immensely, which he repeated in several interviews over the years following his own piece on Swedish cinema from 1920, and again emphasized in his talk when he was on the verge of leaving Denmark for Sweden.

The listing of Dymling and Sjöström makes it plausible that Dreyer had been encouraged by Svensk Filmindustri to come to Stockholm for reasons besides trying to find a distributor for *Day of Wrath*, which turned out to be impossible. In a letter from Dymling to Dreyer dated 15 May 1944, when tensions were building, the former described the working process concerning what was to become *Two People*, itemising it in nine points. The first states that 'You approached Victor Sjöström proposing engagement as director', followed by, 'Sjöström answers that we were interested in your proposal regarding M. Lambert[h]ier.'

Subsequent visa applications for extending the stay proves that Dreyer was hired by Svensk Filmindustri to prepare a scenario based on a play by the Swiss writer W. O. Somin. This was by default since Louis Verneuil's play *Monsieur Lamberthier* was unavailable; Warner Bros. had already purchased the rights, and the film was released in 1946 as *Deception*. Both plays operated with only two characters and relied heavily on information slipping in from the outside via radio, telephone or other sound cues or occurrences visible from inside the apartment.

Dreyer prepared a scenario by adapting Somin's play together with a Danish exile, Martin Goldstein. Eventually the scenario was approved by the producer as a basis for a film to be directed by Dreyer. The collaboration between Dreyer and Goldstein was nothing but frictionless however, and culminated in Dreyer writing a letter to Dymling, voicing his concerns regarding 39 points, most of them, according to him, undermining the tone of the dialogue or the psychological interplay between the characters, making them more banal. The letter, available at the Danish Film Institute, has been reprinted by Edvin Kau in his book *Dreyers filmkunst*.

The studio was not pleased with the first manuscript version prepared by Dreyer and Goldstein and had ordered the latter to rewrite it. Dreyer wanted to keep to the original version avoided signing a contract without the guarantee that he could direct the film. He wanted to make sure that Svensk Filmindustri did not turn the assignment over to someone else. The signing of the contract for the script was therefore postponed, and when Dreyer exerted pressure on Dymling regarding the contract for directing the film, Dymling was annoyed, which provided the background for the letter in thirty-nine points from mid-May 1944.

A week later, Svensk Filmindustri was ready to offer Dreyer the contract to direct the film. In a letter from 23 May, Dymling detailed four conditions for the assignment, the most important being that the shooting script prepared by Dreyer must be based on the revised scenario version, and that casting the right actors for the project was crucial. Dymling proposed Wanda Rothgardt for the female lead. Dreyer's preferred leading lady, Gunn Wållgren, is not mentioned in any of the documents. His preference of her was not documented until the conflict arose, in 1948.

A week later, Dreyer received the revised scenario and was asked by Dymling to make notes of his objections. This is the background for the letter reprinted by Kau. Dreyer reiterated his preference for the first version of the script and apparently many of his objections were noted. Furthermore, during the rehearsals with the actors, he continued to change the script, seemingly trying to work his way back to the first draft.

Dreyer's interest in Anders Ek for the male lead is documented in a letter from 3 June. The personality profile that Dreyer described in all subsequent discussions of the film's characters was already full-blown here. Interestingly, Dreyer seemed to accept Rothgardt for Marianne's part: 'He [Anders Ek] and Wanda Rothgardt will match each other excellently – nobody can be a better partner for her. I don't think she will be perceived as older than he is – but if so, it's of no consequence. On the contrary! It only explains her passion and motherly affection for him.' It is clear from the letter that Dreyer had been in touch with Ek several times, but after this letter, there was no written communication between director and producer concerning casting. The hiring of Georg Rydeberg gave the studio an actor of prominence, which was stated as Dymling's prerequisite already before the contract with Dreyer was signed. And already at that time, Rothgardt was more or less a fact.

Dreyer described the characters in the article from 1948. The male lead was more or less identically characterised already in the letter to Dymling from 3 June 1944. The description below is from Robert Hughes' 1959 anthology, *Film: Book 1: The Audience and the Filmmaker*:

> He has to be young, with a pure mind and heart – without guile or deceit. An idealist so immersed in his studies that he sees nothing but his work, he is an assistant physician at a mental hospital. He loves his wife and blindly trusts her.

For this part I was given an actor of an utterly different kind: mysterious, intriguing, cunning, and even demonical.

She, his wife, should be young, warm-blooded and sensual, with a slightly tarnished past. On the other hand, since she has met her husband she loves him with such complete devotion that she is in constant fear that he may discover her earlier affairs. As a character she is insincere, she has no difficulty in pretending or lying. She is theatrical and a little affected, with a definite inclination to hysteria.

To play her I got a sweet, natural and uncomplicated housewife not at all harmonising with the personality of the woman in the script. In both cases I got the exact opposite of what I wanted.

Late 1943 was a time of reappraisal in Sweden on several levels. Culturally, Sweden had strong ties with Germany, which had facilitated a cooperation with the German film industry within the International Film Chamber; a body dominated by Joseph Goebbels' corporative control efforts of the German film industry. When anti-German films began to surface in France and the US, Sweden as a member of the Film Chamber was obligated to castigate the films if the Germans so wished. Eventually, the organisation became inefficient and politically compromised outside Germany and the occupied countries. The CEO of Svensk Filmindustri, Olof Andersson, was one of the organisation's vice-president during the 1930s.

A German victory seemed likely in 1941, the summer when the leading CEOs of the Swedish film companies – Svensk Filmindustri, Sandrews and Europa Film – visited Berlin for a meeting within the framework of the Film Chamber. The same summer Sweden allowed Germany to use Swedish railroads for moving troops from Norway to Russia. In 1942, Germany's prospects for victory looked bleaker. It seems as if Olof Anderson was replaced as Svensk Filmindustri's CEO in 1942 mainly due to his close affiliation with the Film Chamber. His, successor, Carl Anders Dymling, was a Shakespeare scholar and anglophile, with an impressive artistic track record as head of the theatre division at the National Radio Corporation. His tenure at Svensk Filmindustri led to a slow change of focus for the company's production. Allegorical criticism of foreign oppressors was launched in historical guise in a film like *Rid i natt* (1942). In 1943, abandoning the historical backdrop, contemporary clashes between an occupational force and the local resistance movements was featured in *Det brinner en eld* (1943) – a film set in a thinly-disguised Norway; the success of this film gave rise to a handful of other Swedish features about occupation.

To invite a renowned director from an occupied country, a filmmaker with a reputation for uncompromising artistic ambitions, could be seen as part of Dymling's political strategy. Even if this was the case, a political reading of *Two People* might be as pointless from Dreyer's perspective as the psychoanalytical reading dismissed by him in 1948. Then again, directors are not the only arbiters regarding a film's meaning, which is never a phenomenon in singular. It is tempting to ally Marianne with the entrapped heroines in the occupancy films forced to sacrifice themselves and their love for a bigger cause. Few protagonists have suffered from a more circumscribed chain of irreversible entrapment than Marianne and Arne; no options for anything but futile agency are offered the victims of this chamber setting. Psychologically hounded, they desperately cling to each for love, comfort and normalcy in the face of impending disaster.

The misgivings Dreyer voiced concerning the personality profile of the male lead for *Two People* pitted a decidedly idealist figure against a ruthless power player. Such a personality backdrop no doubt carries potential political overtones. With Rydeberg cast as Arne the conflict took on radically different implications.

Dreyer's ambition was to direct a film based on a spatio-psychological concept: two characters confined to one specific space more or less in real-time in a situation of acute crisis. The gradual revealing of information from the outside world via various digetic forms of communication, the foremost being the radio, defined the *dance macabre* between the couple moving from emotional blackmail to academic scandal, from homicide to double suicide. The fact that Marianne is the killer is suppressed for most of the screen time. Instead Arne, the husband, seems to be the likely killer or at least the main suspect.

Edvin Kau's discussion of *Two People* is the most informative and ambitious to date. Bordwell is more casual in his dismissal, even if he is impressed with the introduction of the characters and reads the camerawork in some scenes, particularly towards the ending, as a precursor to the fluid mobility in Dreyer's *Ordet* (*The Word*, 1955). Kau is more generous, both in terms of analytical energy and in his assessment of the camera style. Moreover, Kau describes the psychological interaction between the characters as motivated by a set of oppositions, all more or less variations on tranquility and harmony versus turmoil and threats.

Kau translates the plot into seven stages framed by the tensions exacerbated by these psychological polarities: the academic scandal is introduced – Marianne calms and encourages the depressed Arne; Sander's death is announced on the radio. Slowly the couple regains equilibrium; information over the radio that Sander's death was not accidental, he has been murdered. Arne seems implicated. Eventually, Marianne's lullaby reframes the situation; additional information on the radio points towards Arne as the perpetrator; Arne finds a love letter from Sander to Marianne. This leads to violence and harsh words, but they decide to start afresh; it is announced that a woman has murdered Sander. Marianne confesses. Escape is planned; Marianne takes poison, and so does Arne. The film comes to an end with Marianne's final rendition of the lullaby before both die.

Bordwell describes the introduction of the characters when they enter the apartment as on par with Hitchcock's dexterity. Respectively, their faces are reflected in a brass plaque, with Arne's name on the door, when they fiddle with the keys. Kau's discussion is more in-depth and overall more complex. He details the camerawork in several scenes and convincingly shows how Dreyer amalgamates character and camera movements into a versatile choreography, which might have been more powerful if reinforced by a different set of personality traits and emotional underpinnings; that is if Dreyer had been awarded his desired leads.

The integrity of the space is preserved except for the scene that Dreyer had removed, in which a flashback shows Marianne's meeting with Sander; the latter only visible as a shadow on the wall. The apartment is roomy with a living room, bedroom, kitchen and a little laboratory. A few temporal gaps in the plot are cued by wipes and sometimes fade out. At one stage Arne leaves the apartment to pick up a newspaper, off-screen, otherwise the protagonists remain in the apartment throughout the film. While Kau does not try to whisk out the film's failure status, his line of reasoning fits nicely into the defalcation discourse – but with a radicalising twist. His thesis, that a failure by a master is more interesting than a success by a lesser filmmaker, sounds like a Cahier-like politics of authorship singling out auteurs from *metteurs-en-scène*.

The embodiment of the dialogue and the violent shifts in atmosphere in the closed quarters required bewildered innocence on Arne's part, and a desperate disavowal of guilt on Marianne's. The moving camera and the fluidity of the edited space highlight an ongoing reframing and repositioning working on several levels. Overall, we learn, Marianne has tried to clear her past by using it in the service of her new love. Such an engineering of happiness is, however, way above her head. She totally misreads Sander's intentions and therefore instead of helping Arne ruins him.

The film is primarily a love story, albeit devoid of passionate expressions. The emotions are kept in check, quoted rather than acted upon, apart from in the scene where Arne discovers Marianne's affair with Sanders. Kissing, for instance, seems here to be a decidedly platonic activity. The two characters are playthings in the hands of a ruthless authority figure out to ruin their happiness and Arne's professional achievements. Sander's malice turns the world against them by using Marianne to ruin Arne in a game she totally misreads.

The chamber-play concept underscores that the two are trapped in their shelter from the outside world, enclosed between despair and hope, and forced to a heightened semiotic awareness in reading what they hear and see. The gradual elimination of evidences pointing towards Arne offers no way out for them; it only transfers the burden to Marianne until she breaks down and spells out her fruitless attempts at orchestrating Arne's career. Deprived of his love and professional achievements, Arne has nothing to live for and thus without hesitation shares the poisonous cocktail with Marianne.

Obviously, the film ended badly for Dreyer, but he managed to keep his emotions under control until he felt publicly betrayed by Dymling, and then chose to give his version and in the process distanced himself from the actual film. Dreyer instead shouldered responsibility for a phantom film shot from a different script, and featuring the actors he did not manage to get. He apparently accepted that *Two People* was a failure, but within Dymling's oeuvre rather than his. Thus, *Two People* turned into yet another one of Dreyer's unfinsihed projects.

Jan Olsson

REFERENCES

Almqvist, S. (1945) 'Två människor', *Aftontidningen*, March 24.

Björkman, C. (1945) 'Masterpiece or Pompous Trash', *Veckojournalen*, 24.

Bordwell, D. (1981) *The Films of Carl-Theodor Dreyer*. Berkeley: University of California Press.

Dreyer, C. T. (1948) 'Debate article', *Aftontidningen*, 12 December.

Hughes, R. (1959) *Film: Book 1: The Audience and the Filmmaker*. New York: Grove Press.

Kau, E. (1989) *Dreyers filmkunst*. Copenhagen: Akademisk Forlag.

Keil-Möller, C. (1945) 'Två Människor', *Morgontidningen*, 25 March.

Lill (1945) 'Två Människor', *Svenska Dagbladet*, 25 March.

Sarris, A. (1967) *Interviews With Film Directors*. Indianapolis: Bobbs-Merrill.

Ulrichsen, E. (ed.) (1963) *Dreyer, C. Th Om filmen*. Copenhagen: Gyldendal.

KAMPEN OM TUNGTVANNET OPERATION SWALLOW

TITUS VIBE-MÜLLER, NORWAY/FRANCE, 1948

On the night of 27 February 1943, one of the most famous sabotage operations during the Second World War took place in southern Norway. Saboteurs from Kompani Linge – The Linge Company or Norwegian Independent Company No. 1 – blew up Norsk Hydro's laboratory for making heavy water, deuteriumoxide, intended for the manufacture of an atomic bomb in Germany. Three months after the sabotage, production of heavy water began again at the Vemork plant in the Rjukan valley, but after an unsuccessful air raid, when 161 American airplanes dropped nearly a thousand bombs over the factory, without hitting the target, the Germans decided to move production to Germany. On 20 February 1944 one of the saboteurs blew up the ferry steamer that shipped the heavy water from Rjukan, and the equipment for production of heavy water, thus ending Germany's hope of producing a bomb during the war.

These two successful operations, by the same local saboteurs, have become something of a national myth in Norway. They have become *the* symbol of the resistance against the five years of German occupation. This resistance became, and still is, one of the 'national grand narratives' of modern Norway, a narrative that has contributed to the legitimation of values and the forming of a modern national culture.

Many books have been written about the operations, and two feature films, one Norwegian and one American, that used the event as source material, were produced in the post-war years. Today, it has been turned into a 'heritage event'; and the two feature films are used as heritage films. Between 1990 and 2001 the tourist industry in Norway offered so-called 'Heavy Water Marches', turning the past into an entertainment experience. In 1990, approximately three thousand people took part in the first 'Heavy Water March', following in part the path taken by the saboteurs when they blew up the laboratory at the Vemork factory, and then taking part in an event at the factory itself; with military music, speeches and singing the Norwegian National Anthem as a concluding symbolic gesture.

The Occupation drama genre in post-war Norwegian film production included symbolic stories of heroism, combat, resistance, gender, ethnicity and identity, staged in highly symbolic national landscapes; often the barren mountains. The most important of these early films was

Kampen on tungtvannet (*Operation Swallow*, 1948) the Norwegian film about the heavy water sabotage operations.

After the war, the Norwegian people felt an intense need for information about the war and war films were very popular. All radios had been confiscated by the Nazis in 1941 and newspapers were heavily censored during the war years, creating a craving for the depiction and discussion of wartime events in the initial post-war years. At the same time, a new generation of filmmakers made pioneering advances in Norwegian film production, while providing the hungry audiences with authentic stories from the Occupation. These Occupation dramas helped shape public opinion while going some way to explaining the war. The pictures used the war as the basis for exciting stories, but at the same time they were disseminating information about it and establishing a context of interpretation, mobilising public opinion for peace.

Operation Swallow was the most popular of the early Occupation dramas, and most influential in terms of style as well as content. It was a Franco-Norwegian co-production, and given the French title *La Bataille de l'eau lourde* on its initial release in 1948. When the film was released in England in the early 1950s it was given the title *Operation Swallow* after the sabotage operation itself organised and directed by the English Special Operations Executive. Directed by the Norwegian director Titus Vibe-Müller and supervised by the French director Jean Dréville, the film depicted the two operations. Norwegian saboteurs are trained in England and then parachuted into the Hardanger plateau, to carry out their mission to blow up the factory where the heavy water was produced.

By the time shooting began in 1947 the screenplay had been worked on by several writers. The credits finally attributed the screenplay to the French writer Jean Marin, who had been the French 'voice from London' during the war, but as early as 1945 the Norwegian writer Arild Feldborg had written a first complete script. Originally the shooting of this script, loosely inspired by the sabotage operations in Rjukan in 1943–44 but taking many liberties in the depiction of the events, started early in 1946, but production was stopped due to problems with the co-production deal that had been agreed with a French film company.

The first script was not only a depiction of the operation, but also a vehicle for the Norwegian-American actress Sigrid Gurie. She was a minor Hollywood star in the late 1930s and early 1940s, starring in films like *The Adventures of Marco Polo* (Archie Mayo, 1938) and *Algiers* (John Cromwell, 1938), but she had never acted in a Norwegian film. Her real name was Sigrid Guri Haukelid, and she was the twin sister of Knut Haukelid, one of the saboteurs. When shooting began Gurie was playing one of the major roles in the movie, as an English radio operator who falls in love with one of the saboteurs hiding in Norway, and keeping in touch with him by morse code throughout the operation.

This first script differed greatly from the finished film as well as the first 'wave' of occupation dramas, being more melodramatic and 'fictionalised' than the other Norwegian war films. Shooting took place in the Sandrew-Baumann studio in Stockholm in early 1946, until the producer was contacted by the French production company Le Trident, which wanted to make a feature-length documentary about the operations, inspired by the success of the semi-documentary study of the French resistance *La Bataille du rail* (René Clement, 1946).

The co-production deal between Le Trident and the Norwegian production company Hero-Film Inc. left director Vibe-Müller out of work for some time, so he directed another Occupation drama, *To Liv* (*Two Lives*, 1946) in Norway. At the same time, a new script was commissioned, first from Diana Robertson, but later a third and final script was completed by the French writer Jean Marin, working with Arild Feldborg and the saboteurs, especially Knut Haukelid, who was busy writing his own memoir.

The second script eliminated all love interest, and placed all emphasis on the production of the atomic bomb. This script opened and ended with the smoke clouds over Hiroshima, dissolving into a montage of reactions from around the world – startled faces and newspaper headlines – with a voice-over in various languages saying, 'Thank God we discovered it first!' In the final film the emphasis on the atomic bomb was toned down, but these three scripts frame the sabotage operations in different ways, presenting quite different interpretations of the event.

Shooting resumed again on 2 March 1947, and the finished film opened in February 1948. It was a huge success in Norway, becoming the biggest box-office success that year. In Oslo, more than half of the population saw the movie in 1948. The critics' reception was also positive, praising the realism and authenticity of the style and its 'thriller-like' suspense story.

Operation Swallow starts with pictures of snow-clad mountains, while a title card ensures us that what is depicted in the film really happened, and that many of the men in the film are identical to the actual saboteurs. Then we move to a BBC radio studio, where a commentator begins the story by presenting the historical background. His voice accompanies the film in voice-over, sometimes explaining the events themselves, sometimes giving voice to the feelings of the saboteurs, and occassionally enhancing the suspense in the action sequences.

The background story starts in Paris in April 1939, and the first French complex, the work of Professor Joliot Curie and his collaborators at the Collége de France with heavy water. The film frames the story of wartime sabotage with the frantic race-against-time scientific and diplomatic activity regarding fission, radioactivity and the struggle to master atomic energy prior to the outbreak of the war. This French connection was the reason Le Trident was especially interested in the events. In the English version of the film, this part of the story was heavily cut, favouring the depiction of later developments in wartime London. Using stock-shots as well as reconstructions and re-enactments, the first part of the film ends with the decision taken that the Vemork factory must be destroyed.

The main section of the film deals with how a collection of Norwegian saboteurs, named 'Gunnerside', who had been trained in England and Scotland, are parachuted into the vast Hardanger plateau, contact a small group of saboteurs called 'Grouse' – later named 'Swallow' – who had been preparing the sabotage behind enemy lines, and waiting in a small stone hut on the barren mountains for the right time to strike against the Vemork factory. The saboteur Knut Haukelid wrote about the planning in London in his memoirs:

> With the help of photographs and drawings we planned the action with Tronstad in the most minute detail. We were to land in the mountains, and after getting in touch with Grouse we were to go down the hillside on the north side of the valley near Vaaer. We were then to cross the Maan river somewhere halfway between Rjukan and Vemork and follow the railway line to the factory, where, according to reports from Grouse, there were 15 men on guard. The work done, we were to return by the same route … After the operation the Grouse and Gunnerside groups were to withdraw to Sweden; but Arne, Einar, Knut Haugland and I were to remain in the mountains to establish a permanent base and organise home forces in the district.

After the succesful sabotage, where the German troops are only seen as silhouettes in the distance, most of the saboteurs withdraw to Sweden. Here, the action is mostly fictionalised, only returning to a more documentary style with footage of Churchill, Hitler, the V-1 missiles and Eisenhower, showing how the war is still raging. In this way the main part of the film is a reconstruction of life on the mountains, and the first successful sabotage, framed by a documentary discourse.

The film ends with a brief depiction of the second operation, when Knut Haukelid places a bomb with a time-release on the ferry steamer Hydro. As with the first operation, the sinking of the Hydro was almost uneventful for the saboteurs, who were safe away in the mountains when it was destroyed. The voice-over briefly concludes with the words: 'On 20 February 1944 the Third Reich lost its last chance in the battle for the heavy water. The battle was won by a handful of men.' The film ends after these words, with a pan over the mountains, and the faces of the saboteurs are superimposed on the snow-clad mountains.

The most striking feature today is the discourse of authenticity used in the film, highlighted during promotions before its initial release. In 1948 the film was presented as a documentary in the newspaper ads, and the assistant director John Willem Gran used the label documentary as late as the mid-1990s. Parts of the film are expository documentary sequences, using authentic stock-shots to explain the wartime events, and creating a frame for the main action. Also, many of the saboteurs play themselves in the film, in reconstructions and re-enactments of the events. However, some of the saboteurs did not want to be a part of the film production, and were replaced by well-known Norwegian actors like Henki Kolstad and Claus Wiese. This has created a situation akin to many historical dramas, when there obviously is 'a body too much' that creates a 'fictional effect'.

The obvious problem with *Operation Swallow*, especially if we compare the film to a documentary classic like *Fires Were Started* (Humphrey Jennings, 1943), is the use of well-known professional actors instead of non-professional actors, and professional actors that had not witnessed or taken part in the events being told. Another complicating feature is the fact that the film depicts one special event, a particular historical moment, and not a generalised example of the resistance. It is a highly specific argument about the sabotage, and not a general argument about the war. *Operation Swallow* is obviously even more creative than the Jennings film in its treatment of actuality, and as a result more problematic.

The film's mixed form, combining documentary sequences and a factual approach with the entertainment values of drama, has never really been the focus of controversy in Norway, yet the film has never been placed in the documentary category by film historians and writers. Film historians have responded to the re-enactments, and the use of well-known actors in some of the major roles, by giving the film the label 'fiction'. Still, the discourse of authenticity has been very important to the reception of the film in the early post-war period, as well as today, in the context of the heritage industry and the struggle over national symbols, because the focus on historically 'accurate' details has been a declaration of faith in a particular way of seeing the past as well as the operations themselves.

Indeed some newspaper critics, after the premiere in 1948, made interesting connections between the stylistic authenticity and the film's advertising. In the conservative newspaper

Aftenposten the critic Einar Diesen wrote on 6 February 1948, 'Stylistically the film is 100 per cent documentary. Nothing is added. No false action is stuck to it … The film is a good advertisement for Norway, it's war effort – and not least for our industry and for Norsk Hydro who gets it free of all costs.'

As a war film *Operation Swallow* is an interesting genre film. Like most other Norwegian Occupation dramas, the film does not demonise the Germans, but unlike many Hollywood films it does not make a distinction between the Nazis and the German people. Indeed, the Germans are without faces, anonymous and distanced, never given individuality or even a special place in the film. This is striking, especially as in the first script recounting the events, a fictional German officer, Colonel Heinz Graumann, is the focus at the beginning. In this version, the events that led up to the war are seen through the eyes of a German prisoner of war after the war is over, creating a quite different dramatic effect and perspective on the events.

In the main part of *Operation Swallow*, Germans are absent most of the time, and the *real* struggle in the film is between the saboteurs and the wild and barren Norweigian landscape. The saboteurs lived for over two years in small stone huts at the Hardanger plateau, and Knut Haukelid presents the stage for this struggle in this way in his memoirs:

> The largest, loneliest and wildest mountain area in northern Europe. Some 6,000 square miles of naked mountains, at a height of about 4,000 feet above sea level. Only for a short time in summer does a little grass and moss grow up among the rocks and snow. No human beings live on these desolate expanses, only the creatures of the wild; there are large herds of reindeer, which shun mankind and whose wants are small.

When the rations in the containers 'Gunnerside' brought with them was eaten, the saboteurs lived again on reindeer meat, and the contents of the stomachs of the reindeers. This made all the saboteurs undernourished and sick, but the film does not present them as they should have been if authenticity was the model in every sense of the word; wearing 'ragged and disgusting' clothes, looking sick, with long beards and skins that 'had assumed a yellowish tinge'. Instead, they look healthy, easily mastering all hardship. This nature theme is reinforced by the film when the Norwegians are not visibly changed by the drastic conditions. They must surely be the ones that have inherited the land, and the only ones that can survive in it. Indeed, the last sequence in the film is a long pan over the beautiful but barren mountains, while the faces of the saboteurs are superimposed onto the mountainside, as if they were an integral part of the landscape.

Operation Swallow is a film about a group, and as such depicts collective action. Although some of the saboteurs are given specific personality and character traits in the film, most clear in the case of the actor Henki Kolstad's portrayal of Einar Skinnarland as a charming and humorous man even in the most desperate situations, they remain anonymous helpers in a collective action. There are no moral discussions of the fight, no 'internal enemies' in the film, or any nerves or doubts, and the collectivity is taken for granted. This is a highly effective ideological position, showing that all 'good' Norwegians just did the necessary job. No questions asked, or needed. Like myth, the collectivity is naturalised, and connected to the role of nature in the film.

The mountains are important here, in an aesthetical as well as ideological sense, and these images are a part of what has been described as a 'grand theme' in Norwegian landscape painting and photography. In the 1840s the painter Johan Christen Dahl formulated a Romantic vision of the Norwegian landscape that has had a lasting influence on both life and art in Norway. Dahl's panoramic and monumental paintings of mountain landscapes conjures a feeling of an overpowering awe of Nature, and these images have been elevated into both the Norwegian national iconography and psyche.

The motifs chosen by Dahl have had a lasting attraction, and have become symbols of *the* Norwegian in the era of mass tourism. The mountains and also the old buldings, like the stone hut Bamsebu where the saboteurs hide from the Nazis, are not just a natural background of unspoilt nature or the romantic 'ruin', but signify true 'Norwegian-ness'. The saboteur's collective fight against the forces of nature is a symbolic regeneration that makes them invincible. No wonder that one of the most outstanding sequences in the film is a dramatic chase between the tired and hungry saboteur Claus Helberg and a German 'alpine ski-master', which ends with Helberg shooting the German soldier.

Operation Swallow, then, consequently exploited the combination of national iconography in combination with the painful contemporary history, but it was not the first Norwegian Occupation drama. Three films were made in 1946. Olav Dalgard and Rolf Randall dramatised the patriotic Resistance in *Vi vil leve* (*We Want to Live*), Toralf Sandø made *Englandsfarere* (*We Leave for England*) and Vibe-Müller directed the Ibsen-like study *To Liv*. However, these films were more action-oriented or more concerned with discussing moral issues. *Operation Swallow* became the model of a more popular semi-documentary Occupation drama, a type of film both culminating in and being questioned in Arne Skouens *Ni Liv* (1957) the most famous of the Occupation dramas beside *Operation Swallow*.

The Occupation drama genre changed dramatically during the early 1960s. The docudrama tone disappeared, women became more important in the stories, and the hero was shown to have his doubts or faults. The heroes were no longer larger than life and perfect, or a part of the Norwegian nature, but human beings like everybody else. The revision of these earlier central themes of the Occupation dramas was important in the 1970s and 1980s, and films like *Belønningen* (*The Reward*, Bjørn Lien, 1980) or *Over Grensen* (*Over the Border*, Bente Erichsen, 1987) show a different side of the Resistance spirit, namely the betrayal and deception not only of the Germans or of the Quislings, but inside the resistance movement itself. However, the last two Occupation dramas made in Norway, *Krigerens Hjerte* (*The Warrior's Heart*, Leidulv Risan, 1993) and *Secondløitnanten* (*The Last Lieutenant*, Hans Petter Moland, 1993), again turned to more heroic and action-oriented stories about the Resistance.

Emphasising collective action, and using a mixed docudrama form, *Operation Swallow* is a very different film from the American version of the operation, *The Heroes of Telemark* (Anthony Mann, 1965), Both films use images of the mountains from the Norwegian national iconography taken on location around Rjukan and the Hardanger plateau, and the brilliant colour photography in the American film version enhances the tourist-like feeling of the film.

Even though Anthony Mann's film is supposed to depict the same historical events, *The Heroes of Telemark* offers a very different version of war, even if the ingredients are the same. The Norwegian film uses understatement and restraint, whereas the American film is more melodramatic and narrative-focused. Differences take place on many levels, especially in the reworking of the events in that the scriptwriters take many liberties with historical accuracy. Factual accuracy, understatement and restraint were scarcely Hollywood's usual methods, and the 'fictionalising' strategy is emblematically signalled in the opening of the film. *The Heroes of Telemark* opens with pictures of the mountains and the Rjukan gorge but then it focuses on several German cars that drive towards the Vemork factory. A small band of Resistance fighters unleash a gigantic rock from the mountainside, nearly hitting the Reichskommisar's car, but sweeping away a small tank that explodes in the gorge. No such event took place during the war, but this scene, coming before the credits as a sort of prologue, signals a more dramatic and fast-paced action film than *Operation Swallow*.

This prologue points to one of the strategies being used in the American film. It uses condensation, creating symbolic but fictional episodes, or changes persons or episodes so that they come toghether in a more fast-paced and dramatically condensed rhythm. This strategy of condensation is linked to an individualisation and personification, that changes the events and the relationship between story and the representation of war and history.

The focus of narrative interest shifts from telling the story about the sabotage operations to the relationship between the saboteurs. Most of all, *The Heroes of Telemark* is a moral duel between the two main protagonists; the strong and unwavering saboteur Knut Strand (Richard Harris) and the selfish playboy Dr Rolf Pedersen (Kirk Douglas). The character played by Harris bears the nickname Knut Haugland used during the Occupation, but the character is a combination of all of the saboteurs. Rolf Pedersen, on the other hand, is clearly modelled on the scientist Leif Tronstad. Professor Tronstad was a leading industrial chemist before the war and had been technical adviser when the Vemork plant was built, so knew the factory inside out, but fled to England where he worked at the Norwegian section of the Special Operations Executive in London during the war. Until his untimely death near the very end of the war, he was operating in London, never taking part in the actual sabotage events.

In Mann's film, Pedersen is the main saboteur, especially in the last dramatic sequence, when he sinks the ferry steamer, but his character is partly fiction and partly taking over the roles and actions of the other saboteurs. In both films there is the depiction of the dramatic ski chase and in *The Heroes of Telemark* Pedersen takes Helberg's part in this chase. Other episodes, like a dramatic escape from German soldiers in a bus, was another of Claus Helberg's exploits transferred to the Pedersen character.

Pedersen and Strand represent two completely different approaches in dealing with the Occupation. Strand never waivers in his belief that active Resistance is necessary, even though it can result in mass executions as a retaliation. Pedersen is presented as a playboy, kissing one of his female students in the darkroom at the University in the scene that presents him to the audience, and not caring about the Resistance, but he makes one of the classic transitions of war films – from an insensitive cynic occasionaly troubled about the morality of killing and the sabotage operations to a brave soldier convinced of the cause.

Operation Swallow and *The Heroes of Telemark* both end with the dramatic sinking of the ferry steamer. The Norwegian film does not mention that, together with four Germans, 14 Norwegians had gone down with her, sacrificed to a greater cause. The American film evades this moral question altogether. While the sinking was only shown as a brief model-shot in the Norwegian film, the sinking is a fictional 'grande finale' in *The Heroes of Telemark*. Up until the last moment Pedersen remains a cynic, but enters the ferry at the last moment, and saves all the children on the ferry in the precise moment the bomb explodes. This sequence, historically flawed, finally resolves the moral dilemma with Pedersen's brave and self-sacrificing gesture. Resistance is depicted as something natural and mythic in the Norwegian film, but in the American version Resistance is an enactment of civic virtue and an exercise in self-improvement.

The Heroes of Telemark takes liberties with the factual historic background, and uses dramatic exaggerations, individualisation and genre-stereotyping to tell the story as exciting and easy comprehensible as possible. The film uses gender-stereotyping in creating a sub-plot where the playboy Pedersen is reunited with his former wife, who is portrayed as a weak and sexy hysteric, and ethnic stereotypes in the portrayal of the Germans as nothing but arrogant cold-blooded killers. While showing the two operations, the two films are so different that one could wonder if they are depicting the same event.

Operation Swallow established a context of interpretation as well as disseminating information about the heavy water sabotage operations. It helped shape public opinion in the early post-war years, when Norway was trying to heal its wounds as a 'split' society during the Occupation. The film uses well-known national iconography to project an image of a society where man and nature are one and in harmony. It uses the language of myth, well suitable for the heritage industry today.

The film emphasises collective action. Germans are faceless and nameless, and there are no roles for women. Although the film obviously wants to depict the operations as truthfully and factually correct as possible – and not only used the actual saboteurs in many roles, but also as consultants before, during and after the shooting of the film – the production history and the three different shooting scripts show that it was quite possible to frame the events in different ways. The end result tells us not only about the events themselves, but also how the saboteurs wanted the events to be represented, and the horizon of expectations of the production company.

The Heroes of Telemark uses fictionalisation, taking great liberties with persons and events, and presents the operations as a background for a moral story about civic virtue and courage. As a big-budget Hollywood genre film, *The Heroes of Telemark* demands conflict, antagonism and action, and therefore needs to invent characters and actions. Pedersen, the main protagonist in the film, is partly fiction, partly an amalgamation of all the individual Norwegian saboteurs. Several minor episodes in the film are examples of how the cinematic demand for action results in factual inaccuracy. An example is the scene where the saboteurs leave the Vemork factory, after the first successful sabotage. Indeed, no single shot was fired, and the German guards did not even hear the explosion because of the humming of the power generators, but in the American film this scene ends as a shoot-out where one of the saboteurs is killed in a dramatic chase.

These two films use the same factual events to tell completely different stories, about a 'factual' and a 'personal' war. In Norway, many have been dissatisfied with the way the events were portrayed in the American film, although the film was quite well received by the film critics, treating the film more as an 'Anthony Mann movie', in an auteurist way, than as a film about the Norwegian resistance movement. However, both films have been used by the Norwegian heritage industry in its recent commercialisation of the past, showing how one event can be and has been appropriated in different ways, but put to the same use in an effort to turn history into artefacts and entertainment experiences.

Gunnar Iversen

REFERENCES

Diesen, (1948) 'Tungtvannsfilmen en seier for norsk film', *Aftenposten*, 6 February.

Haukelid, K. (1989) *Skis Against the Atom*. Minot: North American Heritage Press.

TVÅLEN BRIS BRIS THE SOAP

INGMAR BERGMAN, SWEDEN, 1951

As is well known, screening commercials in film theatres before the feature film has remained a tradition in Sweden, as in many parts of Europe. It may be less well known that some of the most interesting Swedish commercials in the 1950s were directed by a filmmaker who, at least internationally, has almost exclusively (and, thus, quite erroneously) been placed in a purely art-film context: Ingmar Bergman. Bergman made not one but nine commercials for movie theatre release. They were all produced and screened in 1951–52, during the Swedish film industry's ten month-long studio strike, as a protest against the steep 'amusement tax' practised at the time. At the time Bergman, like many other Swedish film directors, faced unemployment, so when Sunlight Soap (on behalf of Unilever, the world's top g rossing seller of soap at the time), asked him to direct several commercials in order to launch the *Bris* (*Breeze*) soap in Sweden, he was 'absurdly grateful'. This was an offer he simply could not afford to refuse.

However, little is known about these commercials, for all the voluminous literature on Ingmar Bergman. And to the extent that they are mentioned at all, they are treated as a peripheral part of Bergman's feature films, sometimes even as an unfortunate mistake, and thus, tend not to be described or analysed at all. A rather typical example can be found in *The Personal Vision of Ingmar Bergman* from 1962 by Jörn Donner, the first Swedish book-length study on Bergman to be translated into English. Donner dismisses the commercials in four lines, although grudgingly admitting that they are 'charming', adding: 'It cannot be denied that Bergman has the ability to create something personal and valuable within the framework of cinematographic improvisation'. Equally reticent was Marianne Höök, another Swedish author who wrote a book on Bergman in the early 1960s. She limits herself to observing that the *Bris* commercials forced the director 'to reflect on his craft … and perhaps to some extent re-examine his own youthful attitudes toward genius', adding, 'Bergman emerged from the soap commercial episode cleansed. He had achieved a new maturity, and perhaps this necessary hiatus had given him the breathing space to enter a new period.'

This approach has not only persisted over the decades but has also been reiterated by international scholars. For instance, Frank Gado's monumental *The Passion of Ingmar Bergman*, almost a quarter of a century later, has only a few words to spare for the Bris commercials. Also, Gado reiterates Höök's comments that the commercials are worth mentioning only to the extent that they indirectly furthered Bergman's film career: 'Of far greater consequence', he wrote, 'than their influence on the future of Swedish advertising … these skits triggered his rise to international celebrity.' This, according to Gado, since then head of Svensk Filmindustri, saw a new and profitable side of the melancholy Bergman, and thus 'coaxed' him into making film comedies, which in turn would enable him to make *The Seventh Seal* in 1957, 'the film that was not only to transform his career but also to establish him as one of the great lions on the world's cultural scene'. In retrospect, Gado concludes, 'it appears *Bris* indeed had wondrous powers'.

Clearly, then, the perspective in all these examples is staunchly auteurist, verging on the romantic. The *Bris* commercials are judged only in relation to the rest of Bergman's oeuvre, and thus deemed only as a mere episode or stepping stone in his cinematic career – but hardly interesting in themselves. However, the *Bris* commercials *are* interesting, in and for themselves. The fact is that at the time they were very favourably received, and were even, according to Bergman himself, considered rather 'revolutionary'. In what way, one may finally ask; what made them so special that it seems they even saved Bergman for posterity?

Let us begin by stating some facts regarding the external circumstances. First of all, the *Bris* commercials were not made hastily and with a small budget, as was common practice in those days. Quite the opposite. The fact is that the Sunlight Soap head office in London had known for some time that their Swedish commercials were poorly made and ineffective. As a result, they ordered Ragnar M. Lindberg, then in charge of the company's advertising, to make drastic improvements. Lindberg proceeded to contact Ingmar Bergman, who, to his surprise, 'didn't tell him to go to hell', but instead agreed to make the commercials. His only condition was that he be given exactly the same technical equipment and artistic freedom he would have when filming a feature-length film. This included being able to continue working in the studios of Svensk Filmindustri in Råsunda, as well as with his regular cameraman, Gunnar Fischer, and – more importantly – retaining full control of the contents of the commercials, from script to final cut. Sunlight Soap in turn agreed to these terms, on the condition that Bergman in each commercial, include a specially-written sales pitch: 'It's not sweat that smells, it's the skin bacteria, when they come into contact with sweat. *Bris* kills bacteria! Thus, no bacteria, no smell!' The length of the films were also agreed in advance: 'I had', Bergman has said, 'exactly 34 metres of raw film to work with – just over a minute – in which the whole sermon had to be squeezed in.'

It is natural to approach the commercials in the order that that they were made, particularly as the first was clearly conceived as some kind of 'prologue' or teaser to the films that were to follow. This is indicated both by its neutral, informational title, *Tvålen Bris* (*Bris the Soap*), as well as by its contents: its primary function was to introduce not only the product itself but also the jovial, elderly actor (John Botvid), donning a hat and a sumptuous moustache, who was to reappear in several of the later commercials.

Stylistically, this teaser contained a preview of things to come, sometimes even literally, since it was a veritable showcase of theatre curtains, movie screens and other visual conceits. The very first image of *Bris the Soap* opens on a young woman, seated at a piano in front of theatre curtains, who, with a quick smile towards the camera, proceeds to play a tune. Cut to a shot of the curtain being raised, revealing behind it a movie screen, upon which a close-up of yet another young woman is projected. Looking straight into the camera she engagingly asks: 'Isn't this an unusually cute package?'

Instead of a continuing this set-up, the curtain quickly lowers, whereupon a slight backtrack reveals a elderly gentleman (Botvid) in front of the now closed curtain, who clearly would have preferred seeing a bit more of the woman on the screen. But he is also intrigued by the object in her hand: 'But what was it…?', he asks. And suddenly, as if by lucky chance, the woman from the screen walks into the shot, cheerfully replying: 'It's the new soap, of course!' Thus fulfilling her role as knowledgeable consumer and a role so easily afforded to young women in commercials.

This is followed by a quick pan to the right, conjuring forth yet another young woman in front of a wash basin, dressed in nothing but a bra and a slip. And sure enough, the elderly gentleman man soon reappears in the left part of the frame: 'Ah', he triumphantly calls out, 'a soap called Buzz!' He is of course depicted as slightly hard of hearing, giving the women cause to correct him, thus constantly reminding him – and the audience – of the new soap's name. Which is exactly what the woman in the bra does, before adding: 'Just watch this wonderful lather', whereupon, in a surprising move, she suddenly splashes it up onto a mirror (which up until that moment had remained 'invisible'), so that she is concealed behind the lather. Not only a visually pleasing conceit but also a, graphically, very efficient argument, as it were.

This is followed by a pan in the opposite direction, the gentleman quickly moving with it, again speaking up: 'A soap called Gust!' The piano-playing woman enters in from frame-left, correcting him in close-up, whereupon he disappears behind her. The woman, who has a bar of *Bris* soap in her hand, has it taken from her by a hand appearing from behind, whereupon she glides out of frame, giving room to the person who stretched out his hand, namely a man dressed in a white laboratory coat, who furnishes the audience with some scientific truths. However, not in the form of a lecture, as one would expect. Instead he walks up to the theatre curtains, visible in the background, finally allowing the gentleman to see the whole film that was cut short at the beginning.

Thus, the woman from the screen is back where she belongs, in close-up. 'Did you know that perspiration in and by itself doesn't smell?', she now asks. A quick pan right to the piano woman who continues the sales pitch: 'It's only when it gets in contact with bacteria that it smells', which is followed by yet another pan, this time to the woman from the wash basin-scene. She has now made it into a shower, where she intones the final part of the pitch ('*Bris* is the only soap that kills germs!'), while working up a sensuous layer of lather on her shoulder.

Bergman had at first insisted on nudity in all the shower scenes of the *Bris* films ('since this is common practice when showering'), but was turned down by the London office of Sunlight Soap. And true enough, the woman's bra from the wash-basin scene is off in this particular shower scene, but due to the modest cropping she remains quite decent. Obviously Bergman hit the bottom line of his deal regarding artistic freedom (unusual as it was in this context), leaving one to speculate whether he would have gotten away with it had the producers been Swedish. After all, this was a time when 'the nude Swedish girl' was starting to become a reality, not least through Swedish films like *Hon dansode en sommar* (*She Danced One Summer*, 1951).

In any case, this first film of the *Bris* series ends with the curtain lowered one last time, and sure enough, up in front of it appears the man in the lab coat to tell one the final truth: 'Yes indeed', he concludes with his sonorous sounding voice, while looking firmly into the camera, '*Bris* is an anti-odour soap'. Then a quick pan left back to our forgetful gentleman, who gets a final chance to play befuddled: 'Well, imagine that, such a good soap... But what was it called...?' Whereupon he gets his final reward, as the woman from the movie screen cuddles up right next to him, supplying the answer one last time ('Briiiiis...') before fade-out.

What is worth stressing here is not so much all the classic tricks of commercials (the half-naked girls and the question, constantly repeated and answered, designed to familiarise the viewer with the product), but the imaginative and skilful use of *mise-en-scène*. This whole commercial contains only two cuts; one at the beginning, and one at the end, both times when the curtain to the film screen is raised, while everything in between is achieved in one long, smooth take. Given the cumbersome equipment at the time, this must have taken a significant amount of plannning.

This intricate *mise-en-scène* would of course later become one of the stylistic trademarks of Bergman's feature films. But equally interesting is the way that it makes these commercials differ from contemporary (both Swedish and international) commercials, made both for television and theatre screening, which almost exclusively rely on short takes and fast editing. Another notable exception is Swedish film director Roy Andersson's commercials and shorts.

The other point worth stressing is the explicit self-referentiality and implicit self-criticism of the commercial. Such self-criticism has naturally been part and parcel of the cinema almost since its inception. It is, however, arguably quite an unusual trait in a commercial from the early 1950s. Let us delve into this aspect further, as the self-reflexivity of this introductory *Bris* commercial is varied ingeniously in the subsequent commercials.

All of the nine *Bris* commercials deal with similarly film-related, theatre-related, or other media-related techniques, including quite radical cinematic experiments and tricks – animation, pixillation, advanced superimpositions, and so on. Of the four commercials that deal explicitly with film as a medium, three are worth describing more closely in this context. The first of these is called *The Film Screening*, and utilises the double-edged concept of 3D in a humorous fashion. The first shot: a movie theatre filled with an expectant audience, all wearing 3D glasses. The second shot: a white, flickering movie screen, a frame within a frame, which gradually gathers itself into a recognisable picture – in this case, a woman's shapely leg. Thirdly, a reaction shot of the (overwhelmingly male) audience, which seems very pleased.

The owner of the legs turns out to be a dark-haired beauty, who now (still framed by a movie frame) is about to take a shower. But turning on the taps, she accidentally aims her hand-held shower at the movie audience, whereupon the water – 'real' and very wet water – sprays out into the movie theater. 'Oh, forgive me', she cries out, 'I completely forgot that this movie is three-dimensional!'

Having passed through the boundaries of fiction, the woman seems to accept the full consequences of what has happened. For she now stretches out her wet arm so that it protrudes outside the frame of the movie screen like a 'real', three-dimensional limb, and in that very same gesture allowing an elderly gentleman (John Botvid once again) seated in first row to eagerly sniff at the soap she is washing herself with. Suddenly the woman slips on the bar of soap, falls and ends up outside the screen, in the arms of the elderly gentleman, who now is positively beaming with pleasure. 'I've always enjoyed three-dimensionality', he muses.

The second of the implicitly self-critical commercials is *The Picture Puzzle*, conceived as a kind visual riddle, and as such perhaps the most ingenious of all the *Bris* films, especially in the way in which it comments on film reception. It begins with a jumble of seemingly discon-nected pictures. We first see a man in close-up, wiping the sweat off his forehead. Then cut to a sniffing dog, in turn followed by a woman shaking her head – an opening which eventually dissolves into an increasingly bewildering fog of fragments and detached symbols, each new image accompanied by a dull drumming sound.

This bewilderment is of course deliberate, for suddenly a window shade is raised – as if the movie screen itself was suddenly being lifted away – and behind it appears, once again, a young woman. 'Was it difficult to understand this little film?', she asks with obvious mock sympathy. 'Well then I'll help you', she continues. 'May we ask the projectionist to run it one more time?' – whereupon she pulls down the movie screen/window shade. The images from the beginning are now repeated on the screen (a veritable instant replay before its time!), while the woman now, standing beside the screen with an indulgent smile, as if speaking to a group of children, explains what each picture 'means'. 'Perspiration', she intones (picture of the sweating man), 'smells' (the sniffing dog), 'but not' (woman shaking her head), 'if you use *Bris*', launching into what, by then, had become the familiar *Bris* sales pitch. What is interesting about *The Picture Puzzle* is that it is nothing less than a lesson on how a film is made, and how it is assembled in the editing process. That is, fragments that in themselves mean nothing, become components of a meaningful whole only when they are assembled into a story.

Naturally, nowadays media or meta-games of this kind are commonplace, indeed only another efficient part of the sales pitch if you will – the medium as well as the product selling themselves in one swoop. But what has become cliché today was certainly regarded as some-thing radically different in commercials in the early 1950s. Indeed, the *Bris* commercials can even be seen as a kind of anti-commercials. For in *The Picture Puzzle* the audience was allowed to follow not only how a film is edited together to achieve a certain effect, but also, in the proc-ess, how a sales pitch is created – and thus revealed as something quite artificial. In that case, an alternative message seems to lurk between the lines: 'As you see with your own eyes, what is said here rests on pure magic, created by these images pasted together – so don't believe a word of it.'

'Magic' is, indeed, the word. In fact, it is the very theme for the third of the self-referential *Bris* commercials worth looking at in closer detail. It is called *The Inventor*, and opens with a man having a dream, conceived as a Georges Méliès farce, including painted backdrops and animated sequences, all rendered in a jerky silent film speed. More specifically, the man dreams that he is an inventor, who has just invented soap (naturally). This is illustrated by means of an animated sequence, seen as if through the round magnifying glass of a microscope, which shows a small man violently hitting a hammer on the head of an ugly looking guy. In the words of the script: 'A small Bacteria killer loaded to his teeth with weapons is performing a massacre on several hideous and trashy-looking Bacteria'!

Hailed as a genius by the Academy of Science, the inventor is triumphantly hoisted in the air – before suddenly waking up. This does not deter him, however: he now goes on to tell his wife that he has invented something amazing while dreaming, bursting into the sales' pitch: 'You see, it's not sweat itself that smells…' – before being interrupted by his bored wife, who of course already knows, as well as recites, the rest of it!

Thus, not only is this commercial conceived as a Méliès pastiche in terms of visual magic and trickery. But so is, in effect, *Bris* the soap itself and the wondrous qualities it is claimed to have: just as fake and unbelievable. In short, the transparent message of the *Bris* commercials is, by various film and media games, cloaked in an alternative message, as it were: that everything in these films is mere hocus-pocus – not least those huge and literally magnified problems that can, as if by magic, be solved by (of all things) a soap.

Maaret Koskinen

REFERENCES

Bergman, I. (1947) 'Det förtrollade marknadsnöjet' *Biografbladet*, 28, 3.

Donner, J. (1962) *The Personal Vision of Ingmar Bergman*. Bloomington: Indiana University Press.

Gado, F, (1986) *The Passion of Ingmar Bergman*. Durham: Duke University Press.

Höök, M. (1962) *lngmar Bergman*. Stockholm: Wahlström & Widstrand.

ELDFÅGELN THE FIRE-BIRD

HASSE EKMAN, SWEDEN/ITALY, 1952

In a chronicle in 1950, Carl Anders Dymling, the head of Svensk Filmindustri, proclaimed a crisis in Swedish cinema. The reason for this sudden alarm was a shock increase of the entertainment tax on cinema tickets from 24 per cent to 39. This, in turn, was a result of the great success of Swedish cinema in the late 1940s. In 1947, no less than 44 Swedish feature films were released – an unparalleled event in the country's film history.

In 1950, only 9 per cent of the films in distribution were national productions. Still, the importance of their role is revealed by the fact that they represented 25 per cent of the total film attendance. In protest, the Swedish film producers decided to close down their studios from New Year 1951. If a Swedish standard feature film was to cover its production costs, it now had to reach an audience of 800,000 spectators. The boycott only lasted for six months, as it resulted in a parliament decision in the spring of 1951 that 20 per cent of the entertainment tax should be used to subsidy film production.

Despite the talk of crisis in 1950, the threat of television that would become a reality in Sweden only seven years later was still non-existent. It was not until 1954 that Sandrews, the second largest production company, produced a series of television test transmissions which were shown in radio and music stores over one week, and regular transmissions began in late 1956. Still, several stylistic strategies developed in the US to combat television – wide screen, colour – were widely adopted in the Swedish film industry as well in the early 1950s, but without any real effect; hence, perhaps, a certain reluctance from some producers, such as Anders Sandrew, to standardise the use of colour.

However, there was more to the films produced than the domestic context. *Hets* (*Frenzy*, 1944), directed by Alf Sjöberg and based on a manuscript by Ingmar Bergman, had reached an international audience (the film won the Grand Prix National at the Cannes Film Festival in 1946) and attracted a fair amount of critical acclaim. Also, Peter Ustinov's play *Frenzy*, based on *Hets*, which had its premiere in London 1948, seems to have increased interest in the film in English-speaking countries. In 1950, three Swedish producers were invited by the Motion Pictures Association of America to study American production and the voluntary censorship practised by Joseph Breen's office in Hollywood. According to one of them, Rune Waldekranz, this trip revealed a clear, albeit modest, new interest in Swedish productions for the American art theatres.

In 1951, Sweden enjoyed another international success, as Sandrews' *Fröken Julie* (also directed by Alf Sjöberg) won the Palme d'Or at Cannes, together with *Miracolo in Milano* by Vittorio de Sica. Moreover, the one film excepted from the production boycott in 1951, *Hon dansade en sommar* (directed by Arne Mattson) won the Golden Bear in Berlin in 1952 and, as a consequence, was widely distributed. Part of the attention is generally supposed to have been due to the sensation caused by the directness of the film's erotic content and its nakedness, in the context of the film, considered as natural. Thus, the situation for film production in Sweden was paradoxical in the early 1950s: on one hand, the economic conditions for national production were hardening; on the other, producers started to nourish a grand vision – the hope of overcoming these conditions with a widened market, by means of a new international breakthrough for Swedish cinema.

Waldekranz, a producer at Sandrews during the 1950s, offered a vivid description of the actual situation of film production in Sweden in 1950:

> On the world map of cinema Sweden had now remained almost as unknown as Egypt or Greece for a quarter of a century. But in film history there were still echoes of the days of glory of Swedish cinema. It was time we called attention to ourselves … To my employer Anders Sandrew, I pointed out that Swedish cinema no longer could be limited only to the domestic market with its preference for cosy popular comedies. In order to make Swedish quality film profitable in a time of increasing costs there was a need for a bigger market, a market outside the country's borders. But we could only compete internationally if we could offer something new and unusual, audacious films that were different, issued from what was specifically Swedish.

What Waldekranz suggested was that Swedish cinema should turn international by way of the national, by returning to tradition and renewing it. It is a striking fact that, although historians in general have mentioned the ambition to create an internationally important Swedish cinema anew, they have barely discussed a central aspect, namely that the clearest expression for this aim was an attempt to revive the 'golden years' of Swedish film of the 1920s. This was to be realised through the shooting of new versions of its greatest successes, among others *Herr*

Arnes penningar (*The Treasure of Arne*, Gustaf Molander, 1954) and *Körkarlen* (Arne Mattson, *Phantom Carriage*, 1958).

However, this grand attempt to revive the Swedish silent film tradition turned out to be a commercial failure. Yet the production companies also tried a different path to reach other audiences than the domestic one, namely co-producing films with other countries, thereby assuring them at least a limited international distribution. During the 1950s, Sweden was involved in no less than 18 international co-productions, five of which were Nordic. Four films were produced in collaboration with film companies in the United States and one with Argentina, whereas the rest, eight films in all, were European co-productions involving different partners: France, West Germany, Italy, Poland, Spain and the UK. Five films no longer exist in any known copy, but as for the rest, they remain an interesting body of films in examining not only Swedish film production in particular, but also ideas of European collaboration and interrelation in 1950s cinema, as well as the relationship to American film. The first of these co-productions, *Eldfågeln* (*The Fire-Bird*, 1952) can be traced back to the period of the boycott.

During the 1951 boycott, the studios did not remain completely empty. Apart from the Nordisk Tonefilm production *Hon dansade en sommar*, Lorens Marmstedt also took the opportunity to produce a twenty-minute film, an experiment with dance and colour. The film was shot in Gevacolor and released as the first Swedish short film in colour; the laboratory work on the film had to be done in Paris according to the *Svensk Filmografi* (*Swedish Filmography*). It starred Marmstedt's wife, Ellen Rasch, the prima ballerina at the Royal Opera. The choreography was by Maurice Béjart. He stayed in Stockholm from 1950–52, following his studies and touring, choreographing for Terrafilm. Together with Björn Holmgren, the first dancer at the Royal Opera, he also danced the male solo parts in *The Fire-Bird*.

Marmstedt was so happy with the outcome of the short experiment that he decided to make a framing story, which was written and directed by Hasse Ekman and shot at the Sandrew studios. The film was post-produced at Denham Laboratories, Middlesex. Rasch played the lead throughout, the ballerina Linda Corina, with Italian opera singer Tito Gobbi in the male lead, as singer Mario Vanni. Marmstedt also added two more ballets by Béjart, all in order to create a dance film for the international market.

An Italian production company was involved in shooting of a number of scenes that took place in Italy. The Swedish production company Terrafilm also concluded a distribution deal with the American producer, Sol Lesser. According to the *Swedish Filmography* an alternative ending to the story – a convincingly happy one – was made on request from the distributor.

This version, however, was never used in Scandinavia. In the surround material, there is a short line written to convince the international co-producer: 'If the American censor should be doubtful about certain short parts of the introductory ballet, reaction shots of Mario in his box can be substituted.' There was also a sheet of paper containing an outline of scenes that were intended for a specific German version of the film.

The original short film, *Meeting with a Stranger*, drew its original inspiration from a song by Edith Piaf: 'Un monsieur me suit dans la rue' ('A man follows me in the street'). A young girl in Montmartre receives a message from a stranger. She leaves her lover and seeks out the stranger, but is unable to find him. Her search transforms into a nightmare, where dark creatures attempt to capture her. When returning to her studio, the stranger is there, waiting for her. Scared, but strangely attracted, she enters into a passionate dance with him – and then sinks lifeless to the ground. The stranger's name is Death. Musically, the ballet is accompanied by a potpourri of French *chansons*. This short film is integrated in the framing story as a film in the film, shown to the Italian singer Mario Vanni, which convinces him to go to Stockholm in order to pursue the leading lady, whose beauty has enthralled and transfixed him.

The two other ballet sequences included in *The Fire-Bird* were *Grand Pas de Deux Classique* (danced by Ellen Rasch and Björn Holmgren), based on music from 'The Nutcracker' and 'The Fire-Bird'. The plot of the latter, however, was changed as to correspond to the plot of the film. An evil queen witnesses in her magic mirror the beautiful Firebird (Rasch) with its shining red plumage. She sends a hunter (Béjart) to the forest to kill the bird – but instead, the hunter falls in love. When the bird flees, he blesses it with an arrow. But the little grey sparrow (Holmgren), which has always loved the Firebird, saves her life.

Swedish film critic Robin Hood (Bengt Idestam-Almqvist), who had a broad knowledge of dance history, commented that *Meeting with a Stranger* revealed Maurice Béjart to be a disciple of Roland Petit and Jean Cocteau, in his avoidance of heavily populated scenes. However, he found that the last ballet functioned brilliantly with its increased scope. Thus, the choreography for *The Fire-Bird* might be seen as a progression in Béjart's work. As he left Sweden for Brussels later in the 1950s, he founded the famous ensemble Ballet du XXe siècle, for which he choreographed over one hundred pieces, several on an epic scale, with stunning effects; a style that he seems to have adopted for the first time in *The Fire-Bird*.

In the framing story, there is no evil queen but a dancer colleague jealous of Linda's success. She wants to hurt her and hides a razorblade in her ballet shoes. Linda has broken off her long-time engagement with the stage manager at the Opera, Frank, and falls in love with a famous Italian singer, Mario Vanni. After a short moment of happiness, he strikes her in anger as she refuses to quit dancing to follow him around the world. As a result, her sense of balance is destroyed and she has to give up working. However, Mario never gets to know about this, as they remain separated. Linda's old fiancé returns and they decide to marry. In the end, the evil colleague who is about to replace Linda in the role as The Firebird forgetfully puts on the shoes with the razorblades. Linda then makes one last comeback on the opening night, which ends the film.

In the *Swedish Filmography*, it is stated that the international version lets the singer get his ballerina in the end. The archive material at the Swedish Film Institute, however, allows for no such interpretation. In the script used by the assistant director, also responsible for continuity, there is a page added in the end with a dialogue sequence, which is not contained in any other script version. In this version, it is underlined – in contrast to the relatively open ending of the original version, which ends only on an exchange of looks – that the original couple, Linda and Frank, are happily reunited. The last lines could not be clearer: 'I love you. – Same here.' This also makes the parallel to the Sparrow and the Firebird in the ballet clearer.

Apart from the 'Fire-Bird' ballet, which is intended to create a *mise-en-abyme* between ballet and frame story, other less elaborated parallels are also established between the stage performances and the screen story. In the first ballet, the girl's meeting with the stranger which results in her collapsing on the floor, could be said to parallel the dancer's meeting with the stranger in the frame story, which leads to her collapsing after having lost her sense of balance. And Mozart's 'Don Giovanni', part of which is performed in the film with Tito Gobbi in the leading role, establishes an almost too obvious connection between the 'Don Giovanni' of the opera and his performer, the Don Giovanni of the frame story.

The most striking aspect of the frame story is the weakness of its plot. Its main function seems to be to transfer between the different stage performances in the film. In addition to the three ballets and the opera, however, there are also a number of performances within the frame story. Already in the first scene of the film, Mario Vanni is rehearsing 'Torna'. When Linda meets Mario at an official dinner party, there is a performance of a Swedish folk song, 'Ack Värmeland du sköna', by the Swedes present (in reality like in the fiction members of the Royal Opera), in honour of the Italian singer.

When the singer discovers that he is supposed to give a speech, he is very embarrassed, and proposes to sing instead, which leads to a long performance of a Neapolitan love song, 'Marechiare' ('Quando spunta la luna…'), while he walks around the room among the dinner guests. In the very short dialogue that follows between Linda and Mario, she asks him to take her to Italy and sing this song for her there. The next scene takes place in Italy, where the sleeping Linda is awoken by a group of men, among them Mario, performing not 'Marechiare' but 'Ack Värmeland du sköna' on the terrace below her balcony.

The night at the opera with Mozart's 'Don Giovanni' provides another elaborated moment of transfer. And towards the end of the film, Linda stands listening for the last time to a record with Mario singing. Already in an early presentation of the idea of the film, before shooting, it is clear that the performance sequences are supposed to last for 52 minutes (the film is timed to 94 minutes). There is a detailed account of the different arias and songs included. These transfers also feature tourist images of Sweden and Italy that were typical of several co-productions from the period. Views of Stockholm are shown, and the beauty of the city is underlined by Mario's impresario, Spinky, who advertises its advantages at the beginning of the film.

According to Leif Furhammar, a Swedish scholar and film critic, the result of the film experiment with *The Fire-Bird* turned out so badly that Anders Sandrew, former partner of Terrafilm, lost his confidence in Lorens Marmstedt, which in turn led to a severe limitation of Marmstedt's possibilities as a producer.

The critical reception of the 1950s in general seems to have been extremely hostile towards the attempts to international collaboration. As the 'threat', or rather the global dominance, of American cinema could no longer be ignored or – like in the 1920s – hidden behind illusions of qualitative superiority, it is obvious that the idea of a Swedish national cinema became all the more central as it was hopelessly marginal. In other words, that the press reception of the period seems to reflect a strongly felt need of defining and redefining the nation by narrating it, both in the films themselves and by commenting upon them in the cultural debate.

The Fire-Bird turned out to be no exception. The film was badly received by critics in Sweden. The frame story was particularly criticised, but neither the dance performances nor their cinematic realisation seemed to impress the critics. Hasse Ekman, the director, was criticised for having overestimated his own artistic capacity. From an *auteur* perspective, however, *The Fire-Bird* may in many ways be seen as typical of its director, who most of all has become known for his directorial ability combined with an unrestrained eclecticism.

Several critics also made the parallel to British or American song- or dance films of the period, like Powell and Pressburger's *The Red Shoes* (1948) or *Tales of Hoffman* (1951). The production of *The Fire-Bird* obviously must be regarded as an attempt to compete with these films. A similar tendency to rely on the likeness to other international successes can be traced in several co-productions. *Laughing in the Sunshine* (Daniel Birt, 1956), for instance, is strongly reminiscent of *Roman Holiday* (William Wyler, 1953).

Swedish critics did not note this similarity. They mostly complained about the obvious banality of the film. In contrast to these two films, the Swedish-Argentinian *Primavera de la vida* (1957) directed by Arne Mattsson and with Folke Sundquist in the male lead, attempted to exploit a contemporary Swedish film, *Hon dansade en sommar*, by the same director and with the same star. This film had known an enormous success not least in Latin America, which obviously made the idea seem particularly attractive to the producers, but not to the critics.

In the case of *The Fire-Bird*, there was one exception to the general criticism towards co-productions. With his broad knowledge of dance history, Robin Hood (Bengt Idestam-Almquist) admired both the choreography and the performances of *The Fire-Bird*. He also initiated a debate in the press where he accused his colleagues of being too negative towards the artistic achievements in the film.

Erotikon (Mauritz Stiller, 1920) also never reached any great fame during the golden years, but contemporary critics have viewed it as one of the greatest masterpieces of the period. Partly, the contemporary rejection was due to the use of the biggest stars from the Swedish Opera ballet in a stunning dance performance integrated as an entire sequence in the narration, which was considered both boring and alien to cinema. Film as performance – this device could on the other hand be true both of *Erotikon* and *The Fire-Bird*, and it reveals a common striving to integrate different media, which remains pertinent throughout several decades of Swedish film production.

Astrid Söderbergh Widding

REFERENCES

L. Åhlander (ed.) (1986) *Svensk Filmografi*. Uppsala: Almqvist & Wiksell.

Dymling, C. A. (1950) *Krönikor 1949-1950*. Stockholm: Zetterlund & Thelanders Boktryckeri AB.

Furhammar, L. (1991) *Filmen i Sverige, En historia i tio kapitel*. Höganäs: Förlags AB Wiken.

Hood, R. (1952) 'Review of *The Fire-bird*', *Stockholms Tidningen*, 13 August.

NISKAVUOREN HETA HETA NISKAVUORI

EDVIN LAINE, FINLAND, 1952

In *Niskavuoren Heta* (*Heta Niskavuori*, 1952) family melodrama meets ethnographic realism, resulting in a classic work of both Finnish cinema and gender history. Like the two previous films portraying the Niskavuori family, *Niskavouren naiset* (*The Women of Niskavuori*, 1938) and *Loviisa* (1946), it is a love triangle and a narrative of desire and loss. Heta, daughter of a wealthy peasant family, marries a poor farm hand, Akusti, because she is pregnant, forsaken by the man she loves and in need to be rescued for the sake of her reputation. For her, this is a humiliation beyond any measure and results in a fierce life-long effort to gain back her class position. Only after her husband's death, at the end of the film, she realises the true loss of her life: the love of Akusti who dedicates his life to Heta without receiving reciprocity, raises a family with three children and becomes the wealthiest man in the village. He is loyally served by a handicapped maid, Siipirikko ('the Broked-Winged'), who loves him but whose dedication is recognised and rewarded only after his death.

Like the two previous and the three following Niskavuori films of the 1950s – *Niskavouren Aarne* (*Aarne Niskavuori* [1954]), *Niskavouri taistelee* (*Niskavuori Fights* [1957]) and *Niskavouren naiset* (*The Women of Niskavuori* [1958]) – *Heta Niskavuori* carries an ethnographic impulse to bring a disappearing peasant culture to the silver screen. Showcasing 'typically Finnish' landscapes and depicting peasant milieu and agrarian work in long montage sequences inserted among the dramatic scenes of suppressed emotions, the film exemplifies a form of cinematic national imagination in the reconstruction period, a Finnish version of the post-war, trans-European *Heimat* genre.

In terms of its visual aesthetic, *Heta Niskavuori* is associated with a number of the post-war books (*Finland in Pictures*, *Finnish Scenes*, *The Image of Finland*, *Finland From a Bird's-eye View*, *Finland in Colour Pictures*, and so on) representing Finland through photographs. These coffee-table books not only featured landscape photography from different regions and seasons, but also ethnological imagery of rural work, as well as pictures of buildings and monuments. Alongside the representations of nature therefore, very importantly, *Heimat* (local societies, peasant literature, films and landscape photography) was imagined in terms of work.

Indeed, *Heta Niskavuori* was characterised as 'imbued with a Finnish settler, a peasant spirit expanding its living'; 'film commemorating real country life and its everyday tasks'. The publicity-stills from fields and forests (often portraying a man with a horse) rooted a reading of the Niskavuori films as ethnological representations of work. In *Finland in Pictures*, a section entitled 'The Main Source of Living' featured photographs of men working in agriculture: clearing a forest, ploughing a field, or driving a tractor, often with a horse. This imagery had been established as typical of peasant culture in the 1943 book *Isien työ* (*The Work of Fathers*) by Kustaa Vilkuna and Eino Mäkinen, and was cited in the montage sequence of *Heta Niskavuori* portraying Akusti's and Heta's toil. Publicity stills framing *Heta Niskavuori* displayed nets and other fishing equipment, Akusti clearing the forest and in a studio portrait of Heta, placing a handle of a hoe in her lap creating the peasant-effect.

Images of rural work linked *Heta Niskavuori* to the aesthetic of picture books, and haymaking was a favourite topic of the publicity stills for all Niskavuori films. The ethnographic and ethnologic impulse also associated *Heta Niskavuori* with the post-war enthusiasm for the 'home-region movement', an emergence of local associations committed to promoting the traditions and values of old peasant culture. Citing Zachris Topelius's *Boken om vårt land* (*Our Country*, 1875) in their rules, these associations attempted to restore, after the lost war, an emotional attachment to the 'home-region' as a ground for identity. The movement defined the 'sense of home-region' as a sense of belonging 'to the soil, nature, the people, and culture of the home-region'. This was the ethos of *Heimat* films.

Like the other Niskavuori films, *Heta Niskavuori* was based on a play and was preceded by popular and critically-acclaimed theatre performances. Transposing the stage production of *Heta Niskavuori* to the screen involved re-staging the narrative for outdoor scenes with a significant emphasis on landscape scenery. This included, certainly, the idealisation of countryside as the locus of Finnishness and even 'a desire to return to the rural hearth'. The centrality of the landscape imagery could, however, also be read in terms of genre memory; from this perspective, the 'Finnish feeling' was an effect of familiarity – constructing a *particular* kind of landscape; coded, sedimented and reiterated as 'national', a landscape 'close and dear to us', 'thoroughly our own and familiar to us'.

The power of tourism, travel and visual art in generating 'the national sentiment' had been emphasised in cultural nationalism since the nineteenth century, and the imagery of *Heta Niskavuori* can be read in relation to this rich intertextual framework. Furthermore, in the post-war context, the borders of the Finnish nation-state were once again renegotiated and half-a-million Finns lost their 'home-region'. In this acute situation, the interest in such a concept of *Heimat* can be read as a need for readjusting the national imaginary.

With her Niskavuori family saga, Hella Wuolijoki (1886–1953), the Estonian-born playwright, businesswoman and later politician, created a trope for the national imagination, which the popular film adaptations of the 1930s–1950s brought to life first in cinema, then in television. In addition to being a locus for imagining national communities, it also offered a timescape, as it tells the history of the powerful and wealthy Niskavuori family from the 1880s to the post-war era. In so doing, the film series comprises both the emergence of Finland as an independent nation and its political, economic and cultural modernisation.

In this analysis, however, the popular appeal of *Heta Niskavuori* both in the 1950s and later, as well as in innumerable theatre productions, is first and foremost based on the film's representation of 'Finnish gender' and with its engagement with culturally resonant images of femininity and masculinity. As a narrative of desire and loss, the film encapsulates powerful cultural discourses on 'Finnish women' and 'Finnish men' that were circulating in the postwar era and that have continued to frame identity narratives of many Finns. Tellingly, in 1988, a feature article in *Teatteri*, the Finnish theatre magazine, when presenting the Niskavuori plays as 'the common national memory' and a self-evident intertextual framework for any talk on 'Finnishness', saw a perfect fit between sociological analysis of Finnish life stories and the Niskavuori saga.

In this taxonomy, Heta and Akusti were seen to personify the imperatives of peasant life in which 'external forces influence life, exceeding the will of an individual who nevertheless reconciles herself'. Heta's and Akusti's marriage, furthermore, was identified as a plausible scenario, a 'straightforward family hell'. As an imaginary trope for Finland, then, Niskavuori as a familial metaphor – in the story of Loviisa and Juhani, the protagonists of *Loviisa*, as well as in that of Heta and Akusti – articulates an image of the nation as filled with tensions. The nation's unity, here, is founded on humiliation, negation and submission.

The character of Heta Niskavuori has become a cultural image; in journalism and everyday speech it circulates as a stereotype of the 'strong Finnish woman', the proud and relentless woman who is less a mother and wife than a matron, who commands and controls and who cannot recognise or display any signs of weakness. This image, however, is older than Heta Niskavuori: the image of 'the hard-working peasant woman' occurs recurrently in writing about 'Finnish women' since the nineteenth century. In 1890, The Finnish Women's Association (Suomen Naisyhdistys) published *Portraits of Peasant Women's Lives in the Countryside*, and during the first half of the twentieth century, the importance of women's work was the political argument the different associations of agrarian women (Martha Association, Agricultural Women) used to gain visibility and political power.

In post-war Finland, again, the discourse of peasant culture gained a distinct, political momentum as the resettlement of 480,000 inhabitants from the areas ceded to the Soviet Union was organised through the Land Acquisition Act (1945). With the execution of this act, a large number of new small farms was established. In this context, the images of the matron-woman had also special relevance. A 1949 publication called *The Finnish Woman* monumentalised the agrarian woman as an exemplary 'Finnish woman' through whose efforts and achievements, it was implied, *all* Finnish women were rewarded with 'equality' – as Anni Voipio-Juvas and Kaarina Ruohtula write:

> The barren northland has not pampered its sons or daughters. The latter have always had to toil beside their menfolk to wrest a living from the soil. Finland's geopolitical position is such that nearly every generation has been obliged to wage war, and Finland has often been a battlefield. While the men fought, the women tilled the soil, brought up the children, and fostered culture. Moreover, after the devastation of war, both men and women have worked shoulder to shoulder to rebuild. In this hard school the Finnish woman has learned to be independent and capable of taking the initiative; and in many things the Finnish man has been in the habit of regarding her as an equal.

Both in publications such as *The Finnish Woman* and framings of Niskavuori films, folklore of the *Kalevala* (1835), the Finnish national epic, has been frequently invoked as an argument for and as evidence of women's authority. As the character of Louhi, the mighty witch-like mistress of the North, implies however, the character and its legacy are highly controversial. While in many feminist-nationalist representations of the 'Finnish woman' Louhi stood out as an admirable monument, in the post-war era of reconstruction – not only of economy, but also of gender – Louhi was evoked a *monstrous* figure. In reviews of the radio production of *Heta Niskavuori* in 1955, Heta's 'hardness, heartlessness and greediness were conceived to exceed those of Louhi'. This ambivalence, admiration and rejection, is also evident in the public reception of the film.

Rauni Luoma's performance of Heta was described as 'monumental', embodying all the desirable qualities of a matron-mother: she was characterised as 'grand, voluptuous, vigorous and stately, looking so that one believes that she both rules and does the work herself if necessary'. One reviewer summarised the character as a 'beautiful' image of 'an unabated woman' and as a 'peasant woman imbued with the spirit of the land'. Publicity stills also suggested this reading, as they portrayed Heta in postures signifying determination.

For example, a close-up also published on the cover of *Elokuva-aitta* from 1952 emphasised her dark eyes as she gazed straight at the viewer. In several medium shots, she posed with her hands crossed over her chest stressing her posture, her sturdy body and her command of the space she occupied. In several publicity stills, she was positioned to highlight her physical height. Significant, however, is her consequent portrayal without a smile on her face. Luoma, one of the most prominent female actors in 1950s Finnish theatre and film, received a Jussi prize (the annual film prize awarded by Finnish film journalists) for her role and in an annual *Elokuva-aitta* poll, she received the most votes for the best female role in a Finnish film.

While Luoma's performance was applauded, critical if no less engaged voices were many. The character of Heta was read as an icon of 'the propertied class'. In 1950, theatre reviews interpreted her to embody a heightened 'pride in ownership' and a 'lust for property', and hence, an 'aggressive peasant consciousness of class' and its characteristic conservatism. Furthermore, Heta was not read only in terms of class and social positioning, but she was also framed in psychological terms, as a personality who refuses to regret, to be humble, or to forgive. Both theatre and film reviews described her character in terms of 'pride', 'selfishness', 'hardness', 'coldness' and 'harshness'.

Later, over the course of the film's afterlife in television and the play's continuous life on stage, the readings of Heta have multiplied. In the 1970s, when *Heta Niskavuori* was staged in the National Theatre (Helsinki), Heta was termed 'a female tyrant' and 'a woman despot from Häme'. With regard to a television play produced in 1987, the reviewers' characterisations were equally harsh and colourful in tone. They described Heta as 'the most malicious and evil woman in Finland', 'an unparalleled bitch', 'hard as a rock', and 'a horrible hag'. In 2001, theatre reviews framed Heta as 'a Finnish she-devil', a bitter and unscrupulous woman who leads 'a pitiful, cold and hard life'. The hardness, coldness and strength attributed to Heta were the very qualities which were seen to make her so 'melodramatically interesting'.

Already in the early 1950s, critical readings of the image of Heta provoked discussion and counter-arguments, witnessing the affective force of this image of femininity. Some defended Heta as 'a proud woman but not hardened into a stone'. She was described as 'not a callous monster but a living and plausible being with special qualities'. Not merely a monster, she was also understood as showing compassion and a sense of humour. Film magazine readers, too, participated in discussions of Heta's character. In a letter to the editor of *Elokuva-aitta* in 1953, a reader called 'Everyman' opposed to the readings of Heta as a monster, pointed out that Heta 'did suffer herself as well'. In *Kotiliesi* in the same year, a reader underlined that Heta was, in fact, a perfect wife for Akusti, motivating him in moving up the social ladder. Furthermore, the *Kotiliesi* reader opposed the framings of Heta as a bad mother.

In the narration of the film, the character of Heta was juxtaposed with that of the maid Siipirikko, played by Mirjam Novero. Publicity stills, too, suggested such an interpretation as they connected Heta's children to Siipirikko who stands out as a positive 'other' of Heta. In one scene in the film, the children in fact refer to Siipirikko as their 'real' mother, and in the closing scene, they denounce Heta twice.

Both theatre and film reviewers read the Siipirikko character, the disabled servant of Heta and Akusti, as an image of victimised femininity, as her name 'the Broken-Winged' literally suggests. Portrayed as passive and powerless, weak and unappreciated, Siipirikko was viewed as a melodramatic character in a classic sense. She prompted sympathetic readings and invited pity. In these sentimental framings, she was described as one who 'remained pale in the shadows of life' and 'reminiscent of a featherless chick, whose whole being startles'. Reviewers described Siipirikko intertwining melodramatic and sentimental expressions ('crippled, fragile crofter's daughter') with references to the real world ('there are many like her').

According to Martha Vicinus, characters like Siipirikko were frequent in nineteenth-century melodrama: 'Their weakness made them vulnerable to the villain's worst designs, but their purity made them triumph, in heaven if not here.' In her analysis, 'One of the most popular elements in melodrama for a working-class audience was the theme of the mighty brought low'. For many reviewers as well, this theme was the main message of the closing scene of *Heta Niskavuori* in which Akusti prioritises Siipirikko and shows his power over Heta in his will. In that scene, the victimised maid defeated the monument-woman, at least momentarily.

Visual framings portrayed Siipirikko in an album-like photo with both her face and blond, plaited hair accentuated by the lighting. They depicted her in the kitchen interacting with the children Heta is shown to ignore and working outdoors with Akusti and Heta. Although her relationship to Heta in the publicity stills suggests fear and condemnation, she, unlike Heta, is portrayed with the children. A magazine advertisement showcased a publicity still in which Akusti and Siipirikko were framed as a couple, though separated by the fishing net. The framings of Akusti and Siipirikko, however, lacked romance and erotic coding. In addition, a publicity photo in which Akusti carries Siipirikko in his arms connotes illness and weakness more than anything else. In these framings, then, Siipirikko not only functioned as a negative of Heta, but also as a projection of Akusti's goodness, serving as a visible sign of his choice and good nature.

Whereas the character of Heta engages viewers through its ambivalent relation to the image of the 'strong Finnish woman', the character of Akusti Harjula (Kaarlo Halttunen) questions the stereotypical image of 'the weak Finnish man' that the male characters of Niskavuori films are usually seen to embody. In the 1930s and 1940s, both theatre and film reviewers expressed – repeatedly – discomfort and even resentment towards the Niskavuori men, Aarne and Juhani, deeming them 'nebulous', 'inconsistent' and 'implausible'. In contrast to these ambivalent and often disturbing figures of the Niskavuorean man-in-crisis, film and theatre reviewers have unanimously praised Akusti, the working-class male protagonist in *Heta Niskavuori*, as the only 'decent' male character in Niskavuori fictions. In the early 1950s, moreover, the interpretive framings of Akusti coincided with a redefinition of both 'the ideal Finnish man' and the nation.

It can be argued that the Finnish cinema of the 1950s concentrated almost obsessively on images of men and the male anxieties about social and cultural modernisation. Not only military farces, but also, vagabond and log-floating comedies, folksy buddy-comedies and crime films foregrounded 'male trouble' and imagery of consoling or utopian male homosociality. Film scholar Kimmo Laine suggests urbanisation, industrialisation, the ongoing reconstruction process and the traumas of the lost war as explanations for this obsession, but historian Matti Peltonen argues that there was, indeed, a conscious effort to formulate a new male ideal for post-war Finland.

Civic organisations promoting good manners and 'moral rectitude', academics and cultural critics as well as *auteurs* of popular culture participated in a debate which articulated several ideals: at least the conflicting images of *gentleman*, *folksy man* and '*jätkä*' ('logger') were offered. A manual of good manners from 1952 proposed a gentlemanly ideal, rooted in aristocratic notions and upper-middle-class decorum. Virtues included politeness, tact, honour, moderation, chivalry, sportsmanship, impeccable manners and appropriate clothing in different situations.

Ethnologists such as Sakari Pälsi and Kustaa Vilkuna, on the other hand, formulated a different ideal, that of a folksy man, based on peasant traditions and values. The two key criteria of this ideal included simplicity in the sense of being folksy and '*rehti*', connoting both honesty and integrity. The third male ideal, the *jätkä*, Peltonen argues, was rooted in the culture of the landless rural population and workers, and it was articulated in different forms of popular culture, in films and popular music identified as 'rillumarei'. The *jätkä* ideal prioritised fairness and equality above everything else.

In the reading offered here, the public reception of Akusti, the working-class hero turned landowner, is to be understood both in relation to the trouble with the images of Niskavuori men as well as the contemporaneous discussions of masculinities. Already in 1950, as *Heta Niskavuori* premiered on the stage, many writers expressed a sense of relief – 'a proper man at last!' Indeed, reviewers expressed affection and movement: 'It is hard for a viewer to disengage oneself from an emotion based sympathy for this character.' At the same time, reviewers celebrated Akusti's 'masculine boldness and endurance from a slightly insecure, but brave farmhand and groom into a wise village councillor'.

The idealising reception of Akusti thus implicitly welcomed him as the Missing Father of the Niskavuori saga. Fathers are generally absent from the Niskavuori narrative; Juhani's father figures in the storyline merely through his absence and reputation; Juhani himself, as Aarne's father, is described as alcoholic and unhappy in *The Women of Niskavuori*, and Aarne, having returned to Niskavuori (*Aarne Niskavuori*), repeats his father's fate and finally dies in war (*Niskavuori Fights*). In the Niskavuori saga, Akusti stands out as the only male figure who connotes qualities of 'heroic masculinity' other than virility and sexuality.

Whereas the male protagonists of the Niskavuori films of 1938 and 1946 were condemned for not knowing their path, Akusti was enjoyed as a protest against such un-heroic masculinity. In film advertisements, *Heta Niskavuori* was framed as 'a story about a proud woman and the hard-working, gentle Akusti', who was read as a counter-image of both Niskavuori men and his wife Heta. These definitional 'others' resulted in an interesting variety of framings.

Reviewers characterised Akusti as an ideal Finnish man and a 'manly' man. He was ascribed both qualities of a man-of-the-people and the logger, as readings emphasised his diligence, energy and his economical skills as well as tolerance and freedom from prejudices. This reading was established by theatre reviewers who saw an ideal hard-working man in him and called him 'good-natured, diligent and resourceful' and someone whose rise in social class was exemplary. For example, Martti Savo wrote of the theatre version:

> Akusti is not a gold digger, he just desires land of his own, and he admires Heta as a farmhand and as a daughter of an estate, but he does so without any sense of inferiority. Akusti, a wonderful dramatic persona, is a gifted and capable man, and with his own

hands, he, starting from scratch, clears the large Muumäki farm for Heta, breaking the soil with a mattock and sowing, buying more forest and land and participating skilfully in the management of village issues.

Akusti's rise in social class was idealised, but he was not regarded as an upstart figure – the class rise did not invite judgement, criticism or distance; quite the contrary. Instead, reviewers framed him as a 'farmhand who throughout his life became a finer and finer person'. In this reading, he was a thoroughly sympathetic figure; in one reviewer's words, 'one loves him as the villagers do'. Many characterisations of Akusti linked him to representations of 'the folksy man'; writers described Akusti as 'undecorated', 'authentic', 'stubborn, a resilient man of the people', 'heart-warming', 'sympathetic', 'simple' and 'warm'. For the reviewers, he passed as a peasant hero; as a responsible and industrious settler, Akusti even corresponded to the ideal male of post-war reconstruction policies.

What is noteworthy in terms of gender politics is that the character of Akusti was described with words and expressions underlining the classic masculine virtues of 'character', 'endurance' and 'strength' that, until now, had been evoked to characterise the idealized matron-mother Loviisa. In this manner, then, the male norm against which Akusti was measured in the Niskavuorean world was embodied by a female figure. Furthermore, Akusti was also defined in terms of 'feminine' and 'maternal' qualities in contrast to the 'hardness' and 'coldness' of Heta as he was called caring and nurturing. In poetic terms, he was read as 'a success of an unyielding, humble, and righteous Finnish man, radiantly good, quietly wise, skilfully steering his family through the sea of life.'

The ideal qualities ascribed to Akusti resembled post-war discussions of a new male ideal, discussed by Matti Peltonen. Bishop Eino Sormunen emphasised in a text from the 1940s the need to renew educational ideals in the light of history; in his formulation: 'the Finnish man is, in terms of outer appearance, slightly clumsy and undisciplined, but tough, deliberative, responsible and ready for sacrifices'. Literary scholar Eino Krohn also sketched an ideal man who 'is willing to forget himself and sacrifice himself for the sake of humanity by refusing violence and, instead, serving others and suffering in their place'. Krohn noted that his proposal foregrounded what has often been dismissed as a sign of weakness. In the portrait of Akusti, these virtues were heralded.

As for visual framings, the publicity stills portraying Akusti shared little with the aesthetic that structured the narrative images of the erotised Niskavuori males. In stills of Rauni Luoma as Heta and Kaarlo Halttunen as Akusti, their difference in height was emphasised. Several publicity photos and the film poster offered a narrative image of an unequal couple in a comic framing. One album-style photo displayed them both standing, Heta in the front and Akusti, the shorter one, behind her with a genial and clever smile on his face. Several other publicity stills reiterated this comic tone. A still referring to the scene in which Heta and Akusti arrive at Muumäki featured them in the foreground. Heta is placed close to the centre of the frame, while Akusti is positioned standing on the side. He is posed carrying a potted plant in his arms, suggesting a subordinate rank to Heta. Akusti's mother and Siipirikko are seen standing behind them. They all are depicted looking at Heta who, again, is not smiling.

Another publicity photo further underlined the difference in height and, hence, the implied mismatch between Heta and Akusti as it represented Akusti standing behind Heta, who is gazing longingly out the window towards Niskavuori. One still featuring the naked bodies of Heta and Akusti in the sauna framed Heta from behind and showed Akusti's illuminated face. While the publicity stills, in the cases of Aarne and Juhani Niskavuori, eroticised the male body, the lobby cards of *Heta Niskavuori* featured a severe-looking man at work (clearing wood, working with fishing equipment) wearing loose work clothes which did not emphasise muscularity, but covered an ageing body. Two publicity stills even framed Akusti as a comic body; in the Muumäki drawing-room filled with the high society, he appears, first, with his dirty working clothes and, second, with his upper body naked. From this perspective, Halttunen's depiction of Akusti connected him more to the loggers, vagabonds and *jätkä*-figures featured in other contemporary Finnish films, as discussed by Anu Koivunen and Kimmo Laine, than to the tormented and/or spectacularised romantic lovers of the two earlier Niskavuori films.

When emerging in 1950, the characters of Heta and Akusti were profoundly embedded in current debates on gender. They also cited and evoked powerful cultural imagery, stereotypes and debates, capitalising on the political passions as well as on the affective forces, desires and frustrations that discourses on femininity and masculinity mobilise. While representative of the 1950s *Heimat* genre, *Heta Niskavuori* engaged viewers by addressing an issue at the heart of modernisation – that of gender and power – via its melodramatic aesthetic of contradiction as characterised by Laura Mulvey. The discourses of 'Finnish woman' and 'Finnish man', those of strength and weakness, both empower and coerce, create and constrain. As the multiple public readings indicate, *Heta Niskavuori* (together with other Niskavuori films) has served as a meta-text for figuring gender and nation and it has enabled and invited multiple, contradictory readings. The popular appeal of the film is therefore founded not on easy stereotypes but, on the contrary, the film's emphasis on ambivalence. Therein lays the resilience of the notions of 'strong woman' and 'weak man', and their continued, if contested appeal later on. As *Heta Niskavuori* was screened on television for the first time in April 1963, YLE, the Finnish Broadcasting Company, reported having scored one million viewers. This indicates that there were more than three people sitting in front of each television set in the country.

Anu Koivunen

REFERENCES

Koivunen, A. and K. Laine (1993) 'Metsästä pellon kautta kaupunkiin (ja takaisin) – jätkyys suomalaisessa elokuvassa', in P. Ahokas, M. Lahti and J. Sihvonen (eds) *Mie-heyden tiellä*. Jyväskylä: Nykykulttuurin tutkimusyksikkö, Jyväskylän yliopisto, 136–54.

Krohn, E. (1948) *Henkisen kulttuurimme kohtalo*. Jyväskylä: Gummerus.

Laine, K. (1994) *Murheenkryyneistä miehiä. Suomalainen sotilasfarssi 1930-luvulta 1950-luvulle*. Turku: SETS.

_____ (1999) *'Pääosassa Suomen kansa'. Suomi-filmi ja Suomen Filmiteollisuus kansallisen elokuvan rakentajina 1933–1939*. Helsinki: SKS.

Pälsi, S. (1942) 'Isäntämieltä ja palvelijahenkeä', *Suomalainen Suomi*, 8–9, 443–7.

Peltonen, M. (ed.) (1996) *Rillumarei ja valistus. Kulttuurikahakoita 1950-luvun Suomessa*. Helsinki: Finnish Historical Society.

_____ (2002) *Remua ja ryhtiä. Alkoholi ja tapakasvatus 1950-luvun Suomessa*. Helsinki: Gaudeamus.

Savo, M. (1950) 'Review of *Heta Niskavouri*', *Vapad Sana*, 19 November.

Sormunen, E. (1948) *Miehen ihanne kautta aikojen in his Eurooppa valinkauhassa*. Helsinki: Kirjapaja, 108–14.

Vicinus, M. (1981) '"Helpless and Unfriended": Nineteenth-Century Domestic Melodrama', *New Literary History*, 13, 1, 127–43.

Voipio-Juvas, A. and K. Ruohtula (eds) (1949) *The Finnish Woman*. Helsinki: WSOY.

DET STORA ÄVENTYRET THE GREAT ADVENTURE

ARNE SUCKSDORFF, SWEDEN, 1953

When the Swedish director Arne Sucksdorff died in 2001 he left a prodigious and impressive filmmaking legacy. His films spanned from an Academy Award-winning short film about man in the city, to full-length fiction about orphaned children in Copacabana. However few films represent his career better than his work on and around the theme of nature.

From early in his career, Sucksdorff's strength was the short film format. He had made 16 shorts by 1951. His passion for nature and interest in man's interaction with it proved perfect for recording on film. The topic was well-timed, in that the environmental movement was just dawning in Sweden and films about nature could easily find their way on to cinema screens.

Sucksdorf's genuine interest in nature traced back to his childhood, where the fascination for nature did not equal preservation, but interaction. Thus the hunt for nature and the animals could be done both with camera and gun. The perception of nature was unsentimental and Sucksdorff's eye for drama always found ways to present the environment dynamically.

During the Second World War Sucksdorff made several important short films including *En sommarsaga* (1941) and *Trut!* (1944). The latter focused on the natural habitat of the Swedish coastal region, but also contained political statements about human conditions during that period. Thus, the cliff where the birds nest is possible to read as an allegory of the world where the (political) threat in the guise of a seagull is preying on other birds and their eggs. In this film Sucksdorff also made use of contemporary composed music, speaker narration and – most importantly – a brilliant editing technique with which he dramatised the life of the fauna. All were ingredients that would become important in his coming projects.

The American film director Robert Flaherty had made feature-length documentaries about nature, and Sucksdorff followed in his footsteps. He had a clear vision of what he wanted 'his' nature to portray. But how to get the nature to come to him and let itself be directed – that was the question. He knew from experience that the task would be difficult. It would take time before the project could be realised, but in 1949 he felt it was time to make a full-length film.

In order to find the motive for such an enterprise, he drew from his memories of childhood. In his youth, Sucksdorff had been given a live lynx from the Skansen zoological garden in Stockholm. The Sucksdorff family belonged to the upper classes of Swedish society, and the young Arne therefore enjoyed considerable privileges and advantages in fulfilling his ambitions, especially in the early stages of his career. The boyhood adventures with the half-tame cat remained within him, and a vision of a lynx wandering southwards from the north of Sweden and a story based on a series of its encounters with man became the basis of the film's narrative. Sucksdorff was left with the question of whether the idea could be transformed into a full-length film.

Dag Hammarskjöld – who was later appointed to Secretary General at the UN – was the chair of the Swedish Tourist Council during this period. He had been involved in the production of Sucksdorff's Academy-awarded short film, *Människor i stad* (*Symphony of a City*, 1947). In this capacity – as well as a personal friend – he suggested scenes for the film that would present Swedish nature in a sufficient manner. Sucksdorff also established a relationship with Anders Sandrews, the film mogul, who had shown interest in the film. The support of Rune Waldekranz, production manager at Sandrews, would prove vital to the completion of the film. For instance, large parts of the film were shot in Waldekranz's childhood home outside Stockholm.

Up to this point Sucksdorff had been devoted to Svensk Filmindustri, but the head of the company, Carl Anders Dymling, could not see how, in spite of the fact that he was an Academy Award-winning filmmaker, he could be able to make a full-length picture out of documentary material. Sucksdorff was upset by this and broke away from Svensk Filmindustri in order to begin working with Sandrews' film company.

With the necessary institutions behind him and with a strong vision of the completed film, he gained access to Bommersvik in the Södermanland region. The difficulties Sucksdorff had anticipated at the beginning of the project became worse than anticipated. The production was delayed for more than a year due to problems with finding the lynx he wanted as the main character of the film. The animal, imported from Norway, proved more difficult to handle than expected, and the half-tame birds purchased for the production preyed on each other. Their nature was still very wild and would not let itself be directed by Sucksdorff. Worse still, having spent countless days and nights outdoors in the Swedish countryside, Sucksdorff became ill and had to be hospitalised with a severe case of meningitis.

During his stay at the hospital Sucksdorff was able to gather his strength. It was not until then that he conceived a new theme for his film that was to be realised during the years 1951–53. It was to be a film about the life of man and nature at a time where agricultural life still prospered, but whose obsoletion was in sight. This was to be a film where the perspective is perfect for the drama: animals tending their new-borns and the humans their children. It was to depict the time in everyone's life which later will be remembered as *Det stora äventyret* (*The Great Adventure*).

This black-and-white film – cut down to ninety minutes from 80,000 metres of raw film – was awarded the International Prize at the Cannes Film Festival in 1954. It is called a documentary film but as with many documentaries, its fiction cannot be excluded. It would be more accurate to call the film a semi-documentary. The film consists of two stories carefully interwoven: the first part has its focus on the animals, whereas the second one concentrates on the human beings – all in settings that depict the Swedish nature over a year.

The Great Adventure begins with a series of stills and a soundtrack that in themselves capture the essence of the Nordic nature with its flora and fauna. It is daybreak in the spring, spider webs glitter in the early-morning sunshine, and the sound of the awakening nature fill the air: crying loons, debating nightingales and robin's drills mix with blackbird melancholy. The sounds of nature are combined with music from Swedish pastoral composer Lars-Erik Larsson, with comments from a speaker in voice-over that leaves no room for the spectator's own fantasy.

Life equals spring but death is never far away, threatening the harmony of the new-born cubs, playing in their innocence around the fox's lair. Initially, the foxes are established as the main characters and protagonists of the film, and their struggle for survival depicts clarity and freedom from guilt in nature. The lynx, which in the director's early vision was thought to be the leading 'character' throughout the film, is now reduced to a sudden smell that the mother fox senses as something new and disturbing in the forest. The speaker tells us she would rather move to a new area, but her instinct and the new-born cubs force her to stay. The lynx that wandered into her familiar woods from the North remains a deadly threat. And there is another threat awaiting.

The struggle for survival is represented by the mother fox who, after leading the cubs through the woods, attempts to steal a hen at the house of the farmer living next to the forest. The drama plays the fox needing to support her cubs against the struggling farmer trying to earn the day's bread for his children; a clever set-up by Suckodorff displaying the conflict between man and nature.

Herein lies the conflict of the film and its statement over the capacity of man. The death of the hen gives life to the fox and her cubs, but ultimately it also leads to the death of the fox, as the farmer finds her catching the hen. The voice-over of the speaker tells us that 'from that moment on the shotgun would be present throughout the summer', and the spectator sees both in close-ups and at a distance the two-barrelled rifle – ever-present no matter whether the farmer is herding cattle or harvesting. Planted in every scene with the humans, there is always a reminder that the man will not forget, and that the inevitable is about to come.

That day comes in August. The search for food has led the mother fox to the field where the farmers are harvesting. A lonely hare is hiding in the hay. We see the fox approaching the spot where the hare is, but only hear the attack. The director is aware of the fact that it is not necessary to spell out everything in detail. This is an understanding he has developed after much of the 'in-your-face narration' in his earlier films. As the fox with the hare in its jaws works its way back to the forest from the open and precarious field, a boy cries out that the fox is present. One of the farmers, introduced as the most aggressive, grabs his shotgun and gives chase.

The music accompanying the chase reaches a crescendo as the man closes in on the fox. The camera follows the animal, while the voice-over tells the spectator that in spite of the situation, the hunger takes the best of the fox and she stops to take a few bites of her prey. She knows that there will not be much left after feeding the hen to her hungry little ones at the lair. The man with the shotgun catches up with the fox, aims his gun and fires. The perspective then changes dramatically. The director is acquainted with the relationship between the drama and the reality and the last-minute rescues he treated the audience to in his earlier short films are now gone.

Sucksdorff used the capacity of the film medium perfectly, from objective point-of-view to subjective perspective. We now see the world through the eyes of the confused, shocked and fatally wounded animal desperately trying to reach safety in the forest where the cubs wait for food. After the shaky movement, conveying the drama of the chase, the camera tilts back and all the spectator can see is the sky and high trees, as they slowly go out of focus in a blur, descending finally into darkness.

However, the drama is not over. No sentimentality is offered as a refuge from the event as *The Great Adventure* completes the Sucksdorffian angle of nature's inevitable mercilessness. In another of his films, *En sommarsaga*, a fox is presented as a main character, but it takes a position of the antagonist as it snatches an egg from a loon. In this earlier story, Sucksdorff decides that the jaws of the fox are too week to crack the eggshell. Life wins. However, only a few years later in *Trut!* the crude reality has found its way into the Sucksdorffian narration as a seagull is successful in doing what the fox was not able to do in *En sommarsaga*: by dropping the egg against the rocks.

As the farmer, turned into hunter, reaches the dead fox, he is disappointed. The fox is too thin and scruffy after all the work she has endured in nursing her cubs. Even her skin is worthless. The hunter's thoughts become known to us through the voice-over. But the director does not allow the spectator to leave the scene quite yet. A weak sound is heard, a soft cry; the hunter reacts, follows the sound and indeed, finds the lair with the cubs. No sentimentality, no compassion is present, just the hunter's ambition to take the cubs out as well as the mother fox. He has to finish the business and eliminate the threat to his livelihood. But how is he to do it? The man has the means. In painful clarity the voice-over explains: 'Thread, ignite and dynamite, that's all that is needed.' The simple clarity in nature is interfered by the innovations of man annihilating the fair play.

A new dawn announces another day, the sun is warming the tree tops where a squirrel finds his food, the birds' serenades and the pastoral scene from the beginning of the film is almost repeated. It is, however, a deceptive calm. From a distance comes a faint roar, like the sound of a waterfall, barely breaking through. Growing in strength, it shows that man, once again, makes his mark on nature. The fighter jets practise high above the woods, picturing yet another evidence of the fight between man and nature.

The next scene is composed of montage editing. The farmer that the spectator now knows is a hunter, runs for cover behind a tree. We see a close-up on his face as he watches the fox's lair, and then a close-up with a sparkling noise of the thread burning its way to the dynamite buried in the lair with the cubs inside. Now follows cross-cut images alternating the burning thread and the hunter. As the explosion finally erupts over the lair, it is to the sound of falling bombs and roaring fighter jets. The camerawork exaggerates the commotion and the rapid montage shows fleeing animals. Even the powerful lynx is scared, chased up a tree. The war is over and the battlefield is calm for the time being, but the director has made a clear statement regarding man's relationship to the nature.

The following scene closes the chapter about the fox and the first part of the film. It starts off heartbreakingly but ends in hope. Once again the voice-over leads us through the scene with just one sentence as a frail fox comes up from the lair in the early sunlight: 'A lone survivor.' The little cub makes sobbing sounds and sees the dead mother lying outside. Its instinct is to play and wake up what it sees as the sleeping mother. He nibbles her playfully and licks her mouth as the canine family does to show support. It is a short but highly emotional scene that ends with the young fox leaving the lair to explore the world on its own. 'In the forest sorrow is short, and life always finds its way', comments the voice-over: a new generation is ready to take on its great adventure.

Up to this point the film has more or less been a film about nature. We have followed the daily lives of inhabitants in the forest and the humans as well. The narration has been dominated by a low-key observing style of narration, except for the hunting scene, which has a political commentary within it. The montage technique, slow tempo and few voice-overs have created a dramatised documentary. What follows is more a conventional, fictional film where humans play the important role. The main characters are two boys – the farmer's sons – and the otter one of them manages to capture.

No Swedish film about nature is complete without the seasonal changes: representing the cycle of life is perfectly easy since the four seasons are clearly distinguished in Sweden. The segment with the children and Utti, the otter, takes place in winter as the snow lies deep and tracks of animals are seen all over the snowy landscape. There is also another animal leaving bigger and clumsier tracks than any other of the inhabitants of the forest, namely man. The otters play in the snow but they are also constantly on the hunt for food: fish. One of the otters finds an open hole in the ice where a trapped pike serves as an early lunch. A low thump is heard and the animal reacts. Not far away we see a man driving a stake through the ice. Is he after fish, too?

Sucksdorff takes the spectator, with the help of inter-cuts, closer and closer to the man. He is dressed in big dark clothing and his lurching moves reminds the spectator of a hunch-backed Mr Hyde. He cannot be up to any good. And sure enough, to the accompaniment of dramatic crescendo in the musical score, the man opens a trap with a saw-tooth in which he places a small fish and puts the trap over the trail the otters use. The occasion is observed, from a distance, by the two children. No speaker tells us why or what will happen.

We have all this in mind when Sucksdorff presents one of the most intense montage sequences in the film. Night falls over the countryside and the people in the little community gather in the church for mass. Outside, nature experiences the darkness while man listens to the word of God. The montage consists of cuts between the church, where the people and especially the children, are introduced singing a hymn, and scenes of nature.

The two otters are seen playing. Then we see shorter clips between interior and exterior. In the church the people are still singing and the otters now play in the water. Outside, music is barely heard from the church. One of the otters dives and stays underwater while the other waits on land. Only bubbles reach the surface, and no otter comes up. Once again Sucksdorff does not have to explain what happens. There is no sequence showing the otter being caught in the trap, no speaker describing such a thing. Just a glimpse of a chain hanging from a branch into the water.

The next scene is in daylight. In the foreground there is the saw-toothed trap, now closed and hung up on a pole by a house. Although the film up to this point has been subtle in its message, it now becomes weaker and too obvious. The poacher is depicted as a stereotyped villain – all that the farmer/hunter in the beginning of the film is not. He is pure evil. His motive for killing the otters is not dictated by his need to protect his livelihood, like the farmer's pursuit of the foxes, even if that, too, might seem unsympathetic.

The two children rescue the surviving otter and keep it hidden from the adults during the winter. The narration has to be different compared with the adventures with the foxes. It is the contrast between the documentary style of the first part of the film that makes us doubt the verisimilitude of the latter part. The film becomes more or less a conventional adventure film showing the children struggle as they try to hide their secret from the adults, not to forget their homework and school and, at the same time, trying to provide the ever-hungry otter with fish.

It could be argued that the film successfully portrays the difference between man and nature, and that the adventure of the children consists of ideas and fantasy while the adventures of the foxes are unintentional and left to the mercy of the world. The otter is the symbol of the children's great adventure, but the film raises the question of whether such a great adventure can be kept in a cage? Such an adventure must come to an end and as the seasons turn it is time for the otter and children to part. The painful insight that the otter is wild and is seeking its own adventure is difficult to accept for the children, but the film ends by them letting the otter free and rejoicing over the arrival of spring which thus completes the cycle of seasons in the story. The Great Adventure never ends, it always begins.

Henrik Schröder

TUNTEMATON SOTILAS THE UNKNOWN SOLDIER 13

EDVIN LAINE, FINLAND, 1955

At the end of September 1954, the author Väinö Linna sent a manuscript he had entitled 'Sotaromaani' ('The War Novel') to his publisher, Werner Söderström Company (WSOY), in Helsinki. It was his third novel, following *Päämäärä (The Goal*, 1947) and *Musta rakkaus (Black Love*, 1948). Linna had hoped that the manuscript would be read and checked quickly so the book itself could be published before Christmas. After a brief delay, Linna's wishes were followed, cuts and changes suggested and reworked by the author in order for the book to be published with the first print run of five thousand copies in December 1954 – now with a new title given by Linna's friend, Veikko Pihlajamäki: *Tuntematon sotilas (The Unknown Soldier*).

The production history of Linna's book has been well-documented by several scholars. The manuscript of 'The War Novel' (including the original cuts and changes undertaken by the publisher) was published in 2000. It included introductions by Yrjö Varpio and Yrjö A. Jäntti, the head of WSOY in the 1950s. Several of the cuts testify to the ideologically radical aspects of Linna's text, and also of the issues that the conservative 'public sphere' of mid-1950s Finland still suffered when having to deal with anti-war criticism. The cuts perhaps made the book a better novel, but also made it look less oppositional towards the idealistic war-enthusiasm and patriotic rhetoric of the period. Linna, nevertheless, succumbed to them (with objections) in order to get the novel published.

Another interesting aspect of these cuts was the willingness of the publisher to censor the sections where Linna uses explicitly sexual associations and religious parody. In Finland, during the public debate early in 1955, two themes were mentioned most often: Linna's assumed negative attitude towards officers and the role of women – especially the female frontline servant, Raili Kotilainen, who appears (briefly) near the beginning and again near the end of the novel. The argument was that in her Linna offers an extremely derogatory, even impious image of all those women who worked near the trenches. At the beginning of the film adaptation there are only a couple of brief images of a woman (supposedly the same Raili Kotilainen) smiling gently at one of the protagonists, Lieutenant Lammio. Her absence in the film was the only major schism between Edvin Laine, the film's director, and Linna.

The book became an immediate success among the reading public. In less than half a year, by March 1955, its print run had escalated to 100,000 copies. The book was widely reviewed and fiercely debated in the press; the critical reception was not unanimously positive. The amount of copies sold, however, prove that the 'common people' in Finland loved it.

The most prominent critical voice was Toini Havu, the literary critic of the largest newspaper, *Helsingin Sanomat*, in Finland. Even though Havu recognised the 'literary values' of the novel, she maintained that the image of war presented, particularly the role of the officers and the leaders, was misleading. The words Havu coined to express Linna's viewpoint – 'the frog's perspective' – came to epitomise the value of the novel itself. For some (like Havu) the term could also be read as derogatory referring to 'low', 'small' and 'slimy'. For others (the majority of reviewers) it meant a more correct view in relation to historical events still fresh in the collective memory. The 'frog's viewpoint' was also the people's perspective.

In Finland, the book's reception escalated into a debate about the 'correct' image of Finnish soldiers at war, though elsewhere the theme has been significantly wider: on what kind of grounds can *The Unknown Soldier* be considered pacifistic? Linna himself always thought that his intention was to 'speak for the living force, but against war'. In another context he expressed this tendency differently: 'More and more clearly I began to see *the human being* as the central agent of this happening. And in this particular case the human being equated the Finnish man.'

During the first weekend in 1955 Edvin Laine, together with his scriptwriter Juha Nevalainen, travelled by train to Tampere to meet with Linna and discuss the film rights. Linna's price was higher than producer T. J. Särkkä of Suomen Filmiteollisuus Oy had agreed to pay. Laine, however, was already an established director-actor with some twenty directed films under his belt, so he had enough courage to promise the one million Finnish marks Linna had asked for. The filming itself started in April 1955 (the final manuscript was not finished until May) and lasted until November. After a hectic period of post-production the premiere took place on 23 December 1955 in six Finnish cities.

As the book had changed the direction of not only the literary but also the entire cultural scene in Finland, so did the film. The 'golden years' of Finnish film production essentially culminated with *The Unknown Soldier*. The black-and-white film that lasts nearly three hours and would cost some 50 million Finnish marks to produce not only saved Suomen Filmiteollisuus from bankruptcy but also made a profit of over 200 million marks within a year. This, however, meant that due to tax reasons the entire income of the company had to be invested during

1956–57. Therefore Suomen Filmiteollisuus produced lots of films, some of which were not premiered until in 1960. This period of 'overproduction' began the end of Finnish cinema's 'studio era' as it had been developing since the mid-1930s.

One of the most important rivalling factors during this changing period was television (the first public television transmission in Finland took place in 1955). The first television screening of *The Unknown Soldier* did not take place until in 1968, gathering almost 2.3 million viewers, that is, half of the entire population. During the 1990s it became customary for YLE2 – the other of the Finnish Broadcasting Corporation's channels, housed in Tampere – to air the film on Finnish Independence Day, 6 December. *The Unknown Soldier* remains the most widely seen Finnish film, both in Finland and abroad. During the first ten years the film was sold to over forty countries. The novel even became a favourite for many 'summer theatres' – most notably the one in Tampere where *The Unknown Soldier* was performed for nine summers in succession after its premiere in 1961. Edvin Laine also directed this theatre performance using several of the actors from the film.

In the memory of post-war generations in Finland *The Unknown Soldier* is essentially a 'hybrid text'. The novel and the film have been intertwined, though, for the advantage of the film. As Juha Seppälä, a Finnish author born in 1956 writes in his introduction to the latest printing (the 56th) of the novel: 'The film versions, especially Laine's direction together with the enormous selling figures of the novel, support the canonisation of *The Unknown Soldier* as a monumental cornerstone of Finnish identity and national history. The images projected from the book ate up the novel.' For those who have seen Laine's film, it has been impossible to read the novel without being influenced by the film's images. This must have been one of the major reasons why the second (colour) film version directed by Rauni Mollberg and released in 1985, still remains in the eyes of the audiences as merely an 'interesting experiment'. This in spite of the fact that it in many respects it is more faithful to the novel than Laine's version.

The Unknown Soldier is not only a hybrid but also a rhizome with several roots extending to the present day. Separate sentences have a life of their own. When Matti Pellonpää – the major male protagonist in several of Aki Kaurismäki's films – was asked about his working ethics he used to give the answer in the mode of a quote from Koskela, the leader of the platoon in *The Unknown Soldier*: 'Asialliset hommat suoritetaan, muuten ollaan kuin Ellun kanat' ('Accurate business will be taken care of, but otherwise we behave like pigs'). Koskela says this to Rahikainen, who asks for permission to leave the tents (and meet women at a nearby work-camp) while the others stay and continue celebrating Mannerheim's birthday. In the film the discussion occurs but without this particular line. No matter how the spirit of *The Unknown Soldier* is interpreted, in its many variations and forms, it still lives.

The Unknown Soldier is a description of a group of machine-gun company men during the war between Finland and the Soviet Union from the summer of 1941 until 1944. This – the so called Continuation War – followed the first conflict, the Winter War (1939–40) in relation to which there are, of course, lots of references in the story. Rather than a 'traditional' narrative built around a continuous plot, the novel, as well as the film, is constructed around a collection of episodes. Moreover, instead of a few individual protagonists, the description concentrates on a *group* of men. From today's perspective this structure can be seen as 'cinematic'.

In the novel the characters are developed much more widely and extensively than in the film, where they are treated almost like comic-strip types. Generally this might be a restriction but one has to remember that at the time of the film's premiere Linna's soldiers were already familiar to tens of thousands of his readers in Finland. The core group of men in the story includes Hietanen (Heikki Savolainen), Lehto (Åke Lindman), Lahtinen (Veikko Sinisalo), Vanhala (Leo Riuttu), Koskela (Kosti Klemelä), Rokka (Reino Tolvanen) and Rahikainen (Kalervo Halttunen).

In a text from 1955 Linna gives quite explicit descriptions of all of his major characters including both physical and psychological features. These descriptions were made as guidelines for the filmmakers even though they seemingly have not followed them to the point. As a type each figure represents the part of Finland the character was born in, epitomising the manifold nature of the Finnish folk. In his descriptions Linna uses the 'age-old' classifications already made by Zachris Topelius in his book *Boken om vårt land* (*Our Country*, 1875) which was widely distributed and consumed for generations in schools in Finland.

In addition to Topelius the novel relates to other core literary texts in Finland, most of all to Johan Ludvig Runeberg's *Fänrik Ståhls Sägner* (*Second Lieutenant Ståhl's Stories*, 1848) and Aleksis Kivi's *Seitsemän veljestä* (*The Seven Brothers*, 1870). Actually to many of the first reviewers Linna's book was 'the seven brothers at war'. There are references to both Runeberg and Kivi in Linna's novel – and therefore in Laine's film as well. These books also have been widely read among schoolchildren in Finland. Therefore, 'ideologies' in relation to issues of honour, freedom, the nation, heroism and masculinity propagated in these books have had a strong foothold in the minds of Finnish people.

Importantly, in his novel Linna not only describes ideologies 'at work' but most of all sets them in ironic contexts so that they begin to look ridiculous. Those who did not like Linna's novel thought of this as sacrilege concerning 'national values'. A case in point could be the scene in the film when, after a long march and a short nap, the company is urged to start moving forward again. Hietanen tries to wake up the sleepy privates by shouting freely cited slogans that remind of Runeberg's heroic poetry: 'Third platoon, wake up! You've rested enough. Rise and show the world the awesomeness of the Finn warrior! Rise, you roaring Finnish lions! The battlefield's rumbling, the cannons are thundering! Put aside your plough, pick up your sword. Turn a new page in the amazing pages of Finnish history!' These shouts, however, have no effect on the soldiers. They only start moving quickly following the call off-screen of 'Chow-time!'

Laine's film opens by concentrating on four of the men in the group. They are the talkative but slightly naïve Hietanen (with his favourite idiom, 'It's mind-boggling!') who is from the Turku area in the southwest of Finland; Lehto, the stern, stone-faced and emotionless soldier whose background remains unrevealed (and is the first of the group to die); Lahtinen, the hard-headed communist, an enduring opponent and griper from northern Tavastlandia; and Rokka, the experienced joker from Karelia. What unites them, despite their personal differences, is the fact that they are all very good soldiers, each a war hero of a kind. Moreover, three of them die, with sole-survivor Rokka leaving the battlefield wounded. Their centrality to the film is motivated by both their heroism and fate. The more the group is reduced in number the more Koskela, the leader of the platoon, and perhaps the most sympathetic of the characters, comes to the foreground. In the production notes Linna describes Koskela as 'a typical "eye-person", a spectator with a strong personality which, however, is not revealed as movement or gesture, but as radiation'.

One of the most evident means of distinguishing the soldiers from each other is the use of speech dialects in Linna's novel. This was seen as perhaps the most realistic aspect of the novel. The use of different Finnish dialects created an interesting schism between the author and the publisher. Linna did not want to use the written forms of spoken dialects faithfully, but instead thought that some kind of a hybrid form – half spoken dialect, half standard Finnish – would work best. The publisher, however, wanted to emphasise the 'documentary' aspect of the novel's language and twisted the spoken lines more away from the standard language forms and norms. The modernist trends in the literary culture of Finland were growing strong in the early 1950s; in relation to this background Linna's use of realistic speech patterns was not only exceptional but also unfashionable.

When one watches the film it is hard to imagine that the way in which the men speak could have been a problem. In Finnish films similar patterns had been quite common for decades and for the film-viewing audience it was no big problem. The same audiences had been accustomed to seeing men in uniforms in the many military farces – one of the most popular film genres in the country. The 'first wave' of these farces in Finnish cinema came at the end of the 1930s, the second one right before the release of *The Unknown Soldier* in the early 1950s. Many of the actors Laine had chosen for his film had actually been wearing uniforms in these: above all Heikki Savolainen (Hietanen), Kaarlo Halttunen (Rahikainen) and Jussi Jurkka (Lammio).

A detail worth noting about the characters and the acting is the age of the male actors. In Linna's novel they are, like most soldiers in the war, youngsters in their twenties. In this respect, in Laine's film all the major characters are over-aged. The coarsest example (often pointed out in reviews) is Rahikainen played by Kaarlo Halttunen who was 46 years old at the time of filming. A slightly milder case in point would be Vanhala played by Leo Riuttu who was 42 years old. One common argument has it that it is impossible to consider the film 'realistic' because of this fault. Again, Rauni Mollberg's version from 1985 aimed at fixing this problem by casting the film with 'correctly aged' actors.

Laine's choice, however, can be accounted for in at least two respects. Firstly, he used actors who were extremely familiar to Finnish film audiences. Of the major characters only Rokka is not a professional actor. Thus the well-known faces carried with them several traces from earlier roles into *The Unknown Soldier*. Hietanen, Lehto and Lahtinen are the roles that perhaps benefit from this most. Therefore, it is not surprising that Laine concentrated on these figures in the first section of the film. Secondly, the real age of the actors related to the documentary material used in the film that at *The Unknown Soldier*'s release was approximately ten years old. The suggestion here is that even though the actors look too old in the fictional sequences, their age would match quite well with the documentary ones. In this sense the age of the actors functions – as so many other features in the film – in a 'double register': both estranging from the supposed realism of the representation and connecting the different elements with which the entity of the film is stitched together.

An interesting aspect in the discussions about *The Unknown Soldier*, then, concern its assumed 'documentary' nature. This was mentioned already in the first (unfavourable) report written by (an unknown) reader at the publishing house: 'The manuscript in question is rather like a documentary reportage.' Linna's intention, however, was not to write a 'reportage'; his original title, 'The War Novel', points to this. Nevertheless, both the reading public and often also the reviewers willingly interpreted the book as a report from the war. Thus, for example, Yrjö Varpio refers to a Danish review from 1955 which also compares Linna to Erich Maria

Remarque – a reference which seems to have been quite common in the Nordic reviews. Linna himself had been at the front as a private and the events described were easily seen as documenting those experiences. Moreover there were speculations about the images of soldiers and their real-life correlations.

In the novel, distinct sections are constructed according to the episodes in such a way that they outline an entity within which the main themes (and therefore also the main figures of style) progress. In the film the shifts between major episodes are marked by images of soldiers marching attached to sequences of documentary footage inserted between the fictional material. This might be seen simply as the director's input into discussions of *The Unknown Soldier* as documentary reportage. In the rhythm of the film, however, these sections perform other functions. As documents they are reminders of the 'real' events of the war. Their visual outlook clearly diverges from the fictional material based more directly on the novel. But this difference also creates a kind of audio-visual link that binds the fictional material more tightly. In the end, more than a comment or the director's word in a public discussion, the documentary footage aims at increasing the level of credibility in general. In this sense the documentary footage – as document – works as if using citations from a historical event. In this sense the documentary footage participates in the film's entire operation as a 'documentary recording' of the lines of speech, characters and episodes of the novel.

Moreover, the documentary footage includes images of explosions, battle-actions, flaming buildings and firing cannons offering elements of spectacle that work as breaks – almost like the dance sequences in musicals. This association is not as farfetched as it might first seem. After the troops have invaded Petroskoi and settled down in the city there is an episode in the film where Hietanen, Rokka and Vanhala visit a couple of local women. One of them (with a stereotypical Russian name, Vera) dances and sings not only for the attending men but also for the film viewers. In the sense mentioned earlier this episode relates to the documentary material. Yet from another angle it is an estranging contrast to the everyday battle of life and death among the soldiers. Without the documentary material Laine's film would be a very different, and one could suggest, a much 'smaller' film. This material not only 'fills the breaks' when moving forward together with the platoon from one episode to another; the 'documents' establish another level entirely, the level of reality, in relation to which the rest of the film is to be seen.

When talking about *The Unknown Soldier* in his memoirs, Laine never mentions the documentary material. However, Åke Lindman (later an established film director who plays the role of Lehto) talks about this material in his memoirs. According to Lindman, Laine assigned to him the watching of a huge amount of documentary footage filmed during the war, possessed by the film archive of the Defence Forces. Lindman collected three hours of film sequences from this material of which Laine then made the final selections. The key criterion was that the landscapes and scenerios depicted in the documentaries should match with the action of the fiction film.

Another aspect to the frequent use of documentary material in *The Unknown Soldier* connects the film more tightly to its production context. The Ministry of Defence caused one of the big problems in the production of the film in 1955 when it refused its co-operation, preventing the filmmakers from borrowing the materials utilised by the military. The reason for this unwillingness was probably Linna's controversial representation of the 'military order' in the source novel.

A more crucial reason might have been that the head of the Defence Forces, General K. A. Heiskanen, was 'deeply hurt' by a military farce, *Majuri maantieltä* (*The Major off the Highway*) produced by Suomen Filmiteollisuus in 1954. The problem with the lack of materials was solved by the Frontier Guard which also has a small unit in military training and which in Finland belongs to the Ministry of Domestic Affairs, being thus out of reach of the Defence Forces.

Moreover, after having seen some rough-cuts of the film, the prime minister of the cabinet, future president Urho Kekkonen, guaranteed that Suomen Filmiteollisuus could borrow a tank from the brigade in Parola and use it when needed. With the apparent lack of equipment available, the documentary footage was necessary to show the larger context of battle. The use of documentary material, together with the rather straightforward way in which Laine turns Linna's philosophical novel into an adventure story, meant that the military circles in Finland preferred Laine's film to Linna's book. The Defence Forces even purchased copies of the film to use as 'teaching material' later.

Irony, parody, farce and humour in general were the elements most praised in the reception of the story from the beginning. Undoubtedly these characteristics also had their part in the wide popular success of both the novel and the film. In many ways the military farces had already dealt with the conflicts between officers and regulars. Their comic constructions, however, were situated in the context of military training and therefore peacetime conditions. Of course, *The Unknown Soldier* is not a farce in the sense that its settings are on the frontlines (not the army barracks) including soldiers getting shot, wounded and killed. Laine uses a lot of footage to depict these death scenes and openly dramatises them both in image and sound as well as in underscored, at times almost melodramatic, acting.

The film still clearly emphasises particular qualities of the novel: the comic, spectacular, dramatic and especially the adventurous. This can be seen in the way the film gives space for the different stages of the events. As such these events establish a standard model of a journey. First the platoon attacks and invades an area. Then it stays there trying to hold its positions, until it has to fight again and retreat. The film uses about an hour and a half for the first part of the journey and only some thirty minutes for the last one. Moreover, the retreat – which in the book is full of violence and which raises questions concerning the rights for war and the patriotic heroism – is covered in the film merely as a series of random deaths.

After a few winter scenes (among them, most importantly the one during which Rokka eliminates an entire Russian company and gets wounded for the first time), perhaps the most famous episode of both the novel and the film takes place. Soldiers are celebrating the birthday – 4 June 1942 – of Carl Gustaf Emil Mannerheim, the leader of the entire military operation. While the soldiers get drunk from self-made hooch ('*kilju*') by their tent, the officers get drunk by cognac and whisky in their dugout. The episode builds into a strange carnival oozing out modes of extreme behaviour by ripping off the last remnants of civilised customs.

In his Bakhtinian study of Linna's novel the literary scholar Jyrki Nummi concentrates on the elements of grotesque, and the drinking sequence is, of course, a key example of this. Even though the grotesque features of the story are on the surface in this episode, they actually exist throughout the novel in one form or another. Laine's film is not straightforward in this sense. Rather, and again, it mixes more crudely different generic characteristics by shifting quite abruptly from grotesque comedy to melodrama to documentary – and back. One of the aspects in which Laine follows Linna's intentions quite closely is the avoidance of gore elements. In *The Unknown Soldier* there is very little 'blood' for a war film. The violence is diluted rather than graphic and even though the deaths depicted seem melodramatic, Laine does not linger on them, but proceeds without hesitation.

The 'hooch' sequence signifies a halt both in the film and actually in the war since it marks the beginning of the so-called 'trench war' period. The film introduces new recruits – the strange Honkajoki (Tarmo Manni) who claims to be an inventor working on a perpetuum mobile and the young Hauhia (Veli-Matti Kaitala) who then gets killed at his first assignment. The rest of the trench war is covered by montage sequences mixing brief scenes of various seasons broken by an episode in which Rokka gets into a serious conflict with the commanding officers. He, however, saves his skin by catching a Russian prisoner of war.

Finally the retreat from the lines begins after a documentary sequence showing bombers and fighters in the air, and tanks rolling in the sand and forests – as though an attack arranged by a huge flock of machines had begun. The quantities here signify the scope of destruction. Explosions caused by the enemy machines are continuous and manifold, generating an enduring chaos during which many of the men whom we as viewers have become acquainted with lose their lives. At this point, near the end of the film, an episode is repeated from the beginning of the film: the platoon carries a wounded soldier (Ukkola) on a marshland and then buries him underneath the moss.

A dried branch of wood that looks like a crooked cross is placed on the grave (in Germany Linna's novel was published with the title *Kreuze in Karelien* in 1955). Since this episode is also at the beginning of the film (together with the *Finlandia* hymn by Jean Sibelius on the soundtrack), its repetition at this point marks the entire structure: the two hours in the film and two years of the war between these episodes have been in vain. The only accomplishment has been yet another body to be buried. Immediately after this Koskela, the charismatic 'eye-person' is killed in destroying a Russian tank.

The film begins in black with the tunes of *Finlandia* on the soundtrack. The first image is of clouds from which the camera pans and tilts down to show a piece of marshland. Walking feet with boots (which will be a recurrent image in the film) appear from right to left, the camera pulls back a bit and shows a ragged company of soldiers. They wander quietly in a line carrying wounded men on self-made stretchers. The group pauses since apparently one of the wounded has died. They bury him quietly in the moss and Vanhala places the cross on the grave. During this ceremony the camera is on the ground, from the 'frog's perspective'. This makes the men look statuesque. Finally the group of men leaves the place, moving back to the same direction they arrived. The camera halts on the image of the cross and all the successive credit titles appear on this single image.

When the sequence is repeated, neither the cutting nor the images are exactly the same and the repetition is shorter. But again the key image of the wooden cross signifies the event – together with the music. The rhythm, mood and perspective of the scene create a very devout atmosphere with a sense of loss. To place this sequence (from the tail of the story) at the beginning clearly tries to set the tone for the entire film. On the other extreme there is the 'hooch episode'. This time the film is not signifying the voice of mourning and loss. Rather, the mood speaks for joy, hilarious madness, loud courage (of Koskela, an otherwise quiet man fighting with the other officers), and the long tradition of male behaviour in Finnish literature and film: getting drunk, singing loudly and out of tune, dancing and giving muddled speeches to the buddies.

According to Nummi this episode in the novel is actually a collage from Kivi's *The Seven Brothers*: Linna picks a line from here, a motive from there, and in both books the founding theme is similar, namely the relationship between an individual and the collective. And along this theme, in Linna's novel the political creeps into the grotesque, but again, in the film this political aspect becomes muffled. The film records an event (familiar) from the book without framing it in a context the way the storyteller does in the novel. In this way *The Unknown Soldier* is both a serious film and a comic farce, definitely in this order according to the filmmakers.

The effect at the very end of the film grows from such an underlying contrast. First we are in the middle of a massive series of explosions, which seem to rip off an entire forest from the ground: 'The felling of trees by sustained bursts of mortar fire seems to emphasise that, like the men, Finnish nature too is a casualty of war,' as Peter Cowie writes. Suddenly everything goes quiet, men climb up from the trenches and hear in the silence that the war has finally ended. Vanhala declares: 'The Union of the Soviet Socialist Republics won but second was stubborn little Finland!' Men gather by the fire to have their last meal. The film ends with images of destroyed landscape, finally resting on a shot of the sun shining through trees in the forest.

Jukka Sihvonen

REFERENCES

Cowie, P. (1990) *Finnish Cinema*. Helsinki: VAPK & SEA.

Havu, T. (1955) 'Review of *Tuntematon sotilas*', *Helsingin Sanomat*, 24 December.

Lindman, Å. (1992) *Åke ja hänen maailmansa*. Helsinki: Tammi.

____ (2000a) *Esseitä. (Kootut teokset VI)*. Helsinki: WSOY.

____ (2000b) *Sotaromaani*. Tuntemattoman sotilaan käsikirjoitus. Helsinki: WSOY.

____ (2000c) *Tuntematon sotilas (Kootut teokset II)*. Helsinki : WSOY.

Nummi, J. (1993) *Jalon kansan parhaat voimat. Kansalliset kuvat ja Väinö Linnan romaanit Tuntematon sotilas ja Täällä Pohjantähden alla*. Helsinki: WSOY.

Varpio, Y. (1979) *Pentinkulma ja maailma. Tutkimus Väinö Linnan teosten kääntämisestä, julkaisemisesta ja vastaanotosta ulkomailla*. Helsinki: WSOY.

TORGNY WICKMAN, SWEDEN, 1969

In the canon of Swedish film history, the 1960s have traditionally taken on a mythical aura. The decade is often identified as a turning point in a long tradition of conventional film production in terms of financing and production methods as well as cinematic styles. It is also considered a period of far-reaching structural changes, reflected in the establishment of the Swedish Film Institute as one of the main features of the 'film reform' of 1963. The 1960s are also viewed as the decade that saw the emergence of a new generation of film directors, including Mai Zetterling, Bo Widerberg and Vilgot Sjöman.

Such features have been seen as resolving the prolonged crisis that hit the Swedish film industry during the late 1950s. Another solution to the crisis was the exploration of new thematic fields, possible due to increasingly liberal views in society at the time. Thus, for instance, when influential filmmakers exploited erotic imagery in films like *The Silence* (Ingmar Bergman, 1963) and *491* (Vilgot Sjöman, 1964), the Swedish Board of Film Censors was forced to change its previously restrictive stance. When the censors initially tried to use their power to prohibit or cut such films, the filmmakers cited their (artistic) freedom of speech and won over public opinion with their arguement. Less influential producers were quick to take advantage of the change.

Yet it is still an indisputable fact that much of the structure of the Swedish film production industry remained unchanged. Since the 1930s it had been a heavily monopolised business ruled by three major companies – Svensk Filmindustri, Sandrews and Europa-Film. These companies were in control of the three classic segments of the film industry: production, distribution and exhibition – particularly in the main urban areas. Almost all film production was dependent on the decisions made by these companies. In cases where minor producers had access to production facilities of their own, they were still dependent on the theatre chains owned by these companies. This was in spite of the fact that there were also a number of cinema owners in need of films made by independent producers. To a certain extent, these owners also contributed to production costs with what in the early days were called '*biografväxlar*' ('cinema bonds').

In order to survive in the shadow of the majors, the minor companies were compelled to find marketing niches that would be of interest to distributors and cinema owners. From the 1930s to the 1950s, some small companies managed to survive by producing cheap comedies while others specialised in producing industrial documentaries, newsreels and commercials. The production company behind *Eva – den utstötta* (*Swedish and Underage*, 1969) was a true heir to such traditional, small-time business. The company itself, with the striking name of Swedish Film Production Investments, was brand new in 1967, but it still had its origins in the small-time showground. One of the owners, Inge Ivarson, had been a managing director and producer for a number of companies in the preceding decades.

Another owner, the distribution company Svensk Talfilm, had produced, among other films, the long-running series featuring a hillbilly character called Åsa-Nisse. Such films were scorned by the critics and shunned by the high-brow cultural elite, but loved by the 'common audiences'. However, by the 1960s the attraction of the Åsa-Nisse series was also waning and the company started looking for new areas of interest. The new sexual liberalism appeared to open up new avenues.

Swedish Film Production Investments became immensely successful with its film *...som havets nakna vind* (*...as the naked wind from the sea*, 1968), directed by Gunnar Höglund. Their success would increase with the release of an educational film, *Ur kärlekens språk* (*Out of the Language of Love*, 1969) and its sequels. The genre it created would turn out to be lucrative enough for Ivarson to dedicate the rest of his professional life to it, and in February 2004, at the age of 86, he was still active, presenting a 95-minute film, *Language of Love 2000* (Anders Lennberg), whose financiers included the National Federation for Senior Citizens, the National Corporation of Swedish Pharmacies, the Society for the Young Quadriplegics and the Swedish Federation for Lesbian, Gay, Bisexual and Transgender Rights.

Swedish and Underage was the company's third feature-length production and was a combination of two other pioneering strands of film production: a mixture of sex and social issues. The film was directed by Torgny Wickman, who had made his name in the production of industrial films, travelogues, journals and newsreels, as well as a handful of feature films in the early 1950s. Over the span of his life, he produced and directed more than a thousand films – most of them unmentioned in filmographies. At the end of the 1930s, Wickman produced short nature documentaries – such as *Fågelvår i Tåkern* (*Bird Spring by the Lake Tåkern*, 1936) and *Sommardag i Lövängen* (*A Summer's Day in Lövängen*, 1938) – claiming later that they were innovative in their genre and immediate predecessors to the famous Arne Sucksdorff films.

Wickman was also proud of the fact that he was one of the first directors in Sweden to leave the film studios for on-location filming at the beginning of the 1950s. The way many of his scenes are shot – in a clinical manner, at a distance and in flat light – may have derived from his background as a documentary film director.

In an interview with Per Lönndahl in 1995, the then 84-year-old Wickman discussed the impetus behind the production of *Swedish and Underage*. His new friend Inge Ivarson once visited his home for dinner, asking at some point whether Wickman had any ideas for a new film. Wickman then told Ivarson that he had been reading a book about a trial in Hjo, a small town in southwest Sweden:

> A story about a girl from Stockholm who becomes an outcast and shunned by everyone, and whose only means of contact with adults is to offer them sex. She does it very successfully and when it all comes into the open, there was not a single person on the City Council who had not fucked her, the county doctor, everyone … no person of any significance had not been involved with that girl. I said I could write a script, and Inge thought it sounded fine. The next day when he came by, he told me that a German distributor had visited him at his office … and Inge told him about the girl in Hjo. So I got two weeks to write the script. Which I did.

The co-operation between Wickman and Ivarson had started a few months earlier:

> [The sound technician] Åke Brandhild called, telling me I should go and see Inge Ivarson, who wanted me to make a big sexual movie. Ivarson was an important producer at that time so I went to see him, looked at the script and told him that I really could use the money but I couldn't do the film unless I was allowed to re-write the whole thing and he said, fine, go ahead. And I did. I knew … that it all came from the deep interest in sexual matters I had had all those years. I had read everything … and I was damn well informed about sexual techniques and problems like that … And I wrote a script for *Out of the Language of Love* – 'Out of', you see, because it was such an enormous field … in fact, three films came out of it. And still, the topic was not exhausted!

As for *Swedish and Underage*, the intentions of Wickman seem to have been quite decent, and twenty-five years later he remained sincere and matter of fact when he talked about his deep interest in 'sexual matters': 'Sure, there is a lot of sex in the film but then again, it was a sex situation we were supposed to film. The story of the poor unhappy girl. Actually it was not about porno ... the films were just quite free. There is plenty of nudity in them – but no actual sex scenes. I made a real porno movie just once towards the end of this sort of career. It was called *Ta mej I dalen* (*Country Life*, 1977).' The working title of the film was 'Eva: The First Stone', referring to the story in the Bible where Jesus urges anyone who is without sin to cast the first stone at an adulterous woman. Another title under consideration had been 'Tistelängen – The Thistle Meadow' – the name of the dump where the main character Eva Blom (Solveig Andersson) has made herself a hideout.

However, far from being marketed as a social report entailing criticism of smalltown bigotry, *Swedish and Underage* was promoted as 'a film about forbidden love – impudent! hot! tender!' and with images showing Solveig Andersson with her breasts bare or, at its best, dressed in a transparent baby-doll nightgown. Abroad, the film was clearly marketed with references to the porno genre, 'The most sensual SWEDISH film. A story of a lonely girl ... created by God and destroyed by lust!' (In the UK it was promoted as *Diary of a Half Virgin* and in the US as *Eva Was Everything But Legal*).

The handful of articles published during the shooting of the film present Solveig Andersson as an upcoming star in the line of Greta Garbo and Ingrid Bergman. She had graduated from a famous acting studio headed by Calle Flygare, who had trained many distinguished theatre and film stars in Sweden, among them Mai Zetterling. The 21-year-old starlet was depicted either wearing mini-skirts and white knee-high socks – perhaps more a fashion of the day than a conscious appeal to paedophiles – or showing off her breasts as she does in the first scene of the film. A couple of newspaper articles included the views of Andersson's parents: they would have preferred her playing Strindberg instead.

The young actress herself said in an interview that she actually thought acting was more interesting when actors had some clothes on and told how she dreamt of a career on stage rather than in film. Andersson starred in a number of porno films until 1975 when, according to Wickman, she became religious. This appears to be correct, because she was not seen in another film for twenty years, when she played a minor role in a short called *Stengrunden* (*Stone Basement*, Rolf Hamark, 1996), financed by a publisher of religious books.

The film opens with Eva, her breasts exposed, standing before a man and a young girl. The girl (Inger Sundh) soon runs from the site. When she is back home, her mother wants to know where she has been and the girl finally tells her about Eva's strip. The raging mother calls for the police – not because she is upset about child abuse but rather Eva's shameless manner. Eva is eventually interrogated at police headquarters. In a rather innocent way, the girl talks about the men she has been in contact with, saying that sometimes she received a little money or a chocolate bar for her 'services'. Later, a psychiatrist asks whether she knew that the sexual acts she had been involved with were illegal. Eva answers that she thought fucking was for everyone. She never thought of herself as underage as she had been abused by men since she was nine.

The police pick up the men Eva has identified while a series of flashbacks gives an account of their activities with her. In a similar manner, the flashbacks show Eva wandering about the streets, humiliated in every way by her schoolmates. At home, her foster parents curse her and her foster father threatens to beat her because she keeps missing classes. The affair makes big headlines in the local newspaper. The editor-in-chief discusses the case with a young journalist, Lennart Swenningson (Hans Wahlgren), who sympathises with Eva because he has seen how lonely she is. Swenningson tells his boss that he too was once solicited by Eva, and he certainly would have given in to her had he not had a young wife waiting for him at home.

Eva finally identifies Gustaf Bolinder (Göthe Grefbo) – a distinguished member of the community and her original guardian – as the first man to take advantage of her when, at the age of eight, she arrived in town. In the resulting trial, Bolinder's counsellor for the defence does his best to put all the blame on the girl. His argument is supported by a succession of witness testimonies, illustrated in another series of flashbacks.

Between the two court sessions, Eva is approached by a female psychiatrist, Jenny Berggren (Barbro Hiort af Ornäs). The woman asks questions about her family, her hopes and desires. Outside the courthouse, Swenningson discusses the trial with the police superintendent. They both agree that the atmosphere is 'uncanny' and that Bolinder's counsellor is manipulating public opinion. Like a *deus ex machina*, Lennart then pleads to take the witness stand. He says that under other circumstances he too might have been one of the men on trial. He talks about his own childhood when he stole cigarettes and was involved in a homosexual relationship. Despite all this, he did not become an outcast in society like Eva. He believes it is because he never reacted to life's injustices with aggression or by developing a 'free mind' as Eva has. Lennart's testimony is greeted with applause, and the case takes another turn. The men involved in the paedophile ring are sentenced to prison and Eva is to be sent to a reformatory. In the last minute, when the girl sits in a train waiting to be sent away, Jenny Berggren turns up and tells Eva that she has applied for custody of her. The two hold each other and Eva smiles happily as the train leaves the station.

Despite the fact that the producer did not invest much in the marketing of *Swedish and Underage*, it attracted a quarter of a million viewers in Sweden during its first year. Contemporary critics, however, immediately recognised the film's double standard. They wrote about a 'disgusting Peeping Tom mentality' and criticised the speculative and poor nature of the film. Jurgen Schildt, one of the best known Swedish film critics of the period, refered to Wickman's earlier career, calling him a Fellini of power plants and tin cans – but ends by claiming that Wickman does not seem to have learned much during his twenty-odd years in the field.

In 1972 Harry Rolnick wrote in the *Bangkok Post*: '[*Swedish and Underage*] is hardly a smorgasbord of sexual delights: it's a Swedish meatball of unfailing vapidity. And of course the point of the film is that though Eva may have done wrong, the townspeople are so hypocritical that they shouldn't cast the first stone anyhow. But this kind of stuff gets all mixed up with some extremely poor voyeuristic shots of Eva herself, lifting a blouse here, wiggling a breast there, and showing that she's got what it takes, even if she allegedly uses what it takes in the wrong place.' The critic finally wrote that he doubted if the director of the film knew much about making movies.

The morally confusing double standard expressed in the film may be regarded as a conflict between image and sound – or action and dialogue. Middle-class intellectuals such as the journalists and the psychiatrist – along with the police superintendent – are given ample opportunity to vent their liberal ideas in long speeches: Eva is a victim of ignorance, bigotry and unhappy circumstances; she should be given a fresh start. They outline the authoritative moral voice of the film. Similarly, the soundtrack gives expression to the actual feelings – hunger for love and caring – that Eva has in scenes together with the young Kenneth (Conny Ling), who is in love with her. On such occasions, the music is restrained and downbeat. The same music returns in the closing scene when the psychiatrist tells Eva she will take care of her in the future.

By contrast, the flashbacks involving sexual exploitation of the child are accompanied by up-tempo melodies. Such a discourse, however, is undermined by the voyeuristic camera positions, clearly exploiting the child-woman's body. Firstly, the camera spies on Eva and any man she is involved with behind corners, doors and storage shelves. In one scene, the camera even uses the point of view of a young boy, who is spying behind a window. Secondly, when Eva undresses in situations that do not involve sex *per se*, her exposed body remains in the centre of the image, with her face in a shadow or hidden behind the dress she eagerly lifts over her face. Thus – effectively decapitated and depersonalised – she loses any compassion there might be for her from the audience. Such a tendency is further reinforced by a lengthy dance-hall sequence where the camera, at waist-high level, focuses on the rhythmically shaking hips and breasts of the dancing women.

Even though Bolinder and the other men abusing Eva are portrayed as negative characters and finally convicted of their crime, the film's moral point of view reflects a positive attitude towards sex with underage children. Eva is depicted as an unharmed, innocent object of nature who does 'what she always has done' and 'cannot be seen as immoral because she has no morals'. What prevents the film's hero, the journalist, from taking advantage of her is the fact that he has a wife who is almost as young and willing waiting for him at home – not the fact that Eva is a child. In discussing the case with the editor-in-chief, the journalist states, 'There is something so temptingly forbidden with the underage!' And the two men agree that they are actually envious of the men who have been involved with Eva. 'Perhaps that's why we get so morally upset when it happens!' says Swenningson, while the editor-in-chief corrects him, 'Enviously upset, you might say!'

Eva is ultimately depicted as an innocent, unspoiled, 'open-minded' and 'naturally free' creature who, as a result of such idiosyncrasies, is socially shunned by women and sexually exploited by men. The moral discourse in the film casts her in an aura of saintliness of sorts, which is clearly illustrated in the last scene of the film. It begins with a close-up of a hand that collects a couple of railway tickets. Then a full shot depicts an expressionless woman – a guard sent to watch Eva – who takes the tickets and walks to a waiting room where the girl is sitting with a black scarf over her head, her face glowing, illuminated as in the portrait of a saint. In another corner, two women exchange meaningful glances while staring at her. A ringing bell marks the departure of the train. In this context, it sounds like a fragile church bell marking a rite of passage in life.

In the next, lengthy, shot, Eva and her guard walk in the bare, bleak winter landscape. In a shot from inside the station, the window frames creates a pattern of bars through which a woman is seen leaving a car in a hurry. There is another shot from inside the train, where Eva and her guard – looking just as expressionless as before – sit across from one another. The stationmaster signals with his flag, and the next shot shows Eva's questioning face as Jenny Berggren enters the compartment, the girl smiling for the first time. Jenny embraces her and explains how much she has been thinking of her. She has decided to try to persuade the authorities to allow her to take responsibility for the schooling that Eva has been sentenced to. Eva smiles happily and the long final shot depicts the train leaving the station and disappearing into the distance. The wintry landscape has an overtone of sadness to it, but the train's movement out of the frame contains the promise of a better future as well.

The final scene of the film is interesting for its change in terms of gender and parenting. On several occasions, Eva has been seen cherishing the Jean Webster novel *Daddy-Long-Legs* written in 1912. Young Kenneth has given her the novel, and Eva is seen reading it in bed at night. *Daddy Long Legs* is a classic youth novel about Jerusha Abbott, an orphan girl growing up in an asylum who is unexpectedly sent to college. Jerusha calls her mysterious benefactor 'Daddy Long Legs'. Eva, too, talks to an imaginary Daddy Long Legs, wishing that he would come and take her away. However, it is not a Daddy but a Mummy who finally assumes the position of saviour and takes the girl away from her barren existence.

Interestingly enough, in this film the position of an unhappy outcast depicted by Eva is not described as a result of the sexual abuse committed by men, but more as a result of the behaviour of the women in the town. Swenningson's wife, Maria, calls her 'a little magpie with too much make-up' and one of the younger wives says that the 'little slut' should be sent away to some correctional institute where people would 'whip some decency' into her. The mothers prevent their daughters from playing with Eva and openly show their contempt for her. Clearly, it is her association with sexual 'freedom' that places her at one end of a binary opposition between vice and virtue. The only woman obstructing this pattern is the female psychiatrist, the only professional woman in the film. Thus placed in the same category with middle-class men, Jenny Berggren, as a model of an ideal mother, repairs the damage caused by the other mothers – less educated, less rational and less tolerant.

Per Olov Qvist and Tytti Soila

REFERENCES

Rolnick, H. (1972) 'Review of *Swedish and Underage*', *Bangkok Post*, 11 March.

Schildt, J. (1970) 'Review of *Eva – den utstötta*', *Aftonbladet*, 24 April.

Webster, J. (1964 [1912]) *Daddy-Long-Legs*. New York: Penguin.

Wickman, T. (1995) *Berättar filmhistoria: Interview by Per Lönndahl*, NFTU CA project, The Swedish Film Institute.

MAZURKA PÅ SENGEKANTEN BEDROOM MAZURKA

JOHN HILBARD, DENMARK, 1970

In 1970, the first in a stylistically and thematically concomitant series of Danish popular soft porn films, starring Ole Sølstoft as main stallion, was filmed in Denmark. John Hilbard's *Mazurka på sengekanten* (*Bedroom Mazurka* a.k.a. *Bedside Mazurka*), which was based on Danish novelist Soya's short erotic novel *Mazurka*, and which was unquestioningly well received by the Danish audience, opened up a genre that has come to be known as Danish *blød porno* ('soft porn'). The Danish *blød porno*, by the Swedish audience referred to as Danish *gladporr* ('happy porn'), constitutes a genre of its own, and as such it would come to dominate the Danish (porn) film industry for almost a decade. A characteristic of this genre was, besides its inexhaustible emphasis on the comic and the farcical (which have a close affiliation to the traditional Danish erotic comedies called *lystspil*), the always lascivious stallion Ole Sølstoft who appeared in the majority of films produced.

Sølstoft had previously appeared in Annelise Meineche's erotic movies *Sytten* (1965) and *Sangen om den røde rubin* (1970), the latter filmed just before *Bedroom Mazurka*. Yet it was as the innocent and sexually inexperienced teacher Max Mikkelsen in Hilbard's cardinal film that Sølstoft would rise to the position of king of Danish soft porn film. Prior to this, the 1960s had seen a few Danish erotic films being produced, either in the form of frivolous, simple-minded erotic comedies or as erotic, explicit argumentative films concerning sexual freedom and a woman's right to her own body (as in Swedish director Mac Ahlberg's *Jeg – en kvinde*, 1965).

These films, however, had reached only minor audiences, occupying the periphery of Danish film production and culture. With *Bedroom Mazurka*, comic soft porn – dealing with exceedingly simple narratives framed by nudity and explicit allusions to sexual activity – became established as a Danish genre, if not as Danish cinema altogether. As such, it would reach outside of Denmark and become a commercial hit for years to come. In Sweden, for example, *Bedroom Mazurka* was a huge success, and one of the few pornographic films that made it to regular theatres.

The film premiered in Sweden in 1970, and the Swedish critics were united in their appreciation of the film: seeing in it a new freshness it was first labelled 'elegant porno', and when the sequels appeared, it was given its epithet *gladporr*. *Bedroom Mazurka* had very little to do, the Swedish critics argued, with 'the mechanical hard core pornography' that had dominated the industry during the 1960s. The new Danish comic porno, then, was understood to be 'innocent' porno for everyone, and indeed, in the midst of a sexual revolution of the 1960s, comic porn held a high attraction value. Popular with the Swedish audience, and with the critics, *Bedroom Mazurka* screened in several Swedish cities and continued to draw people to the cinema theatres for over a year, attracting about 1.5 million Swedish spectators.

Bedroom Mazurka was the first film in a series of eight films made by director Hilbard starring the always quite ridiculous and displaced Sølstoft as the main protagonist. *Bedroom Mazurka*, then, together with its sequels within the same 'Bedroom' series of eight Hilbard films in all, belongs to – or creates – its own sub-genre. However, as a sub-genre it must not be understood to be subordinated to, or dependent on, the larger genre of Danish comic soft porn. Rather, it must be seen as its origin and cause, if not as its paramount body of work. For the 'Bedroom' films have come to reach a larger audience than have other sub-genres of Danish soft porn, and it has come to be seen as the epitome of this specific 'national' genre.

Aligned with the 'Bedroom' films is the slightly more sexplicit series *of I … tegn* (*In the Sign of...*) – for example *I jomfruens tegn* (*In the Sign of the Virgin*), *I lovens tegn* (*In the Sign of the Lion*) and *I tvillingernes tegn* (*In the Sign of the Gemini*). This series consists of six films filmed between 1973 and 1978. The first of these films, *In the Sign of the Virgin*, was directed by Finn Carlsson and the following five were directed by Werner Hedman. In all of these six films, the main stallion is again played by Sølstoft, further placing or constituting him as the male signature, the sign, of Danish cinematic erotica. What differed the 'In the Sign of...' films from the first 'Bedroom' films was the inclusion of explicit straight intercourse, and of endless close-ups of male and female genitals, that is, of more 'hard core' sexual portrayals. Yet the frivolous, comic character and the unmistakable reference to the old Danish *lystspil* was as strong as in the 'Bedroom' films.

In June 1969, Denmark became the first country in the Western world to abolish film censorship and the distribution and sale of pornographic material in public was legalised. With film censorship abolished, the previously peripheral erotic film could suddenly enter the mainstream, just as other pornographic material now slowly entered all corners of mainstream culture. The abolishment had been anticipated for some time: the 1950s and 1960s had witnessed a long, and at times fervent, debate on the use of censorship. Like all disputes revolving around the subject of censorship, this one was much constructed around two almost irreconcilable positions: one stressing the absolute necessity of censorship, and the other refuting and condemning its supposed limitation of freedom.

Authors and cultural radicals Ove Brusendorff and Poul Henningsen, proclaiming the necessity for free distribution of erotic portrayals, would in their *Erotik for millioner: kærligheden i filmen* written in 1957, conclude with saying that 'for he who believes that every human being can be his own master if given the right opportunity and the freedom to be so, it is never too late to fight for freedom on all levels … Those of us who believe in freedom must unconditionally believe in it now, today rather than tomorrow.' The freedom referred to, of course, was the freedom to produce, distribute, consume and take pleasure in erotic and pornographic material.

Criticising what they referred to as the 'mental-hygienic censorship', Brusendorff and Henningsen argued that it was up to every Danish citizen, every Danish individual, to fight the politicians' 'apparent incapacity to understand the necessity of [pornographic] freedom', hence ascribing to the Danish government a certain 'dictatorian' mentality. And twelve years after the publication of their manifesto, the newly-won freedom gave way for pornographic representations and materials in mainstream culture, bringing nudity and sexual portrayals into public cinemas. *Bedroom Mazurka*, then, must be understood as a seminal and pivotal text: not only was it the first in a series of nationally and internationally successful films, it was also the one text that first portrayed what the upheaval of censorship would bring with it: an opening up of pornography in the Danish mainstream.

With the pro-censorship (and anti-pornography) forces now defeated, and the 'moral' panic held at bay, one would perhaps have expected a veritable explosion of explicit and hard core portrayals of sexual activity. Interesting, however, is that all of the 'Bedroom' films kept their focus on the comic and the soft (although they became more and more sexually daring as the series prolonged). Once the juxtaposition of eroticism and comedy had proved a commercial success, first in *Bedroom Mazurka* and then in its subsequent sequel, *Tandlæge på sengekanten* (*Danish Dentist on the Job*, 1971), it would of course have been risky to depart from the winning formula. It was obviously clear that the mainstream audience appreciated the more innocent combination of comedy and sex. This combination, much framed by 'softness', opened up for an all new audience: having been absent in the pornographic audience, yet constituting pornography's most required and most visually present object, women were now implicitly targeted as a new possible audience group. And already with *Bedroom Mazurka* did the constellation of the pornographic audience change: for the first time, in public, men and women enjoyed pornography together.

Whereas most nude films produced in Sweden at this time took on a blatantly instructive character, as in Torgny Wickman's *Kärlekens språk* (*Language of Love*, 1969) (Joseph Sarno's *Fäbodjäntan* from 1978 proves to be an exception), Danish pornography was more in line with the tradition of *lystspil* that had developed during the eighteenth century, a form of theatrical plays that belonged within the rural, working-class setting and culture. It was, indeed, the people's theatre.

Like the old *lystspil*, the genre of *blød porno* was structured on rather simple narratives which included rather detached erotic scenes displaying (and sometimes only alluding to) heterosexual intercourse. Like the *lystspil*, the Danish soft porno film of the 1970s had quite a strict framing with certain established ingredients. Besides the often ridiculously simple and straightforward narrative, it included stereotypical and simple-minded characters, lots of allusions to, or actual portrayals of, nudity emphasising the female breast and bottom, and several scenes including awkward and comic sex (with the butt of the joke almost always being the man, in the case of film, Sølstoft) and – which is crucial – a happy and romantic ending.

The comic, then, was created by the pleasure and fun with which these films represented sexual desire and sexual acts. Sex, within this context, was much aligned, if not equalised, with naïveté and laughter, smiling faces and unquestionable indulgence. Any explicitly visual connection made between sexual pleasure, violence and pain, so central to more contemporary pornography, was non-existent within this genre. Yet in many of these films (as well as in the old *lystspil* plays) sexual intercourse was – by its characters – explicitly interpreted as rape, and vice versa. However, taken that the atmosphere and the storyline all presented happy, sexual people, rape came to equate love-making, and hence, something that women and men alike desired.

As previously mentioned, the films produced within the 'In the Sign of…' series were from the beginning more hard core than were the 'Bedroom' films in their portrayal of sexual activity. However, following the public demand and the more general development in porno films and pornographic material, the two last 'Bedroom' films include more explicit portrayal of sexual acts. Both *Hopla på sengekanten* (*Danish Escort Girls*, 1976) and *Sømænd på sengekanten* (*Bedside Sailors*, 1976) diverge quite clearly from their forerunners, even though the traditional *lystspil* structure with its comic elements, was still dominating.

Bedroom Mazurka was indeed so *blød* as to offend nobody, and contained only five shots that show nude breasts and buttocks, and there are no images of genitals. Further, the few sex scenes portraying intercourse are all filmed under the cover, that is, with the actors slowly 'bumping' under the blanket. A film like Werner Hedman's *I tyrens tegn* (*In the Sign of Taurus*) from 1974, on the other hand, is more hard core. The film contains several scenes with women performing felatio on male actors, scenes with women being instructed how to masturbate using bananas as dildos, and there are numerous close-ups of male and female genitals, both isolated and in close contact with one another. Also, it includes a long scene portraying a white and a black woman engaging in oral sex. Here, the narrative has indeed become subordinated to the sexual content. At this point, then, the story was no longer needed as the prerequisite to show nudity and sexual acts, rather, the story here functions as a loosely constructed link between the various portrayals of explicit sex acts.

Bedroom Mazurka follows a straight and simple narrative line, offering few surprises as it develops. The story takes place at a conservative boarding school for upper-class boys, seemingly aged between 8 and 18. The school, which reassembles a little castle, is situated in the Danish countryside, and given that the story takes place in the summer, nature plays a central role. Not only is nature connected to sexual activity (the film opens with the school's young maid having sex with one of the older students in the nearby forest), it is also used as a backdrop for class differences. Thus the upper class (to which the old, all-male trustees belong) drive in fancy cars, whereas the modest people (such as the maid and the village people) walk, indicating that they are more in touch with the ground, nature and, hence, with their sexuality).

The initial problem is presented early on in the film: the school's present principal, Mr Bosted, has been elected minister of the Danish government and is about to leave his post. However, he cannot leave his position before finding – together with the trustees – a suitable follower. Working as a teacher at the school, is Max Mikkelsen (Sølstoft), a nerdish 30-year-old virgin dedicated to his profession, and also, it is pointed out, to science. Early on it becomes clear that Max is liked by his students, and also, that he is the one preferred by the trustees and the principal, who see in him a good and trusty follower.

Subsequently, as we already know from an early state, he is very likely to become the new principal. However, the school has certain rules that must be followed, and these rules constitute the structural hindrance in the narrative for any quick solution and ending. Hence, these rules help establish the very starting point for its development. According to them, the principal must be married – as in heterosexual – and if not married, then at least engaged to be married. As Max has never even been close to a woman, the prospects seem poor at first.

It soon becomes quite clear, however, that it will only be a matter time before he loses his virginity: his more experienced students try taking control over the situation by finding him a suitable woman. After long discussions they agree to invite a prostitute, a foreign girl who does not speak the language and would remain silent. At the same time, the current principal's wife, Mrs Bosted, who is portrayed as a sex-hungry middle-aged woman, tries to seduce Max. Furthermore, one of the trustees at the school, Mr Barnewelder, has two beautiful daughters, who both are introduced as Max's possible sex/love object, and also as a possible wife.

The sisters are presented as each others' definite opposites, thus underlining the cultural dichotomy between bad woman/good woman. The youngest of the two, Line, is a 'Nordic' type; she is blond and down to earth, lacking any mannerisms. In addition to this, she is politically active and presented as an intellectual, which allows a certain depth to her character. The older sister, Renate, in contrast, is dark-haired and very stylish, caring more for her looks than for her brain: she is all surface. Furthermore, as to support her deviance from Line, she is an unhappy divorcée, who has developed a craze for men and sex.

Max falls in love with Line from the moment he lays eyes on her, but it is Renate who seduces him. Before the seduction occurs, however, Line advises Max that if he wants to win a woman's heart, he must try and become more self-assured, more confident in his masculine role. Max interprets her advice in sexual terms, and sets off to acquire knowledge about carnal love. He seeks help in a porno store located in the nearest village, where he gets instructions (from a nude female employee) about the various ways of gaining sexual pleasure. After having acquired the theoretical knowledge, he tries to find his male confidence by putting theory into practice.

He soon starts – as if by accident – to have sex, first with the principal's dark-haired wife who more or less forces herself on him. Later he encounters a foreign, dark and mysterious prostitute who also forces herself on him (just as she's been instructed and paid to do). A third woman who forces him to have sex is Renate. In front of our eyes, then, Max suddenly blooms into a sex-stallion, apparently finding his masculine 'confidence' through sexual activity.

Although he now has overcome his virgin status, he still has no fiancée, and therefore his chances for being elected principal, after all, still seem poor. His students, however, who have witnessed the developing romance between Max and Line, make a last effort: they trick Line into a cabin where they lock her up, and then force Max to join her. Confined, the two soon start expressing their feelings for each other, and one thing leads to another: they turn to romantic love-making (a tender love-making that of course differs widely from the earlier sexual encounters portrayed). Before Max and Line have reached nudity, however, the door is flung open and their love is there for everyone to see. They then walk out, announcing that they are engaged to be married. Everyone cheers and applauds and the film ends on a happy note. The principal is replaced by a more worthy candidate; virginity is overcome, masculinity is acquired, and the romantic couple is created.

From the above presentation of *Bedroom Mazurka*, it is clear that non-straight sex and desire is being avoided in the film. When it is referred to verbally, it is in a derogatory and homophobic manner. An initial problem that has to be resolved is the suspicion that the nerdish hero might be gay: since he has had no sexual encounters with women he is at first read as asexual, and in its prolongation, as possibly gay. Further, the main goal of the narrative is an engagement. As principal of an all-boy school, one has to be married, so as to avoid any suspicion of paedophilia. As is often the case in a homophobic culture, paedophilia and homosexuality are treated as equal.

Bedroom Mazurka is thus a staple 'boy meets girl' story, with the only variance that here it is the hero, and not the heroine, who has to get laid (so as to fulfil the story's main goal). Of course, he does not get to have sex with the girl of his dreams until the very end, but he manages to have sex with at least three other women, all of whom desire him as a sexual partner (sexually starved as they are). He loses his virginity, becomes a real man, has his heterosexuality confirmed, and is thereby also being assumed into the Symbolic. And it is not until he is man enough – that is, knowing how to fuck and how to satisfy women – that the hero gets both the girl and the position as principal.

The film presents its female characters according to the general dichotomy dictating Western culture's notion of Woman as either good or bad. The two daughters, Line and Renate, together constitute a prime example of this binary couple: the blond sister is presented as saint, the dark sister as whore. The blond, politically-active heroine, on the one hand, remains untouched until the end, expressing no desire to have sex before she is certain that Max truly loves her. And on the one hand, we have Renate, Mrs Bosted and the prostitute, various incarnations of the whore. These are women characters presented as sexually-starved creatures, seeing in every male a potential lover, and who are more than willing to have sex with any male; more problematically, they are women who express explicit desires of being raped.

The film's portrayal of women as sexually active, getting laid because they want to, must of course be read in connection with the larger political and cultural discussion on the liberation of women's sexuality that was being focused upon at that time. Yet the film's overtly romantic – and indeed unquestioned – equation between sex and rape, transforming heterosexual intercourse into rape, and sexualising rape as something desired by everyone, is of course problematic. Placed within a comic framing, rape becomes fun and its violent connotations are lost. It is presented as fun because there is no 'real' rape taking place in the film: although the (bad) women accuse Max of being a rapist making him responsible for the sex they have had with him, he is – as far as the audience knows – not a rapist.

Max, then, becomes a rapist against his will, due to false accusations. What makes this weird and awkward rape discourse fun and innocent within the film's fictional universe is the fact that all the men surrounding Max applaud him for being so manly and masculine. Therefore rape, it is maintained, is what makes a man a real man. Moreover, rape is presented as something that most women desire, and hence the film helps reinforce the old dominant notion that all women dream about being raped, so as to escape their own (shameful) sexual desire. Within this film, this is presented as truth.

In *Bedroom Mazurka*, as in the other 'Bedroom' films (as well as in the 'In the Sign of...' films) that would follow, the sexualisation of violence is both covered up (by the comic portrayals of sexual activity) and made invalid. Here we have men and women engaging in mutual sexual encounters, and no one is seen forcing anyone. There is no rape in sight, yet the very discourse on sexualised rape (so common in contemporary pornography) is loudly present: rape equated with sexual intercourse, rape as desired by both sexes, rape as the ultimate proof of real manlihood (sexual activity) and acquired womanhood (sexual passivity), and rape as just another word for/way of love-making. Although the representations here are being altered, with women actively seducing men and then accusing them of rape, the actual and real effect is the one and same: a woman claiming that she has been raped is not to be believed.

This chapter has argued that John Hilbard's *blød porno* film *Bedroom Mazurka*, filmed in 1970, only one year after film censorship had been abolished in Denmark, must be seen as a seminal film. It was the first in a series of comic soft porn films that would come to dominate the pornography produced not only in Denmark, but in all of Scandinavia during the 1970s. Connecting sex and comedy, and obviously drawing on the old, popular and traditional Danish *lystspil*, the film instantly proved successful, both commercially and critically. Focusing on comic and soft portrayals of sexual activity, the film, as well as its followers, would prove attractive to an audience that was indeed heterogeneous to its constitution, hence removing pornography away from the tabooed periphery to the more tolerated mainstream.

Yet while being soft, simple, innocent and comic to its narrative as well as to its visuals – its sexual portrayals – the film is far from unproblematic. By equating homosexuality with paedophilia on an implicit level, and by equating rape with heterosexual intercourse and desire on a more explicit level, *Bedroom Mazurka* must be understood, to some lamentation, as both homophobic and misogynist. For while the film can be understood to be in line with Brusendorff and Henningsen's early quest for every individual's freedom, it makes clear that the freedom here attained does not include everyone.

Louise Wallenberg

REFERENCE

Brusendorff, O. and P. Henningsen (1957) *Erotik for millioner: kærligheden i filmen*. Copenhagen: Thaning & Appel.

ELVIS! ELVIS!

16

KAY POLLAK, SWEDEN, 1977

Swedish children's cinema occupies a prominent position internationally. Films like *A Jungle Saga* (Arne Sucksdorff, 1957), *Hugo and Josefin* (Kjell Grede, 1967) and, more recently, *Elina* (Klaus Härö, 2003) have received numerous awards at film festivals around the world as they have been acclaimed as pieces of art that do not shy away from difficult subjects. Death, loss, loneliness, powerlessness and difficulties with coping with the expectations of parents and other adults are, in these films, depicted in both straightforward and poetic ways. Despite this well-deserved attention from critics and audiences, little research has been devoted to the Swedish children's film. It the intention here to contribute, even in the slightest way, to a change in attitudes towards the children's film as being a less important genre, not worthy of serious study. By a closer look at Kay Pollak's *Elvis! Elvis!* (1977), attention is drawn to the richness of the distinctive devices that compose what can be called a children's film aesthetics.

Upon it release, *Elvis! Elvis!* was something of a shock – especially for the parents among the audience. Up until then, ever since *Anderssonskans Kalle* (*Mrs Andersson's Charlie*, 1922), the children's film in Sweden had thematically, with very few exceptions, been rather 'harmless'. The 1950s and 1960s were the decades of everlasting sunshine and flowering meadows within the genre of children's film. The dominant director during these years was Olle Hellbom, whose films all were adaptations of the immensely popular books by Astrid Lindgren. *Ui på Saltkråkan* (*The Seacrow Island*, 1968) and *Alla vi barni Bullerbyn* (*The Children of Bullerby Village*, 1960) are only two examples of Hellbom films that are until today screened repeatedly on Swedish television.

Undoubtely, Hellbom was an effective storyteller, but the quality of his films lies almost exclusively in the stories they tell. Without Astrid Lindgren's exuberant narratives, her unmistakable feeling towards the magic of a child's everyday life and warm humour, Hellbom would hardly have achieved the enormous success he did during his professional life. Aesthetically, his films are very conventional and follow the Lindgren narratives very strictly, without the slightest cinematic digression which, perhaps, would have heightened their quality. This, most likely, is a consequence to Lindgren's iconic status in Sweden. Indeed, it would be fair to say that no one person has had a more profound impact on the Swedish culture of the twentieth century, not even Ingmar Bergman or August Strindberg.

Lindgren's books are universally – and repeatedly – read. The filmic adaptations have beeen seen by as many again. There is no Swede who does not know of *Pippi Longstockings*, *Emil* or *Ronja* and there is not a child whose adolescence has not been influenced by the stories of these figures. One might say that they are part of the Swedish soul in a way that no other social, political or cultural aspect is, and in that way, they are unique. The common understanding seems to be that they should not be adapted by any ambitious film director with 'ideas' either. From this vantage point it is possible to assume that Lindgren's stories have inhibited the artistic development of the Swedish children's film.

To break away from the flowering meadows of Lindgren's stories, then, you have to find another author of children's literature whose books could be adapted into cinema. Maria Gripe seemed like an obvious alternative. Considering the themes she has depicted throughout her long professional career, her works appear as goldmines for artistically ambitious film directors. Loneliness, alienation, frightful imaginations, occultism and fairytales of death and violence are just some of the subjects Gripe has dealt with. Not surprisingly then, the first Swedish children's film which was valued artistically as well as storywise, was Grede's *Hugo och Josefin*, based on a trilogy by Gripe.

Another ten years would pass from Grede's film until Kay Pollak made his debut as a film director. Originally a mathematician, Pollak started working for Swedish television attracting substantial attention for his serial *The Secret Reality* (1972), a story about 12-year-old Anders with problems with school, with friends and parents. The series made a profound impression on Maria Gripe, whose two initial books about six-year-old Elvis had just been published. She soon made contact with Pollak and together they wrote the script for *Elvis! Elvis!*

Elvis! Elvis! is the story of a boy who is just about to start school. He lives with his parents in a typical Swedish small town. Elvis Karlsson – named after his mother's idol – is a lonely boy with no friends of his own age who spends his days strolling outdoors. He has two close friends, both grown ups: Brovall, a sad railway worker and his grandfather on his father's side and an elderly man who lives with his wife in the country. According to Elvis's mum, he drinks too much. Together with these two men, Elvis feels comfortable to speak about love, power and death – things that he spends a lot of time pondering over.

At his first day at school, Elvis finds himself unable to speak when his teacher reads out his name, wetting his pants out of worry – an incident his mother will never forgive him for, while his teacher says it is nothing to worry about: 'It could happen to anybody!' At home again, Elvis overhears a telephone conversation between his mum and one of her friends, his mum telling about the 'catastrophe', complaining how impossible he is. Next day at school, however, Elvis makes friends with a girl called Anna-Rosa, who considers him very brave to have had the courage to wet his pants at school.

Although his mother has decided it would be best for Elvis to start school the following year instead, Elvis continues and finds himself improving with each day. He also spends more and more time at Anna-Rosa's place, which becomes a sanctuary from his mother's supervision. Anna-Rosa's mum, grandmother and great grandmother, who all live in the old house, seem always to be joyful, telling jokes and baking gorgeous buns. When Elvis's mother finds out where he spends his afternoons after school, she forbids him to ever set foot at Anna-Rosa's house again, referring to her family as 'bad people'. Elvis gets very upset and screams out that he wants her to die. Suffering from bad conscience, Elvis then makes his father buy a beautiful ring to the mother for Christmas. The film ends with Elvis lying next to his sleeping mother, whispering 'I will be a good boy, mum, I will be good.'

As may be clear from this summary, *Elvis! Elvis!* is a rather pessimistic description of a child's struggles to become loved for who he is, especially by his mother. Elvis's mother in her turn is a very immature, selfish woman who constantly fails to understand her son's behaviour, wishing he was different, like 'ordinary children'. Elvis is torn between his longings to fulfill his mother's wishes and his urge to follow the voice of his own heart. The depiction of the mother is almost a caricature, but without ever becoming wholly unrealistic.

The 1970s was a time when the nuclear family was a major subject of debate in Sweden. In numerous articles, but also in children's books and films, family life was depicted as a prison, a symbol of oppression and egoism. Gripe's books and Pollak's subsequent film can be seen as parallels to this debate. Elvis's struggle for self contentment collides with the role of the conventional mother. The reviews that followed the opening of *Elvis! Elvis!* are clearly coloured by the offence many adults took from the role of the mother in the film. Many of the critics seem provoked, even indignant, of the way she behaves, and even the ones that praise Pollak's film as a true piece of cinematic art conclude that it is not a film for children. 'A children's film for adults', was a general comment.

But what is a children's film, then? The answer to this seemingly simple question is actually far from given – something that the great number of different definitions found in the literature on children's films demonstrate. Some say that a children's film simply is a film seen by children. Others claim that a children's film is a film about children. To others, it is a film adapted from a children's book. These are just some of the most obvious examples of definitions of a children's film that are either too broad, too narrow, or in other ways misleading.

The British film scholars Cary Bazalgette and Terry Staples have approached the problems of defining a children's film in a somewhat different way, namely by trying to trace aesthetic aspects that distinguish it from a film for adults. For example, they find that casting, camera angles, editing style and music are used in ways that, taken together, create a viewpoint that is mainly or entirely a child's. Although it is more of a sketch than a thorough analysis, Bazalgette's and Staples' reasoning is a useful stepping-stone in trying to draw up an aesthetics of children's films. As Pollak's *Elvis! Elvis!* has been accused of being too difficult for children – a 'children's film for adults' – it is especially interesting to apply Bazalgette's and Staples' thoughts upon it. By looking closer at some of the aspects of the film, we can see how *Elvis! Elvis!* addresses a young audience through its aesthetics, especially by focusing on its use of long takes and static camera, low angles and close-ups, sparse dialogue and sound, as well as non-classical narrative.

Let us take a closer look at one of the key scenes which takes place a third of the way into the film. This is where little Elvis is confronted with his namesake – 'the *real* Elvis', as the mother calls him – for the first time. A giant Presley concert in Hawaii is screened live on television all over the world via satellite. In honour of this special occasion the family has, at the father's disapproval, bought their first colour television. The episode opens with the arrival of the television set; two men carry the huge box from a van into the apartment house, while the mother, very excited, asks them to be careful. She does not notice Elvis, who is just coming home from school and gets the front door slammed right before his face.

In the next scene, the family is seated in front of the television set. The living room is all dark, except for one solemn candle and the flickering from the television screen. The mother, all dressed up and in a state of extreme excitement, is seated right in front of the television, celebrating this moment of magic with a bottle of wine. The father, apparently bored, is sitting in the background, drinking beer, and Elvis sits in an armchair next to his mother, sipping soda and watching the 'real' Elvis and his mother alternately. He is obviously stunned, confused by this strange man on the television, but probably even more confused by the expression on his mother's face: all shimmering, smiling out of love, tenderness and joy – an expression of happiness he himself has never given rise to. Elvis leaves the room to study his face carefully in the mirror. He turns his head back and forth, obviously looking for a resemblance with the 'real' Elvis. This mirror scene returns several times in the film and is an important key to understanding Elvis's thoughts, his doubts concerning his identity, his attempts to find his true self and at the same time satisfy his mother's demands of him.

Elvis returns to the living room and sits down next to his mother again. He stretches out his hand to touch her arm, as if to assure himself of their affinity, but she pushes it away. She is completely absorbed by her idol, her eyes filled with tears. Elvis leaves for bed, lying wide awake staring into the ceiling. When the concert is finished, his mother comes to say good night, asking him what he thought: 'Wasn't he cute?' Vacantly, Elvis answers with a counter-question: 'Whose Elvis am I?' – whereupon his mother says, confused, that of course he is his mother's little Elvis. She then wants him to kiss her, but Elvis refuses turning his head away. Disappointed by this, she firmly places his hands on top of the quilt, as that is the proper way for decent children to sleep. She puts out the light, says good night and closes the door. Elvis lies awake, overhearing his parents' discussion on his name. He shakes his head anxiously, as if this would get rid of his uneasy thoughts.

This passage lasts for seven minutes and consists of 26 takes, with a very small variation in motifs. Almost exclusively, the images show either Elvis' face, his mother's face or the television screen. This creates a slow pace, corresponding to Elvis' pensive way to apprehend his world, and at the same time making it possible for the children in the audience to grasp the full action of the film and also get time to interpret the course of events.

Throughout the film, the camera movements are few, the panning shots even fewer. Most of the time, the camera is placed still to register the action in front of the lens, much alike an objective onlooker. In the television concert passage, this use of the camera becomes flagrant. The first shot is of the apartment house door: Elvis returns from school, visible at the rear of the screen image, while the foreground is occupied by the men bringing in the television set. For a second, the large box containing it will fill all of the image. In the next scene the family is seated on the sofa, watching television. The living room is all dark, except for the light from one solemn candle and the flickering from the television screen. The mother, all dressed up and in a state of extreme excitement, is seated right in front of the television set. There seem to be primarily two reasons for this static use of the camera.

Firstly, it corresponds with the static atmosphere within the family. All three of them are trapped inside their given roles, which no one seems able to break through – although Elvis is constantly making daring attempts. They are all pitiful victims of conventional social ideas about the nuclear family, according to which the mother and housewife is responsible for raising the child, cleaning the house and in other ways keeping the façade to the outside, social world in a perfect state. The father, on the other hand, brings money to the household, but has almost no say, agreeing with his wife or protesting mutteringly most of the time. Elvis in his turn tries heartbreakingly hard to live up to his mothers' expectations of him, constantly failing in his effort. The family is imprisoned, their apartment a prison cell, depicted through a static camera. In contrast, the camera moves more freely whenever outside, as if Elvis momentarily were able to break out of his prison.

The second reason for the static use of the camera is related to the slow editing technique, as it helps the children of the audience grasp everything in the image. André Bazin claimed that the static camera offers a more democratic way of seeing, but you could also say that it offers a more 'childish' way of seeing. The director does not choose for the young viewer what s/he is to see, he does not force upon her/him his own, adult, way of seeing. Instead he leaves it to her/him to focus upon whatever s/he wants to. And, as we all know, adults and children do not always have the same opinion about what is worth noticing in the world.

Related to the two above-mentioned aspects of the children's film aesthetics is the use of low camera angles and close-ups. In *Elvis! Elvis!* the perspective is literally the six-year-old boy's. The camera is lowered down to the level of Elvis' sight, with the consequence that now and then the heads of the adults are missing from the screen image – or that from time to time a large part of the image is filled with the back of a chair or some other 'meaningless' object. This low camera position is maintained even during the dialogue scenes, where alternating point-of-view shots would be expected as in classical continuity editing. At one moment, when Elvis is speaking to his mother, we see her from below, which is Elvis' point of view, while Elvis is seen from beside, at the height of his shoulder. In this way, the camera keeps the child's perspective, never letting the adult occupy a superior position. As one of the central themes of *Elvis! Elvis!* is the struggle for power between Elvis and his mother, this use of low angles makes a central standpoint in favour of the child.

In the television concert scene, we see the set as Elvis sees it, at one point in extreme close-up focusing on the text flickering on the screen, saying 'ELVIS'. Elvis's mother is seen from the height of Elvis's sight, but straightforward rather than from beside, where Elvis sits. This is to emphasise the mother's facial expression, to give the audience a close look at the amorous gaze that she never directs towards her son.

Just like the low angles, the prevailing use of close-ups in *Elvis! Elvis!* could be seen as a device to tell the story from the child's point of view. Children in general – and Elvis in particular – tend to focus upon one thing at the time, their peripheral vision is not yet fully developed and the child's world is small compared to the grown-up's. Considering these factors, Pollak's frequent use of close-ups makes an important aspect of the children's film aesthetics. When Elvis watches television, he sees nothing but the screen, as if the world outside it did not exist – and this is the way children generally watch television. Therefore, the television screen is solely shown in a close-up or extreme close-up, thus filling all of the image. When Elvis plays with his hands on his lap, he concentrates all his attention upon this – and consequently we see his hands from above, in extreme close-up.

In contrast to the classical Hollywood family film, the dialogue in *Elvis! Elvis!* is written for a young audience. The sentences are kept short, there are no jokes over the heads of the children and the vocabulary is simple. It is probably more difficult for an adult to keep up with the dialogue between Elvis and Anna-Rosa, as it follows the logic of children, and occasionally could be apprehended as nonsense.

There are some exceptions to this use of dialogue suited for children, primarily in the discussions between Elvis's parents or Anna-Rosa's mother and grandmother. But these conversations are not meant to be comprehended by children. On the contrary, just like they sound to Elvis and Anna-Rosa – as adult background noise, frightening and unintelligible – these conversations are to sound in the ears of the young audience. One example of this is the discussion that Elvis overhears after his mother has said goodnight and closed the door. In the distance his father makes ironic remarks on his son's name, which, according to him, will be a good laugh at school. This is the starting point of a quarrel which Elvis tries not to listen to, as he probably has heard it before, and most likely does not understand, as he has not yet learnt the art of irony.

Just like the dialogue, the non-diegetic music is used sparsely and suited for children. There are three different music scores appearing in the film, but only very rarely. The film opens with the sound of a music box, a simple melody which will return a few times later on. During a period while Elvis is feeling really happy, in the schoolyard or at Anna-Rosa's house, there is a joyous circus tune being played. There is also a still tune accompanying a few very emotional moments when Elvis and Anna-Rosa are becoming friends. Accordingly, the non-diegetic music is used sparingly and to heighten emotion rather than drama. Most of the time, only natural sound is used, which creates a strong sense of realism. This is not to say that the film is silent. On the contrary, in Elvis' apartment there is an everlasting sound, either from the radio, the television, the record player (playing only Elvis Presley) or from the mother on the phone with her friends. Elvis himself is obviously disturbed by this constant noise that is forced upon him, preferring the silence on his own, or in the countryside. Therefore, the scenes depicting Elvis by himself are often silent, or with just a few distant sounds of cars, birds, and so on. In this way, it can be said that the use of sound in *Elvis! Elvis!* is part of the children's film aesthetics as well. The non-diegetic music is suited for a young audience and the diegetic sounds are all heard through Elvis's ears, so to speak.

Unlike the classical Hollywood film, *Elvis! Elvis!* lacks a fixed beginning, middle and ending, and is instead narrated in a rather fragmentary way. From the seasonal changes in nature one can easily figure out that the story proceeds from late summer until Christmas, but there is no given causal relationship between most of the scenes. The television concert passage considered above, to take one example, could have appeared anywhere in the film. There is neither a previous scene leading towards it, nor a subsequent one emanating from it. Like so many other passages of the film, it is a slice of the life of a boy called Elvis Karlsson. And unfortunately, these slices of life do not lead to any satisfying solution; the closing scene could as well have been the opening one – Elvis begging his mother for forgiveness, promising to be a good boy.

In terms of the different likely reasons for the use of this non-classical narrative structure, one could suggest that it is a structure well-suited for children's films. A child lacks the overview of time and life that an adult possesses. Elvis, together with the younger kids in the audience, has no realistic concept of time. To him, the Presley television concert seems to last forever and consequently, this scene amounts to a seemingly oversized part of the film. In this way one could say that the non-classical narrative structure corresponds to the child's way of apprehending the flow of time and the course of events. One could also say that the children's film is an area freed from the constraints of a classical film. The young audience has not the same fixed expectations of a film as an adult audience. A person who has not already seen hundreds of films is probably more open-minded to an alternative narrative structure, just like a child has no problems apprehending an animated film being as realistic as a live-action film.

From an aesthetic perspective, therefore, Kay Pollak's *Elvis! Elvis!* is definitely a children's film. Through its use of long takes and static camera, low angles and close-ups, sparse dialogue and sound, as well as the non-classical narrative, it entirely offers a child's point of view and thereby primarily addresses children in the audience. Furthermore, *Elvis! Elvis!* is a prime example of Swedish children's film at its best, making clear that it constitutes a valid, sometimes even innovative, form of cinema. Today, the climate for Swedish children's culture is different from the heydays in the late 1970s, but the children's film is still on the side of Elvis Karlsson. Even today, the Swedish children's film does not have to rely on box-office success, as its financial basis is state subsidies, thereby resisting the pressure from commercialism – the force that makes the Hollywood children's film an entirely false story, told at a level high above the heads of the young audience, primarily addressing their parents, who pay the tickets. Whether the kids prefer a Disney reel to a Pollak work – that is an altogether different story.

Malena Janson

REFERENCE

Bazalgette, C. and T. Staples (1995) 'Unshrinking the Kids: Children's Cinema and the Family Film', in C. Bazalgette and D. Buckingham (eds) *In Front of the Children: Screen Entertainment and Young Audiences*. London: British Film Institute.

EBBA THE MOVIE

JOHAN DONNER, 1982

I was nine years old when the film *Ebba the Movie* (Johan Donner, 1982) premiered, regrettably too young to see it at the time. The title of the film, of course, alludes to Lasse Hallström's film *Abba the Movie* (1977). It was not until the mid- or late 1980s, as a young punk in the small town where I grew up, that I saw the film for the first time. It really stunned me, and I was struck by the same thoughts that any person who likes music from an era other than his own has had: why could I not have been born in another time and place? Everything seemed so much more intense in that film compared to the boring smalltown life I was leading. It did not seem fair that I had no opportunity to take part in a movement that was so different from anything I had seen, or heard, before.

The provincial town of Gnesta, the end of the line for the commuter train from Stockholm, did not offer much space for a young punk. Although it was only seventy kilometres from the capital city, it seemed to belong to a different galaxy. We definitely did not share the same suburban environment depicted in the film; we certainly did not have many concrete buildings that could be spray-painted with graffiti. It was all just middle-class, one- or two-storey houses in neat rows inhabited by people like my mother and father – housewives, clerks or construction workers. In this setting, the adolescent period in which I sought identity as a boy, punk music and punk culture became my primary points of reference. Then came The Second Summer of Love, the Stone Roses and Primal Scream and a completely different frame of reference. I grew up and forgot all about *Ebba the Movie* – until now. I bought the film recently and started to ask myself why punk music and punk culture in general, and this film in particular, had such a tremendous effect on a teenage boy like me in a town so far away in time and space from the epicentre of this cultural earthquake. Was it just the music or was it something else that made me connect with the film?

Ebba the Movie is a documentary capturing the infamous 1981 tour of the Swedish punk band Ebba Grön (Ebba Green) and the reggae-rock band Dag Vag (Day Vague) called *Turister i tillvaron* (*Tourists in Life*). The documentary also captures the band in the studio, recording their second album *Kärlek och uppror* (*Love and Rebellion*), which was eventually released in 1981.

The band were arguably the most influential punk band in Sweden and, like the documentary film about them, they were deeply rooted in the social and political context of the time.

During the second half of the 1970s, Sweden was governed by the first right-wing administration in over forty years. The 'Swedish model', known as 'Folkhemmet' (the People's/Citizens' Home), which was the result of four decades of social engineering, ranging from schooling and welfare systems to better housing and city planning, was disintegrating. The housing program ('miljonprogrammet' – the million program), in which previous governments initiated the building of suburbs to meet the need for sound housing following the economic growth and increasing urbanisation of the 1950s and 1960s, had led to social segregation and alienation by the end of the 1970s.

Disappointment with the effects of 'Folkhemmet' was beginning to spread throughout society, not only among its political opponents, but amongst the grass roots of its ideological foundation – the working class. It was in such a context that the band Ebba Grön emerged, or rather, can be seen as a result of these conditions. Their name comes from the code name 'Ebba Grön', used by the Swedish police to arrest the German terrorist Norbert Kröcher and his accomplices in 1976, as they were planning the abduction of the Swedish politician Anna-Greta Leijon, in order to exchange her for imprisoned members of a German terrorist group. This socio-political setting, similar to that of other countries in Western Europe at the time, is a necessary starting point in understanding both the existence and the political significance of Ebba Grön and Swedish punk culture in general.

Ebba the Movie itself is a rather straightforward documentary capturing the band on tour and in the studio: concert footage and scenes from the tour bus are mixed with interviews with the three band members, reminiscing about how and why they started playing punk music. The concert footage blends footage from the vantage point of the audience with close-ups of the band members as they play. The critic at *Dagens Nyheter*, the major morning paper in Sweden, claimed that director Johan Donner had accomplished a film that 'tried to find a structure and an approach to Ebba Grön' and in this way distinguished itself from other filmed portraits of musicians.

The placement of something out of the ordinary and subversive (punk) into an acceptable and familiar context – a mainstream documentary format – may disarm the potentially subversive character of the music. However, the tension between the (allegedly) subversive character of the music performed and the conventional visual form of the documentary create an interesting arena for the conflicting discourses at play in the film. The conventional format also places the film within a long line of music documentaries that date back to D. A. Pennenbaker's groundbreaking documentary about Bob Dylan's tour of the UK, *Don't Look Back* (1967).

Further, *Ebba the Movie* premiered at a time when the opportunities for the exhibition of music on screen (both television and cinema) were very limited. Swedish television, with its non-commercial two-channel system, did broadcast programs containing popular music at the time, but lacked the diversity of contemporary music stations. The film thus filled a cultural gap, or need, that would be commercially exploited a few years later in Sweden by the MTV network. In addition, *Ebba the Movie* is one of the few documents of punk in Sweden during the late 1970s to early 1980s. Today, the only version of the film available in commercial circulation is an edited 'hardcore' variation, released in 1996. This shorter version converges the film further towards music video aesthetics, making it a generically transitive mode of music-film. This later version, according to the records of the Swedish Film Institute, is also more in line with the original intentions of Johan Donner.

An underlying premis of this chapter is that the uneasy relation between the actual male bodies and the stereotyped idea of masculinity may be challenged by individuals as well as groups in society. Therefore, the dominant view of how this relation should be displayed by individuals must be upheld by the society in some way, most likely through representation in the media. Following this, it is fruitful to see *Ebba the Movie* as an intersection of different discourses concerning masculinity, as one of many discursive statements that contribute to constructing our understanding of ourselves, as well as others.

The influence of music and representations in film and other media, such as television, is integral to a gendered self-construction process, as is the case in other identity projects, be they ethnic, social or sexual. Lawrence Grossberg has stressed that struggles of identity no longer involve questions of adequacy or distortion, but rather the politics of representation itself. Politics involve questioning how identities are produced and taken up through practises of representation. The main task at present is to study how such a process may be organised in *Ebba the Movie*. This as a particularly relevant angle because identity is one central aspect of the punk movement; you are not born a punk, you become one.

Liesbet van Zoonen has proposed that we should look at gender as an ongoing process in which we are constituted, often in paradoxical ways. Hence, there are bound to be contradictions in all aspects of gender, and cinematic representations are no exception. This has implications for the analysis of any subculture, but especially when it comes to punk culture, because it has often been characterised as being involved in representing of hetero-sexual working-class men.

Ebba the Movie clearly frames punk music and punk culture through issues of class struggle and suburban life, challenging but also supporting the dominant stereotypes of masculinity. In the opening scene, the spectator is confronted with pictures from one of the working-class suburbs of Stockholm. The first images are accompanied by the song 'Hat och Blod' ('Hatred and Blood') which tells of the hopelessness of working-class youngsters' life. The melody sets the frame of reference for the film, guiding the spectator into the world of Ebba Grön. The scene consists of a close-up of singer Joakim 'Pimme' Thåström singing the song live. This is then cross-cut with images of the suburbs. Tall buildings and a hoisting crane structure a skyline against the rising/setting sun.

Then there is a quick cut to a series of negative images of suburban milieus followed by takes from a concert. The tempo is hectic and the musicians are absorbed in their performance. The bass player, Lennart 'Fjodor' Eriksson, dripping with sweat, counts in German: '… stat und kapitale … ein, zwei, drei …', prior to the beginning of the next song, 'Staten och Kapitalet' ('The State and Capital'). On one hand, the use of German and the way he utters the words connote aggression and a 'negative' affiliation with the historical past (the Third Reich and the Second World War). On the other hand, the choice of language and the lyrics of the song function as a reference point to historical events closer to the time of the performance. A commonly used chant in left-wing demonstrations, 'ein, zwei, drei, Nazi Polizei', identified the police as a representative of the state and government, which in turn was seen to associate them with totalitarian regimes of the recent past; an association that echoed the ideological foundation of left-wing German terrorist groups like Baader-Meinhof.

The next scene opens with a cut to interviews of the band members followed by a shot of the subway station sign for Rågsved, the working-class suburb of Stockholm, the home territory of Ebba Grön. With this link, the band and their music are firmly rooted within an all too identifiable urban space and with the problems experienced within it. In all the interview sequences with the band members, the spectator is continuously reminded of the suburban, working-class perspective, as well as the new freedom of personal expression that accompanied the expansion of the leftist culture of the early 1970s; a feeling that everybody could 'join in'. For the first time, a lack of skill was not an obstacle but a means in itself. This 'do-it-yourself' philosophy was further elaborated by the punk movement and ardently emphasised by the band members as they describe the problems they had had with local authorities in Rågsved since their establishment of the concert and rehearsal venue, Oasen (the Oasis), which played host to numerous punk bands.

The drummer Gunnar 'Gurra' Ljungstedt admits that while establishing their activities in Rågsved, the band members did everything 'by the book', but in what he calls an 'informal manner'. These statements serve as a boundary marker between punk culture and official culture; the founders of Oasen may very well have been working within the system, but on their own terms without conforming to the demands of the dominant society. This dissociation from the society is also made explicit in the film when the bass player emphasises his personal experience of suburban life in the first interview conducted with him: 'We are trying to describe our reality, our friends' reality. What I see with my eyes, that's what I write about.' In stressing this, he makes clear the fact that these (young people's) voices had not been listened to and that their stories had never reached the public before. Although echoing the motto of the feminist movement in the 1970s, this perspective, in which the personal – and the marginalised – becomes the prerequisite for the political, has no other parallel in Swedish society. 'Hat och Blod', with its crude language and naked description of an evening in the life of suburban kids, was an anthem for and the voice of a disenfranchised youth.

Critics did question the portrayal of Ebba Grön as if they existed in a void or vacuum, in spite of the fact that the band members presented themselves as spokespersons of their generation of working class. The fans of the band and the local residents of Rågsved are absent in the film. On a visual level, there is a lack of references to an outside world and there are virtually no women present. The film could be understood as an environment where masculine identity remains as the single point of reference at the level of identification, both for the male participants and the imagined male, or female, viewer.

The reciprocal counterpart for a young (working-class) man in this film is, thus, a void. This 'lack' of women could in itself create an opening for a new way of representing men, and masculinity, without confining masculine images to stereotypes created by the history of gender representation, and in which women work as a sign to reinforce the power of men. However, the discursive insistence on class struggle in the film, supporting the class perspective on punk culture that, for instance, Dick Hebdige in his book *Subculture: The Meaning of Style* emphasises, helps in reproducing dominant society's subordination of women. Ebba Grön and punk in general are portrayed as being against social-conservative values, dominant society's oppression of 'ordinary' people, and are determined to confront them directly, as long as it relates to class. Hence they come to reproduce the most basic oppression of all – that of women.

As Lucy O'Brien has pointed out with regards to trying to become successful in the British punk scene, that, contrary to popular myth, punk was not necessarily woman-friendly. Consequently, women suffered the same discrimination they had always suffered and were treated as a novelty and not as serious musicians.

The film must be seen from a broader perspective that considers the contradictions and struggles embedded in gender representation and gender politics, especially when classes intersect in such a distinct way. A Marxist discourse on the relation between the working-class and dominant capitalist interests constructs a formation of class that excludes questions of other forms of subordination at work in society. The working class, regardless of gender and race, is equally subordinated through the uneven distribution of the means of production.

One effect of this standpoint is that class struggle has precedence over all other social struggles, since it is the root of all subordination. In other words, gender, race or sexual subordination is simply an effect of the uneven distribution of capital. This argument is supported by the fact that the film highlights the song 'Staten och Kapitalet' several times and clearly sets the political frame of the band within the boundaries of Swedish left-wing politics in the 1970s, at a time when different Communist or Socialist parties were increasingly making their voices heard in the public debate and criticised, among others, the Social-Democratic Party for its affiliations with capitalist interests. 'Staten och Kapitalet' is a cover version of a song originally called 'Den ena handen vet vad den andra gör' ('One hand knows what the other hand is doing') recorded by the left-wing political group Blå Tåget (The Blue Train), a cover version now more famous than the original. The lyrics of the song are a fierce attack on the Social-Democratic Party, which had governed the country for most of the last forty or fifty years, and its alleged alliance with the financial powers of capitalist industry.

Although the drummer of Ebba Grön plays the original version recorded by Blå Tåget on a gramophone during a scene shot at his home, the song is synonymous with Ebba Grön. This political framing by Marxist discourse that runs through the film, reinforced by the melody in question and the topic itself – punk culture – overshadows other discourses, including that of gender.

The film's neglect of women is made obvious on the two occasions when reference is made to women in punk culture. The first time is when a concert poster is seen in the apartment of one of the band members. It shows Ebba Grön sharing the bill with female punk band Pink Champagne at the Oasen. The second time is when the same group is featured with the leading singer of Ebba Grön on stage, wearing a T-shirt with their logo in one of the shots. However, these references to women who are active in the production of punk (music and culture) should not be understood as making women in punk culture visible and providing those points of reference mentioned earlier, but rather as a way in which the dominant society handles subversive ideologies. Roland Barthes has referred to this as 'immunisation' or 'vaccination', where presence dismantles accusation, in this case, of gender-biased representation.

One of the key issues in the construction of meaning in, and from, this film, is the concept of subordination. In one scene, we see the bass player sitting alone on the subway, looking out of a window as the train passes tall buildings, probably the suburbs of southern Stockholm. On the soundtrack, we hear the voice of Joakim 'Pimme' Thåström singing, 'Waking up from my dream, to a day like every other day, the same colour as concrete/Don't ask me how I feel when I'm waiting for the subway to take me to work.' The song fades out and we hear a voice on the soundtrack speaking to pictures of tall buildings and construction sites, 'There are a hell of a lot of people living out there.' The next shot is of the singer, sitting in a dark room with everything else blackened out. He keeps on talking: 'But there is … kind of nothing to do … there are really no signs of life … anywhere.' The scene depicts a feeling of hopelessness, or abandonment, as if society has left these people to their unfortunate destiny. It becomes more than a statement; it is a witness to the subordinated position of these men. It is this subordinated position of belonging to, or wanting to be a part of, the suburban working class that is a prerequisite for the construction of gender relations in, and beyond, the film, and perhaps punk culture in general. It is a question of the reproduction of power relations that are basically the same as in society in general. In considering punk culture's insistence on equality, there is a contradiction between being subordinated in one aspect, as working-class, and dominant in another, as a male.

The processes described above are not exclusive to this subculture alone, but could easily apply to society in general. The difference lies in the fact that male punks are regarded by society as less masculine – no matter how tough they look – as a result of them being regarded as punks first and men second. Perhaps the exclusion of women is the only source of empowerment left for this subordinated group of working-class men. *Ebba the Movie* could also be said to render the unknown (punk) through the known (traditional gender representation), in this case, by the exclusion of women. Perhaps this is one of the reasons that this film, despite representing something so far from the life I was living, struck a nerve the first time I saw it.

Peter Lindholm

REFERENCES

Grossberg, L. (2000 [1996]) 'Identity and Cultural Studies: Is That All There Is?', in J. Hartley and R. E. Pearson (eds) *American Cultural Studies: A Reader*. Oxford and New York: Oxford University Press.

Hebdige, D. (1979) *Subculture: The Meaning of Style*. London and New York: Routledge.

O'Brien, L. (1999) 'The Woman Punk Made Me', in R. Sabin (ed) *Punk Rock: So What? The Cultural Legacy of Punk*. London and New York: Routledge.

Van Zoonen, L. (1994) *Feminist Media Studies*. London: Sage.

KAN VI BRY OSS OM VARANDRA? CAN WE BOTHER ABOUT EACH OTHER?

ROY ANDERSSON, SWEDEN, 1988

Films as commercials belong to the alleged periphery of film history, the norm of which is feature fiction films. Theorists of documentary cinema have maintained, and rightly so, that this norm is arbitrary and frequently erroneous, as the majority of films made have been non-fiction. Similarly, if sheer quantity is at least one factor in theorising film, we can easily note that the most seen film of 2003 is neither a J. K. Rowling or a Tolkien adaptation, but more likely a film promoting, say, Budweiser. This chapter is an analysis of a one such film, a Swedish commercial for nationwide theatrical release from 1988.

Forty-five seconds in length, *Kan vi bry oss om varandra?* (*Can we bother about each other?*) is structured as nine tableaux, all with a single set-up and no camera movement. A wide-angle lens is used, rendering each image with great depth of field. Typically, the main characters are positioned in the foreground, framed in full figure or in *plan américain*, but the focal depth reaches to the farthest background. The film is shot in faded, pastel colours, lighting and processing adding a greyish quality. The settings are all different, but they share a certain dullness and a sense of archaism, as something from the past, possibly the 1950s. The actors are obviously instructed to deliver their lines impassionately, almost completely devoid of character psychology. It is as if they are reading their lines out loud, rather than acting in any traditional sense. Each scene or tableau starts with the camera resting on one or two characters, and after a few seconds a short line is spoken. The camera lingers for a while before the next tableau, which follows by a straight cut.

The first tableau depicts a middle-aged man, overweight, with grey hair and thick-rimmed glasses sitting in an old barbershop. He is wearing a cloth, seemingly interrupted by the camera after being shaved. Just behind him stands the barber, of the same age as his customer, wearing a white coat. He is also looking into the camera. The walls are greenish grey, the floor is chequered in pale red and beige. There are a few pictures on one wall. Both men seem neither happy nor sad, tired perhaps. The customer says: 'I want a sailing boat.'

A young chef is standing in the doorway to a shabby restaurant kitchen in the second tableau. Beside him, there is a bucket of potatoes, possibly waiting to be peeled. He looks depressed. In the kitchen behind him, people are working, but slowly. One of his colleagues pauses to look into the camera. The floor is chequered in grey and beige, the walls are grey. The young man says: 'I want a home.'

In tableau number three a military officer in his late fifties is sitting in a crowded train. He has a grey moustache and is wearing dark glasses and a captain's uniform. Behind him a younger man in a suit is sleeping. Looking sad but stern, the officer says firmly: 'I want to have friends. Many friends.' As he speaks, the man behind him awakens and turns his head slightly towards him, then goes back to sleep. This tableau is followed by a scene, which takes place in an almost empty bar. The air is grey with cigarette smoke. A young woman, wearing a business suit, is holding a drink. She is sitting by a table on a man's lap, possibly her boyfriend or a recent acquaintance. Seemingly devoid of emotions, she says: 'I want higher profit.'

In the fifth tableau an elderly man, looking lonely, is sitting by a table in his small apartment. The floor is dark brown and the walls are grey. On them are a few pictures. In the background, the kitchen door is open, through which we can distinguish an old gas stove with a kettle. At the table, there is an empty glass and a newspaper turned to the crossword section. The man is bald and wears a white shirt and braces. Although he looks rather worn out, his voice sounds almost bemused as he says: 'Well, I want to have fun. I enjoy having fun very much.'

The sixth tableau opens with a thin, middle-aged man is standing in front of an old building (obviously a backdrop). He is holding the leashes to two dalmatians. The weather is foggy, adding a grey hue to the beige and brown colours of the building. There are no other people around. The time seems to be early in the morning. The man looks pale, saying 'I want to get well.' As one of the dogs moves, he looks down on it, miserable.

The seventh tableau pictures a female, overweight, middle-aged teacher with her hair dyed red, standing in a school corridor. She looks downhearted, holding a calendar and some notes in her hands, and a purse on her shoulder. She is wearing a beige sweater. The school looks old and rather run down. Behind her are a bunch of children – presumably her students – waiting to be let into the classroom. She is looking down at first, then raising her head to look into the camera, saying: 'I want a man.'

In the eighth tableau the spectator encounters what seems to be a married couple. The scene represents a bedroom, dimly-lit by the sun coming in from the half-drawn curtain. The image is dominated by a bed, in which a bald man with a moustache is lying on his side resting his head on his hand and with his knees curled. In front of him, a woman in a night-gown is sitting on the end of the bed. As she is in the foreground and in the centre of the frame, we might expect her to speak. Instead it is the man, saying in a tired, high-pitched voice: 'I want less tax, taxes are too high.'

Finally, the ninth tableau presents a short, thin, bald man with moustache and glasses, wearing a dark overcoat. He is holding a plastic bag in one hand and a young boy in the other. They are in an unidentifiable public place, possibly a subway, with a grey and white chequered floor and concrete walls. In the background, we can distinguish three other characters of the film: the schoolteacher, the officer and the customer from the barbershop. Behind them, there are more people, impossible to recognise. The boy looks up at the man, as the latter is saying tiredly: 'I want to breathe', and then the title 'Can we care about each other?' appears in white, followed shortly by 'Socialdemokraterna' (The Social Democratic Party) in red letters.

Before the title 'Socialdemokraterna', it is hard to tell that this film is a commercial for the Swedish Labour party. Indeed, it is hard to imagine the film to be a commercial for anything. And, perhaps even more disturbingly, even after we know the ad is aimed to be promoting the Labour party, it is hard to see how it would succeed. Exactly what ideology, policy or specific issues are being communicated?

Traditionally, political campaigns in Sweden and elsewhere have been focused either on concrete issues (longer vacations, lower taxes, better medical care, and so on), or more vague ideologically charged concepts such as equality or freedom. Here we are, instead, with a commercial launched in the midst of the 1988 congressional election campaign, where it is hard to distinguish even between protagonists and antagonists. Only one of the characters, the young chef, seems to express a traditional leftist value: the slogan 'Homes for everyone' has been, and still is, a common issue among social democrats and socialists at least since Friedrich Engels' pamphlet *The Housing Question* (1872).

One of the characters is expressing a traditional right-wing idea (lower taxes), whereas others are maintaining cliché-like bourgeois values of consumerism and capitalism, such as wanting a specific commodity (a sailing boat) or, more vaguely, higher profit. Are these characters the antagonists of this supposedly social democratic commercial? Are they being mocked? The genius of the film, and the reason why it fails to work in promoting the Labour party, is that the answer seems to be no. But if it fails as a commercial, it does this in exact proportion to what it gains in artistic value. All the characters, regardless of their seeming ideological preferences, are being portrayed with equal tenderness, but also – almost paradoxically – with a Brechtian dissociation – *Verfremdung*.

It could be seen that the characters are expressing abstract, apolitical desires shared by us all: for friendship, happiness, health, love. How should these wishes be interpreted in this context? Is the film claiming that everything is political, that even love is governed by a relationship of powers similar to the system of a society? Or should we understand it the other way around, that relationships and personal well-being are the result of specific political decisions? Both these readings, however valid, seem to be missing the point (if indeed there is a definable point to the film). Rather, the film is a treatise on the human condition, and it just happens to be financed by a specific political party. Similarly, class relations, so dear to social democrats (at least in the past), are clearly expressed, denoted by clothing and work-related attributes, but the film does not conform to any notions of class struggle, of rich versus poor, and so on. How come a political party has decided upon such an ambiguous message in the middle of an election campaign?

The director of the film is Roy Andersson, by then well-known by educated Swedes as the maker of two feature films, and notorious for a number of idiosyncratic but successful commercials. When the Labour party commissioned Andersson for a theatrical commercial in 1988, it was their second collaboration. Three years earlier, Andersson had made the widely seen commercial, *Varför ska vi bry oss om varandra?* (*Why should we care about each other?*). This earlier film was similar in construction, if less powerful. However, it was a success in its own way, causing a huge stir among the right-wing press in particular that accused it of intimidating people into voting for the social democrats.

Andersson came to prominence with his debut feature film *En kärlekshistoria* (*A Swedish Love Story*) in 1970. After the commercial failure with his second feature *Giliap* (1975), he took a two-decades hiatus from feature filmmaking, working exclusively with advertising. In this capacity, he promoted the insurance company Trygg-Hansa, *Lotto*, a commercial bank called Svenska Handelsbanken, Air France, Citroën, potato crisps, dairy products, beer, among many other companies and products. Except for one short film, Andersson made nothing but commissioned works until his 2001 feature *Sånger från andra våningen* (*Songs From the Second Floor*).

This film was highly acclaimed in Sweden as well as internationally, winning the critics' award at Cannes Film Festival and gaining wide international distribution. Today, Andersson holds a position in Swedish cinema as one of its most prolific filmmakers. Although his feature filmography is short, Andersson is clearly one of the most distinguishable *auteurs* in cinema today. Like a few other filmmakers, he has developed a style that is as original as it is recognisable, working exclusively with long takes, single camera set-ups and an extreme limitation in camera movements. His actors are all amateurs, performing in a blank, non-realist, Bressonian manner. Refusing almost all characteristics of classical Hollywood cinema, he is arguably one of the most original directors in film history, at least stylistically. Instead of dominant modes of filmmaking, he favours a style which allegedly went out of fashion in the early 1910s: the tableau style of pre-classical cinema.

But if Andersson by now is being promoted into the pantheon of canonised filmmakers, this is a rather recent turn of events. Returning to his less glorious days, it might seem odd for a Labour party to choose a filmmaker whose reputation rested upon commercials, at that for corporations epitomising capitalism, such as insurance companies, banks and *Lotto*. One does not need to be a Marxist to find all these phenomena suspect, profiting as they do on the small savings of the working class, and even luring them into spending it on gambling, with dubious promises of profit. Although the Swedish Labour party, along with its European equivalents, has effectively done away with most of its socialist heritage, it would still seem strange to completely forget that the centralisation of credits into a state-owned national bank with exclusive monopoly has been an immediate socialist task since Karl Marx. And gambling can be seen as a pacifying instrument to prevent revolutionary movements; it also diffuses the old axiom that accumulation of capital rests upon labour.

Of course, these issues would not matter much to modern social democrats, but the question remains: why did the party-owned advertising agency ARE approach Andersson for their election campaign in 1985? The reason no doubt lies in how his commercials for all these companies and products have looked. Already in *A Swedish Love Story*, Andersson had demonstrated an excellent observational talent in depicting a working class increasingly consumed with materialism.

There is a brilliant scene in the film where the heroes, a teenage couple, are at the girl's white-collar parents' house. Her mother is crying in the kitchen, showing all the known symptoms of clinical depression. Her father's diagnosis follows, which he cries out angrily: 'She is poor!' 'Poor', in this case, seems to mean they cannot afford a new car, or going abroad on holiday. In Andersson's debut film, and later in his production, happiness is immediately linked to income. The futility of such an economist philosophy seems to be his idealist message.

But more interesting than his ability to express ideology in a feature film is that Andersson also managed to deliver the same kind of critique of consumer culture in the commercials, hence deconstructing the very logic of the phenomenon, which is of course to uphold consumerism. Whether his clients did not see this or whether they did – but cleverly realised that people would appreciate the irony and paradoxically reward the commercial by buying the product – is hard to tell.

Andersson's commercials, in short, are never mainstream promotions. He never indulges, as traditional commercials, neither in commodity fetishism (think average car commercials) nor in selling a 'lifestyle' (think *Coca-Cola*). Instead, his commercials are characterised by an ambivalence between the product being sold and an implicit criticism of consumer culture in general and sometimes even the specific product itself. As an example, let us consider a commercial for *Felix* frozen potato chips, 'pommes strips'.

The spectator sees a farming couple in their sixties, standing in a potato field. They look into the camera, saying the following:

- Me and the missus have been growing potatoes for 32 years now. And we've delivered them to Felix.
- Not all of them.
- No, we've eaten one or two ourselves. Potatoes are good.
- Yes, boiled and fried, mashed or baked…
- That's right.
- And chips.
- Yes, and chips.
- That's strips, Dad.
- Strips, that's right, strips. Now they're doing that out of all our potatoes. That's what people like.
- They're making strips out of everything.
- Yes, they do, don't they …

If not explicitly critical of potato chips *per se*, the film does seem to express a longing for a time when potatoes were used in a more old-fashioned, and certainly healthier, way. And as with the people of bourgeois values in the *Can we bother about each other?*, the old couple are not mocked or dismissed as reactionary in their somewhat understated assertion that their fine product is turned into something else. Rather, they are tenderly portrayed as representatives of an older generation, whose values are vanishing in the industrial age.

A more explicit criticism of its product is evident in a commercial for *Preppen* light beer. If beer commercial traditionally is selling a lifestyle, where happiness increases to the proportion of beer consumption (which may be true in some cases, in others clearly not), this one takes this concept and turns it around. As most of Andersson's films, commercial or not, it also reflects a stereotypical notion of Scandinavians as shy and gloomy. This *Preppen* commercial presents a middle-aged couple sitting in a couch in a depressingly decorated apartment, looking straight ahead. It seems as if it is their second or third date. They are certainly not living together to judge from the bachelor-like qualities of the flat and the awkward silence between the couple. They are both holding a glass of beer. He asks, with an awkward jestfullness:

–   Who need's a refill?
    (Not waiting for a reply, he fills her glass from a bottle, saying:)
–   So you don't refuse a glass of light beer now and then?
–   No-o.
    (Refilling his own glass as well, he replies:)
–   Good for you. That's something I think one should bestow oneself.
    (Complete silence for a while. As he takes a large gulp, he exclaims:)
–   Yoo-hoo!
    (Another embarrassing silence, and the film ends with the title: '*Preppen's* light
    beer: Lighting up your existence.')

If beer commercials typically show happy, excited people, this one instead seems to say that sometimes not even *Preppen's* beer helps. Neither is it common to portray the consumers of the product as so extraordinarily uncool. The man's 'Yoo-hoo!' does, to put it mildly, not correspond to an objective view of the scene. *Preppen's* is, in a word, associated with the complete opposite of ordinary beer commercials. And if it is a taboo in alcohol advertising to show people getting drunk, or needing a drink to release tension, this film does precisely that, suggesting that beer is necessary only to those who need it to improve their social skills. We can also note how economy is an issue, as in many of Andersson's films (one needs to 'bestow oneself' a beer). In this respect, the *Preppen* commercial is a logical forerunner to the films for the Labour party.

The list of Andersson's deconstructing commercials can be extensive, but we can now turn to his most overtly critical film. It is also a minor classic in Swedish cinema, for a commercial a huge success in its time. Being a young boy then (the early 1980s), I remember how Swedes collectively quoted from it in all imaginable circumstances. Part of a series of *Lotto* commercials by Andersson, it is one of the most remembered. The fact that in despite of its criticism, it helped to increase the sales of *Lotto* coupons significantly proves the point of the ambiguous tension between successful advertising and implicit criticism that is one of the trademarks of Andersson's commercials.

We see a young boy sitting on a sofa before a television set, from which we hear the evening news. On the coffee table in front of him is a wooden plane model he is working on. In a chair behind him, his grandfather is sleeping. His father, dressed in a bus driver's uniform, comes home in a hurry. To his son's 'Hi!', he replies absent-mindedly 'Hi-hi-hi…' As the father sits down, we hear from the television: 'And here are the correct numbers on this week's *Lotto*.' The father cleans the table brusquely, smashing his son's plane in the process, to produce his *Lotto* coupon and a pen. He eagerly listens to the announcer's reading of the numbers, noting them meticulously. Devastated and eager for revenge, the boy runs away to where the grandfather is sitting, pulling out the television cord. As the television dies, the father desperately tries the remote control, until he realises what has happened. As he plugs the cord back in, we hear from the television: 'And now the weather.' The grandfather awakens, asking in a thin voice what the numbers were. His son (or son-in-law) furiosly repeats: 'What were the numbers!' and pulls the old man's ear, who whines of pain.

Lotto, apparently, turns fathers into abusing their closest family, and the unspoiled children react with sabotage. In fact, all of Andersson's *Lotto* commercials end with failure: either, as in this case, by interruption, or by simply not winning. It is hard to see how these films could help sell a product when associating it with its worst possible effects, but surprisingly, they did.

Returning to the commercials for the Labour party, it is perhaps both more and less reasonable that they would choose Andersson for their campaigns. He had clearly made a name for himself as a director, who within a strictly commercial system was able to express opinions that run counter to capitalist values. In this respect, he seemed like the perfect choice for a social democratic party, negotiating between a mild socialism and a market economy. On the other hand, he must certainly have been viewed as unfaithful, constantly biting the hand feeding him. Would he be less critical now? The final reason why he was selected, must have been that he had recently directed three commercials for the Swedish labour union, 'Landsorganisationen' (LO), which were atypically favourable in regard to its client (they showed people having fun at work or the opposite, claiming LO to guarantee the fun).

But given the idiosyncrasy and ambiguity of his commercials, it would seem that Andersson rarely simply sells a product. What, then, are we to make of his films for the Labour party? If not critical, they are indeed ambiguous. His 'conservative' style, austere *mise-en-scène*, faded colouring, grim lighting and archaic iconography could all be read as typically 'social democratic' in the worst possible sense. Indeed, Swedish right-wing parties have always accused the Labour party with social engineering, favouring a 'grey', colourless society where supposed equality reigns over personal freedom.

Hence, it should come as no surprise that at least the 1985 film *Why should we care about each other?*, was read by some right-wing commentators as an accurate description of a social democratic society! Featuring oppression in daily experience (a large man intimidating a young couple away from their table in a bar; a nurse failing to care for her patients; people in the subway morning rush refusing to help a fellow commuter who has fallen, and so on), this film was taken as the perfect example of real socialism, deprived of its utopian wishfulness. One newspaper, for instance, called the film a 'social democratic horror movie'.

These counter-readings were scarce, however. More commonly, conservatives and liberals were appalled by a film that was said to be anything from 'repulsive propaganda' to unconsciously revealing the hidden agenda of the Labour party. However, Labour did win that year's election, although the murder of Prime Minister Olof Palme was probably an immensely more important factor than Andersson's contribution to the campaign.

When for the next election Andersson was once again commissioned, he changed his strategy slightly, making *Can we bother about each other?*: more of human conditions and less of overt political propaganda. Did it work? Well, Labour lost the election to a right-wing coalition, which for the first time in history could form a government with a conservative Prime Minister. This is not to say that Andersson's film was responsible in any way.

In closing, it might be of interest to consider a letter from Roy Andersson regarding the 1985 film *Why should we care about each other?* to the person responsible at ARE, Harald Ullman, dated 5 March 1984:

Dear Harald

I hereby send you a cost estimation for the SAP [Socialdemokratiska Arbetarepartiet] film which unfortunately is not as low as you would like it to be. It is, however, a perfectly reasonable estimation if you would like to reach a very high class, and if you further take into account that the smallest shampoo or toothpaste commercial in a very mediocre execution today averages around 120–150,000 SEK.

Actually, I have thought of pressing the budget by counting on a consumption of film stock of only 2,000 metres, which would save us about 16–18,000 SEK, but I'm waiting for this to be absolutely necessary. Because I think that the idea that we have sketched could reach unimagined heights and it demands a suitable execution. Granted, the approach in this production does not need any expensive actors or expensive constructions, but it demands all the more in the selection of people and places and the possibilities of catching the poetic charm of the moment. This demands that one needs the possibility to return when one does not succeed, change persons and lighting conditions that are misplaced, etc…

Best regards,
Roy Andersson

The amount was 176,220 SEK, and it is to the credit of the Labour party that they agreed to these terms, not only financially, but even to the higher risks at stake: that with Andersson, you never know what you will get.

Jan Holmberg

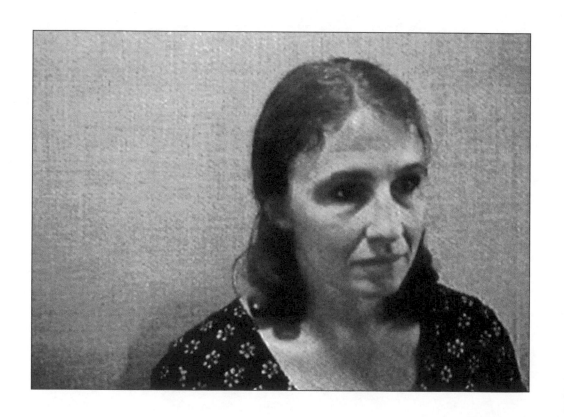

IDIOTERNE THE IDIOTS

LARS VON TRIER, DENMARK, 1998

Since 1995, the year which witnessed the birth of the Dogme 95 movement, Danish cinema has garnered worldwide attention. Danish filmmakers Lars von Trier and Thomas Vinterberg wrote the Dogme Manifesto as a set of rules that were aimed at producing a new kind of cinema. The manifesto called for 'character-driven' films which were simultaneously 'instill[ed] … with a thoroughly cinematic feeling'. While the Danish Dogme films have been widely regarded as constituting the latest new wave movement, protesting the 'decadent illusionism' of contemporary cinema, only recently has the importance of the films' cultural and national contexts been addressed.

Through an examination of Bodil Jorgensen's performance in *Idioterne* (*The Idiots*, 1998), this chapter will place von Trier's filmmaking within the context of Scandinavian filmic and theatrical traditions, and consider von Trier's intimate form of filmmaking that focuses on the actors being closely observed by the director, the co-actors and the spectator. The creation of intimacy in *The Idiots* is linked to the discussion of von Trier's redefinition of the intimate chamber space, realised through his use of empty space in a middle-class living room, and the fusion between the actor's silence and the filmmaker's use of close-up.

What is striking about von Trier's filmmaking career is the profound change in his view of the role performance plays in film. Dogme filmmaking, which demands a filmmaker's total focus on the actor's performance and thus 'gives cinema back to its actors', redefined von Trier's view of performance. Von Trier acknowledges this shift in his relationship to the actors, yet denies that there was a total lack of attention to performance in his earlier work. In Mette Hjort and Ib Bondebjerg's volume, in answer to a question about his apparent neglect of the actor's craft and storytelling in favour of being a 'masterful manipulator of images' in his early work, von Trier states, 'I had my own, very precise interpretation of what I wanted, but that doesn't mean that I considered the acting negligible. The actors' presence was just as important as in other films, but the psychological dimension was of no interest to me.'

When interviewd by Stig Björkman, von Trier admitted that it was his 'conscious decision not to be too close to the actors'. Thus, the short films von Trier made at the end of the

1970s and beginning of the 1980s, such as *Orchidégartneren* (1977), *Menthe – la bienheureuse* (1979), *Nocturne* (1980), *Den sidste detalje* (1981) and his graduation film for the National Film School of Denmark, *Befrielsesbilleder* (1982), are, according to Hjort and Bondjeberg, 'stylistically inventive explorations of themes and symbols which would later play a central role in his feature films'. Likewise, his first trilogy *Forbrydelsens element* (1984), *Epidemic* (1987) and *Europa* (1991) established his reputation as a filmmaker of bold experimentations with cinematic styles, genres and thematic issues. Nigel Floyd argues that the proximity to the actors in Dogme filmmaking reflects the filmmaker's discovery of 'an emotional vulnerability and grasp of human feeling that were barely hinted at in his earlier work'. In Dogme filmmaking, performances are recorded using unobtrusive digital cameras, thus creating a physically close relationship between the camera and the actors. This 'new confluence of emotion and technology' which creates 'intense, riveting immediacy', as Shari Roman describes it, is made possible by the filmmaker's redefined approach to performance.

The novelty and inexperience in this mode of filmmaking is something that Bodil Jorgensen, on of the main actors in *The Idiots*, shared with von Trier. For the theatre actor, performing in this film was a new experience that enabled her to explore the depths of both her character and herself as an actor. Prior to *The Idiots,* Jorgensen had acted in *Planetens spejle* (1992), *Russian Pizza Blues* (1992), *Kun en pige* (1995), *Sunes familie* (1997), *Nonneborn* (1997) and in television series such as *Strisser på Samso* and in the episode titled 'Biblioteket' of a series called *Alle tiders nisse* (1995). Apart from these film and television experiences, she acted mainly in the theatre after her graduation from the National Theatre School in 1990. She was granted a position at the Royal Theatre in Copenhagen in 1997.

In *The Idiots* Jorgensen plays the part of Karen. She joins a group of people who have reunited to discover what they call their 'inner idiocy,' that is inner authenticity – a condition not defined by the behavioural norms or social roles society has imposed upon them. Karen is the outsider in the group. She does not believe that the authenticity of being lies in externalised behaviour. For her, silence is a guarantee of her non-theatricality and authentic existence.

The characters live in a deserted house, where they practice exceeding physical and psychological limitations through the performance of madness. The public spaces function as arenas where the behavioural codes are disrupted and their existence is made aware of. Yet the strength of the characters' beliefs in their project will be tested in the end, when they try to perform madness in more private spaces. The project is cancelled when nobody's actions can live up to this challenge. The film ends with Karen returning home, being the only one of the group who can perform madness in a private space.

When von Trier and Vinterberg wrote the Dogme Manifesto, one question raised upon reception of the manifesto was that of setting limitations on expression. According to the rules, 'Shooting must be done on location. Props and sets must not be brought in. The sound must never be produced apart from the images, or vice versa. The film must be in colour. Special lighting is not acceptable. Optical work and filters are forbidden.' The rules emphasise an authenticity of space used in order to create authentic performances. Authenticity of space helps the actor to live through his/her role and to create the truth of inner reality, thus enabling the Stanislavskian equation between the actor and the character. It is also used to highlight the actor's performance. According to the rules, the space chosen must be simplified and emptied of all distracting elements. The use of simplified space turns the films' focus onto the actors: portrayals of raw emotional states are openly displayed and are made the focus of the Dogme films.

Von Trier's experimentation with simplified, intimate space as a means of highlighting the actor bears fascinating similarities with the Swedish playwright and theatre director August Strindberg, whose experimentation with intimacy of simplified space Scandinavian theatre and film has kept exploring ever since he first wrote for the theatre. The concept of space in Strindberg's oeuvre is inseparable from his redefinition of the actor's craft. Strindberg's modernism redefined staging techniques by simplifying the realistic stagecraft that the Norwegian playwright Henrik Ibsen brought into vogue.

If Ibsen's realism was based on bringing drama into the interior setting, specifically into the middle-class living room, Strindberg's modernism emptied the Ibsenian space of all the domestic signifiers. Strindberg's experimentations with the reconstruction of space culminated at the Intimate Theatre in Stockholm that most strikingly depicted the ways in which the scenic simplification of theatrical expression enhances the focus on the actor and draws him/her closer to the audience. More importantly, Strindberg's use of simplified, condensed, intimate theatrical chamber space illustrated how the minimised amount of distractions helps the actor in his/her psychological introspection. In Stridberg's words: 'With simplicity one wins the solemn calm and quiet in which the artist can hear his own part.' Furthermore, while aiming towards achieving the 'power of poetic and spiritual expressiveness' in the intimate chamber space he simultaneously advocated a less theatrical acting style, one paradoxically filled with dramatic intensity.

The deserted middle-class living room where most of the scenes take place in *The Idiots* push the filmmaker's examination of empty, condensed, intimate space to the extreme, consequently redefining the use of intimate chamber space in Dogme filmmaking. Von Trier's use of intimate space encourages Jorgensen to adopt a Strindbergian mode of acting, one based on subtle, yet intense facial expressions. The goal of this mode is to engage and absorb the spectator into the dramatic mood of solemnity.

The scene at the beginning of the film illustrates the way in which von Trier's use of simplified space, together with appropriate cinematography, aims at intensifying performance. Furthermore, it demonstrates how the emphasis on the actor's psychological introspection and the discovery of a hidden inner reality helps to embody her character's fear of intimacy and hidden anguish. The scene takes place after Karen has arrived in the deserted house with the group. The camera follows Karen withdrawing from the group and retreating into one of the empty rooms to call her husband Anders (Hans Henrik Clemensen). The extreme sorrow and fear that fill her presence are explained at the end of the film when we find out about the loss of Karen's child. It is this experience that made her join the group on the day of her child's funeral. The fact that she refused or could not do what was expected of her led to her exclusion from the family. The time with the group strengthens her discovery of herself and helps her to overcome her inhibitions as well as gain freedom from the previous social roles that restricted her existence.

This scene is an example of the way in which von Trier takes advantage of the actor's background. Von Trier uses Jorgensen's experience as a theatre actor and adjusts it to film by building intimacy through theatrical means. The chosen space mimics an intimate, theatrical chamber space. During the whole scene the camera is relatively static, as if recording the performance on stage. The emptiness and quietness of the room further enhances our concentration on the actor, who is performing for the privileged gaze of the camera. All distractions are absent from the room. The actor's striving towards heightened introspection is further accentuated by her unawareness of the space surrounding her.

Karen stands by the window under the close scrutiny of the camera and dials a number. Her face is filled with subtle, yet intensified expressions. She places the phone against her ear. She stares outside without moving her body, motionless except for her eyes which blink a few times. She is in her own world, one that is disrupted by the voice at the other end: 'Anders speaking.' The camera moves closer to her face, set against a white wall in an extreme close-up. After hearing the voice, her eyes become moist with tears and she tries to hold back her tears by stiffening her mouth. When the emotion overcomes her, she puts her head down, simultaneously hiding her face with her hands. We only hear her crying. The camera does not move. She raises her head and we briefly see her tearful face, while she keeps looking outside, hiding from the camera. She then quickly turns towards the camera, but closes her eyes to retreat to her own world, immediately swinging her head to turn away from the camera's gaze.

In interview, Jorgensen has analysed her performance in the scene and has observed how the use of cinematography is subordinated to the actor's performance in Dogme filmmaking. The lack of distraction makes it easy for the actor to be 'in the moment'. In Jorgensen's opinion, the high footage ratio and the unfelt presence of the cameras enable a continuous, uninterrupted heightening of feeling to become possible: 'In Dogme, there are moments when you are not aware of filming and you are still in the picture. Nothing disrupts the flow of the actor's stream of consciousness. There is space for using your own memory and making pictures in your mind. I've never been so close to what I love in acting.'

The analysis of Jorgensen's performance leads one to consider von Trier's direction of her performance as the clearest example of the adaptation of Strindberg's modernist principles to film. Jorgensen is a Strindbergian modern actor, able to listen to her own performance through the peacefulness of her surroundings. The lack of agitation in the cinematography and the quietness of the aesthetic space add to this feeling of intimacy in the environment. This use of simplified space enables the actor to 'attend to the role, to concentrate all his thoughts on it, and not let himself be distracted from it' as Strindberg writes in *Open Letters to the Intimate Theater*. Jorgensen has 'the imagination or the gift of imagining the character and the situation so vividly that they take shape', thus becoming 'the artist', who 'gets into a trance, forgets himself, and finally *becomes* the person [she] is to play'.

Thus, Jorgensen's performance is an example of the ways in which Dogme filmmaking can be 'liberating for the actors', as von Trier remarks in Richard Kelly's volume on Dogme95. This sort of liberation, which allows for the heightened internalisation in the actor's performance, has not been recognised as an important methodology which Dogme filmmaking also emphasises: subdued expression in the evocation of the vulnerability of being human, or, as Shari Roman writes, 'the exploration of human frailty in [von Trier's] filmmaking process'. Furthermore, this dimension of Dogme filmmaking, which builds intimacy on minimalist performance, is a site where the influence of theatrical modernism in von Trier's filmmaking is particularly glaring.

Strindberg's modernism, embodied by his intimate and condensed chamber space, strongly influenced modernist Scandinavian filmmakers who tried to find cinematic equivalents for his principle. Carl Theodor Dreyer's use of close-up is an example of the way in which Strindberg's process of de-theatricalisation was continued in film. Close-ups were Dreyer's tools for creating intimacy and concentration in the chamber space. His use of close-up reflects, as Dreyer writes in 'Imagination and Colour', an interest in 'the spirit in and behind the things', as well as his belief that the truth lays in quietness, in suggestive expressions. Close-ups capturing the subtleties of expression in the actor's performance were Dreyer's means of emphasising 'the immersion' into the image.

In his book, *The Films of Carl-Theodore Dreyer*, David Bordwell analyses Dreyer's cinematic use of 'chamber-art tradition' – the 'tableau'. Bordwell notes that when Dreyer adapted the principles of chamber art to his films, he also questioned movement as something essential to film, while also calling into question the movement of the actor's body as something essential to performance. Bordwell points out that Dreyer relied on the actor's face in the projection of 'the most intimate human qualities, the "soul"'. Facial expressions were viewed as honest language, thus replacing the spoken word.

Influenced by the performance in Dreyer's *The Passion of Joan of Arc* (1928) Bela Bálàzs states that

In this silent monologue the solitary human soul can find a tongue more candid and uninhibited than in any spoken soliloquy, for it speaks instinctively, subconsciously. The language of the face cannot be suppressed or controlled. However disciplined and practisedly hypocritical a face may be, in the enlarging close-up we see even that it is concealing something, that it is looking a lie. For such things have their own specific expressions superimposed on the feigned one. It is much easier to lie in words than with the face and the film has proved it beyond doubt.

In Dreyer's films, neither language nor body were relied on as a means of expression. The facial expressions alone, while being 'more subjective even than speech' and the 'most individual of human manifestation', to quote Bálàzs, were the filmmaker's primary means of building autonomous characters.

Jorgensen's minimalist performance in *The Idiots* depicts how von Trier further explores Dreyer's fascination with film's unique ability to penetrate into the Bálàzsian 'micro-physiognomy' of the actor's face which alone can express something deeper and more truthful than language or externalised bodily actions can. The way in which Dreyer linked silence and the internal mode of acting with the quest for authenticity is given an explicit statement in von Trier's film. By contrasting two extreme acting modes in *The Idiots* – Jorgensen's silence vs. the other actors' bodily movements and speech – von Trier favours one acting mode over the other in the conveyance of truth.

Karen's suppression of speech, coupled with extreme control over her body, is juxtaposed with the community of other characters whose behaviour is defined in terms of free, playful experimentation of body and voice, what they call 'spassing' – a performance of madness. The close-ups that capture Jorgensen's 'silent monologues' and focus on 'the most delicate nuances' of the actor's facial expressions, as Bálàzs puts it, are juxtaposed to with other shots that, while in constant motion, eschew concentration on the face. The close-ups of Jorgensen's face are stable, tranquil and meditative. They speak to us 'instinctively, subconsciously' and are thus more truthful, since they do not rely on external means of expressions. The other shots of *The Idiots*, recorded by free-flowing digital cameras, keep on finding and capturing externalised bodily movements, which do not conceal the fact that they are 'looking [at] a lie', to follow Bálàzs. The tension between these shots is remarkable.

The inadequacy of the word or externalised body language as a means of authentic self-expression become one of the major concerns von Trier explores in this film. Karen's autonomy and inner strength are built on her silence. This embodies her quest for honesty and her refusal to accept role-playing. For Karen, behind every gesture, expression and word there has to be a meaning. The moral of the film is that the truth lies in silence. Von Trier suggests that truth lies in the acting mode that suppresses the use of verbal language, which simultaneously restricts the actor's bodily movements.

Karen is the only one for whom the whole idiot-project has a meaning. For the others, it is a game that permits them to feel free. Karen's belief in the meaning behind the actions makes it difficult for her to let go; she never takes part in performing madness yet, in the end, it is only Karen who will find the true meaning of freedom. For Karen freedom is internal, for the others external; Karen liberates herself whereas, for the others, freedom does not extend beyond the performance frame and remains a temporary experience. The idiot-project did not encourage them to abandon the limiting norms of everyday life, which had restricted their free spirits.

The major concern, the 'superobjective' – as Stanislavski calls it – in Jorgensen's perform-ance deals with the quest for the authentic being. To accomplish this superobjective, Jorgensen searches for a method other than the use of words to capture truth. Words cannot be trusted as a means for honest expression. According to Jorgensen, Karen's existence is speechless, like a child who is crying, laughing and is *feeling* things. Jorgensen points out that, as an actor, one has the opportunity to convey feelings that cannot otherwise be described in words. Here, Jorgensen refers to performance of a 'dramatic state' and creation of a 'dramatic tension to a mere state or condition, without any external event at all' as, again, Bálàzs would put it.

Like Dreyer, von Trier is fascinated by the actor's silence as conveyed in close-ups that evoke emotional states that are verbally inexpressible. These states of being, that Dreyer masterfully depicted in films such as *The Passion of Joan of Arc*, can be defined as 'the Strindbergian moods in the savagely antagonistic silences of human beings confined together in narrow spaces' to follow Bálàzs; or what Gilles Deleuze calls the passion pointing out the 'expressed of the state of things'. These moments of inexpressible emotional states, evoked by Karen's silent being in the absence of words or gestures, are captured with von Trier's use of 'the affection-image'.

Deleuze's theory of 'the affection-image' is strongly depicted in Renée Falconetti's performance in *The Passion of Joan of Arc*. Jorgensen's performance in *The Idiots*, as well as her own analysis of it, reflects von Trier's continuation of the use of 'the affection-image', where it refers to something that is intangible, unrealisable in the actor's words or gestures, something that is, as Deleuze describes it, 'felt, rather than conceived'. In creating 'the affection-image' the close-ups capture Jorgensen's silent being, like that of Falconetti's, by focusing on 'the reflexive face' that 'expresses a pure quality'.

The previously discussed scene where the close-ups record Jorgensen's silent presence and the creation of Affection, demand from the actor a true talent and mastery of her craft that, according to Stella Adler, is 'what finally transforms the dead factors into living ones – from "theatrical" to human, artifice to art – through the secret ingredient: the actor's imagination'. Jorgensen, the actress, is willing to remain under the close scrutiny of the camera in order to give the camera a chance to record raw emotional states, 'pure affects as the expressed' as Deleuze puts it. In her own words, the director gives her a universe, which she fills in with her 'inner pictures'.

For Jorgensen, these are the moments when pure fantasy and memory dominate, which she uses without limitations: 'Lars knew what he wanted; I knew what the feeling inside her [Karen] was.' Those inner pictures/images that Jorgensen refers to are, according to Stella Adler, the constituents of the actor's 'active imagination'. The inner images are the actor's tools that s/he uses for the evocation of Affect which, to quote Deleuze, is 'something expressed: the affect does not exist independently of something which expresses it, although it is completely distinct from it'.

It is this mode of von Trier's intimate filmmaking that demands an actor's total commitment to the project and willingness to expose one's deepest being to the penetrating gaze of the camera. As Jorgensen recalls, the close presence of the camera makes it impossible for the actor to lie and to pretend to be 'in the moment'. She recalls von Trier saying, 'I don't believe you' if he felt the actor was not in the moment. It is authenticity of being that von Trier is searching for, the sincere exposure of one's deepest fears and desires – the purity of feelings. The actor is asked to let herself be humiliated by the camera's close gaze into the purest, unfiltered, emotional states – to surrender completely to the camera. To use her inner resources at the deepest level, the actor's mental strength is needed. To create these deeply moving and powerful performances takes a combination of strength and humble innocence, freedom and control. These are not only the qualities required of the actor, but also essential traits of the character she portrays.

The intimacy of chamber space in von Trier's treatment in *The Idiots* highlights the actor's performance; furthermore, the filmmaker creates this intimate space for the actor's benefit. The filmmaker's choice of space has a direct influence on the actor's construction of deeply-felt portraits of human beings. Moreover, von Trier questions the authenticity of words when depicting the depth of women's experiences. Silence becomes a strong person's way of building her self-reliance. Consequently, von Trier asks his actor to question the role of words in the performance and to look for other, more authentic, avenues of expression.

This return to the chamber space also evokes a question of how women's status in the domestic sphere has been previously represented and shaped by the use of cinematography, the site wherein chamber drama is translated onto film. Indirectly, then, the analysis performed in this chapter raises further questions of how the relationship between women and domestic space has been examined in film and theatre and renegotiated in the dynamics between these two mediums. The evolution of chamber drama tradition does reflect the process of reconstructing women's identity in the domestic space. Performance is thus a unique tool with which to explore a (re)construction of identity. Furthermore, this analysis prompts a consideration of the significance of contextualising performance culturally, historically and socially.

Hanna Laakso

REFERENCES

Adler, S. (2000) *Stella Adler on Ibsen, Strindberg and Chekhov*. Ed. Barry Paris. New York: Vintage Books.

Bálàzs, B. (1952) *Theory of Film: Character and Growth of a New Art*. Trans. Edith Bone. London: Dennis Dobson.

Björkman, S. (1996) 'Naked Miracles', *Sight and Sound*, 6, 10, 14.

Bordwell, D. (1981) *The Films of Carl-Theodor Dreyer*. Berkeley, CA.: University of California Press.

Deleuze, G. (1986) *The Movement-image*. Trans. H. Tomlinson and B. Habberjaum. London: Athlon.

Dreyer C. T. (1973 [1955]) 'Imagination and Colour', in *Dreyer in Double Reflection. Translation of Carl Theodor Dreyer's Writings About the Film*. Edited by D. Skoller. New York: E. P. Dutton, 174–86.

Floyd, N. (1996) '*Sea breeze*. For actors, working with Lars von Trier is far from a chore.' *Time Out*, 9–16, October, 28–9.

Hjort, M. and I. Bondebjerg (2001) *The Danish Directors: Dialogues on a Contemporary National Cinema*. Bristol: Intellect.

Jorgensen, B. (2001) Personal interview with the author, 26 June.

Kelly, R. (2000) *The Name of This Book Is Dogme95*. London: Faber and Faber.

Roman, S. (2000) 'I Confess', *RES: The Future of Filmmaking*, 3, 3, 46–52.

Strindberg, A. (1966) *Open Letters to the Intimate Theater*. Trans. W. Johnson. Seattle: University of Washington Press.

JUHA

AKI KAURISMÄKI, FINLAND, 1999

Aki Kaurismäki is the foremost auteur in contemporary Finnish cinema. Since his solo debut in 1983 with *Crime and Punishment*, a clever adaptation of Fyodor Dostoyevsky's classical novel, he has directed 14 feature films. Most have been critical successes, with the most recent, *Mies vailla menneisyyttä* (*The Man Without a Past*, 2002), the critical culmination; it received the Grand Jury Prize at Cannes Film Festival. The films have, however, never really been successful at the box office in Finland. Exceptions are the more or less realistic working trilogy *Varjoja paratiisissa* (*Shadows in Paradise*, 1986), *Tulitikkutehtaan tyttö* (*The Match Factory Girl*, 1989) and *The Man Without a Past* whose success in Cannes made domestic audiences curious about the film, but only after it had already achieved considerable attention and appreciation.

The national unpopularity of Kaurismäki's films might be no surprise to the international community of film buffs, since his oeuvre is understood as part of a cineaste culture paying homage to such auteurs as Robert Bresson and Jean-Luc Godard. However, the interest here in the cineaste culture of Kaurismäki is the very special blend of national 'content' and international 'form' that is a common trait running through his entire oeuvre. He is usually able to find a way of his own to convey traditional Finnish values using a highly sophisticated film language. On the other hand, this clash between 'form' and 'content' may explain why his films have seldom translated into commercial successes in Finland.

In 1998 Kaurismäki made a silent film, *Juha*, based on a very classical Finnish novel that had already been adapted three times: twice for the screen in Finland and once in Sweden, by the Finland-born director Mauritz Stiller. To complicate matters further he chose neither to set the film in its true fictive time (the eighteenth century) nor the present day. Instead the film unfolds in a fictive epoch, which can be roughly dated to the 1950s. Kaurismäki, however, does not treat his staged past consistently. As such, the settings represent one (past) epoch. The director introduces objects which are 'out of time' – for example, objects common to the period of the film's shooting such as contemporary money, microwave ovens, and so on. Moreover, as his cinematic mode of expression, the director chose the silent film. No wonder that both the audience and the critics, nationally and internationally, were puzzled.

The original story of *Juha*, the novel, is a story of rural Finland when it was part of the Swedish empire. It tells of an older man married to a much younger woman, Marja, who lives in the woods in the far-east of Finland. This region has always been a natural borderland between East and West, between Finland, Sweden and Russia. One day, a young and handsome Karelian peddler, Shemeikka, arrives to Juha's remote farm. The outcome is obvious: the young wife is seduced and leaves the farm with Shemeikka.

On her arrival at her new home in Karelia, Marja discovers that she is not the only lover there. She soon becomes pregnant, and lives an unhappy life in Shemeikka's harem. Juha, on the other hand believes that Marja was taken by force and manages to trace her and to bring her and the child back to his farm. When realising that his wife had left him by her own choice, his sense of honour and male self-image are so damaged that he chooses to commit suicide and the story ends with Juha hurtling down a waterfall with his boat.

The novelist, Juhani Aho, paid close attention to the portrait of Marja. Throughout the novel she is depicted as having a very ambivalent attitude to her own deeds and feelings. Aho constructed a careful psychological tragedy where everything that is human is neither right nor wrong. The characters are victims of nature, of Juha's old age and disability (he limps), of the geographical landscape (a remote cottage in the wilderness) and the political site (a land in-between Finland and Russia). In the different film versions this force of nature has alternated. *Johan*, the Swedish version from 1921, offers a family melodrama where Juha's inability to show real desire for his wife makes her a runaway. Juhani Aho was very critical of Stiller's adaptation; he maintained that Stiller reduced the complex *mélange* of culture and nature, psychology and external forces, down to a question of psychology. Aho's critique is intelligible: in his version Stiller shows that as Juha finally realises that the reason for Marja's flight had been his lack of feeling and affection, he simply takes her back and everything is summed up with a harmonious and conventional heterosexual happy ending.

At the point of shooting the first Finnish film version, *Juha* had already reached considerable status as a classic story in Finnish culture; two operas had been composed, one by Aarre Merikanto in 1922 and the other by Leevi Madetoja in 1934. In his film version from 1937, Nyrki Tapiovaara presented a handsome and unreliable Karelian, Shemeikka, who threatens Juha's male nationalistic identity. The tragedy is that of a man whose wife does not understand the real nature of his manhood.

The 1957 version of *Juha* once again told the mythic story, this time seen as a perfect opportunity for presenting a big spectacle. The year 1957 coincided with the heyday of Finnish film production with peaks of two premieres a month, and the film was the first widescreen colour release with stereophonic sound produced in the country. It also benefited from added attention during its production process, mainly because of its use of 'Agascope', the new Swedish cinemascope format.

The huge media and marketing interest in the making of the film culminated in the grand premiere, attended by no one less than the president of the republic, Urho Kekkonen, the post-war father figure of Finland. The film, however, was no critical success and found its function as an instrument for marketing Finland internationally. The film does not foreground the narration and is not profound when it comes to narrative structure and plot. Instead, it was obvious that the filmmakers concentrated on the new technology, which resulted in stiff acting and overstated visual imagery. Hence, the characters are treated as narrative functions: a tall blond Finn (Juha), a dark devious Karelian male (Shemeikka) and a blond innocent Finnish woman (Marja).

Both Finnish versions focus on two categorical themes: male honour and national identity. It could even be said that the two films establish a parallel between male identity and national identity. At the time the novel was published (before Finnish independence), it was criticised for presenting an inaccurate portrait of the Karelians, who at that time were part of the Finnish population. After the Second World War, as Finland lost territory to the Soviet Union, that part of the country became a province of the USSR, and the native people of the area moved west, to the remaining Finland.

Against such a backdrop it is understandable that the Finnish versions focus on the nationalistic meaning of the region. That, however, was not only a product of the new situation. In the late nineteenth century, when ethnographers such as Elias Lönnroth were looking for the origin of the Finns, the region of northern Karelia was one of the proposed provenances. The Finnish national epic, *Kalevala*, has its origins in folk tales from the Karelian region collected, edited and rewritten by Lönnroth.

It is therefore clear that the story of Juha has a place and significance in the national psyche. This was not easily dealt with, and might be the reason why all Kaurismäki's predecessors chose to set the story in a mythological time before Finland's independence. Kaurismäki, of course, did it differently. He mixed the time markers, choosing instead the 1950s as the mythological time and space for the story.

Here we shall focus on Kaurismäki's method of treating the representation of history in Juha as 'condensed history', a mode which is especially suitable for the visuals and the setting, but also of greater significance as it raises some key questions about the issue of history and memory; in particular, how does a specific community or society organise and form its history and memory? How do these memories become actualised and used and which ends do these different acts and practices serve? In short, what is the relation between form and function of approaching the past in the present, and the techniques used in the specific case of *Juha* by Aki Kaurismäki?

Juha is interesting because it is a story told at different periods in Finnish history. The topic is especially important with regard to collective memory, as the act of appropriating the past is always a matter of handing over material and forms for understanding, to move such material and modes to the present and thus constituting a basis for the making of the future.

Hence, memory as a human practice implies both a poetics and a politics. Which techniques are used? What is structuring the use of the techniques? It can be argued that, if history and memory have as their necessary counterpart the act of forgetting or leaving and even hiding away certain traces, such a complex practice and situation to act in is especially interesting for the visual as it elicits the possibility of including material from different epochs, in the setting or *mise-en-scène*, of a staged past. Kaurismäki often uses a technique pointing almost directly to the fact that the combination of materials used is the result of an act of exclusion (an act of forgetting in that sense).

In *c* this is very evident by the choice of an already outdated form: the silent film. The question is not only a matter of aesthetics and 'pure' technique in that sense, but also of materiality. The form of structuring an utterance is always a part of material facts, techniques for making meanings. If the material is changed, then the meanings are also changed. Hence, the mode (silent film) and the stylistic choices (condensed *mise-en-scène*) are extremely important.

In the early twentieth century, at the time when the novel *Juha* was published, six years before Finland became independent, such a story clearly had a male and national significance. Shemeikka was an evident symbol of foreigness, easily translated into a representation of Russia: dark with curly hair, lively and talkative and very aware of his appearance. In the beginning of the novel, Juha observes Russian boats on the river, which clearly points to both the arrival of a stranger and to the relationship of the province of Karelia to the oppressive Russian empire. For a contemporary reader it was not far-fetched to transform Shemeikka into a condensed symbol for both the power of Russia and the sexual attractiveness and potency of a male rival. The values attached to that figure were clearly negative and immoral: the Russian empire could not be trusted. It was only looking for new territories to conquer for reproducing and securing its position. This may also be read from Shemeikka's relation to his wives. His lovers do not revolt against him, for example – Juha's wife is only waiting for Juha to save her; they are thus totally in the power of the Eastern male.

As mentioned above, the novel was considered offensive against people from the region of Karelia. That Aho and some critics were blind to this fact may perhaps only be explained by the strong national male drive behind the story: the craving for national independence was so urgent that no one in the centre of literary production (Helsinki and its institutions) paid real attention to the actual conditions in the remote area of Karelia. Neither could anyone imagine that the narrative was not limited to being read as a historical tale with national signification.

Kaurismäki's version is set in another context. He wants his audience to remember the story in a different way because Finland is in a different political and cultural situation. Finland of the late 1990s is an ardent supporter of the European Union and Russia has lived through a turbulent period in its history, providing no concrete threat to Finns. In such a situation and after two different Finnish film versions of the classic, the act of telling the story of Juha is by historical necessity forced to enact a form of remembering of a well-known story. The nationalism has changed both form and content, as it cannot directly be constructed in relation to either a foreign national superpower or to a manifest male worldview.

It seems as if Kaurismäki had actually thought about this, as he chose to form his narrative through a historical aesthetic of cinema, the black-and-white, silent film. According to the press notes for the film held at the Finnish Film Archive, he has acknowledged that he made the film because of his mourning of the loss of the aesthetics of pure visuality, which were destroyed by the sound film, television and commercial filmmaking. This archaic form of film narration attaches a historical vestige on the film, as a director's way of consciously intervening in the process of telling a tale already told making it possible to comment upon both the technique (film form) and the practice (narration).

Through the choice of such a specific historical form of expression, it is further being implied that what will be shown is of historical nature, but not in the sense of what has 'passed', but rather in the capacity of a theoretical and distancing gesture. It is also characteristic for Kaurismäki to use self reflexive techniques in intriguing ways. For example, in his melodrama *Kauas pilvet karkaarat* (*Drifting Clouds*, 1996), he does not represent music directly on screen (as emanating from the diegetic space). Instead the music is filtered through, and mediated via, an old machine (technique) for reproducing music. It is as if the music was played on an old gramophone or heard from an old movie. In that sense, the music represents old film music but it functions also as a background to the melodramatic emotional situation of the characters. In fact, it could be argued that the feeling is heightened, as it points both to a historical state of matters as well as to a present situation. Another example is the dramatic start of the actual narrative in *The Man Without a Past*: when the man is mauled, one of the attackers switches on an old radio and the beating becomes accompanied by the melodramatic music from the radio.

It could be argued that the repetition of a tragic psychological situation and relation in *Drifting Clouds* makes the past present as a fact – and history turns into a story being retold. However, such a notion of history and memory has more in common with the form of melodramatic tragedy and the logic of a returned of the repressed. Instead 'change' is a more sociohistorically accurate notion of history. When something has changed, we know we have reached another time and situation and memory is activated. Therefore, the mode of silent film in *Juha*, for instance, is not so much historical because it is an old form, but because we nowadays have another dominant mode of making film.

The criteria that something has passed, is forgotten and 'not present anymore', is also one of the primary characteristics of condensation as defined by Sigmund Freud. It can be said that the things are often so historical and consciously forgotten, they have to force their way to the present by using other vehicles or techniques or pictures as metaphors and condensed constellations in order to become part of the memory-work.

In *Juha*, the silent film form is used in order to make it possible for the audience to travel back to a mythological period called the 1950s, the epoch before Finland was modernised. Kaurismäki also chooses objects from the present to be able to place his story in a contemporary situation. The mix of time layers makes the return backwards in time credible. A technique and manner which is quite common in several of Kaurismäki's films and the reviewers of *Juha* even referred to it as a Kaurismäki-land, a specific time and space which only exists in his films. It may be preferable to call it 'mythological', as it is not an accurately represented epoch; time and place are not materialised in a unitary space but transgressed and condensed.

Instead, we experience the epoch via objects and things: Kaurismäki can therefore avoid the problem of staging a past. We do not have to experience the past; we only have to reflect on it because the past is represented through its signifiers, its objects and things. The 1950s are thus used to represent an epoch that people can remember or have fantasies about, but which they have left. Hence, it signifies not a certain period (material and fact) but something that has been somewhere, sometime and which therefore functions as a projected space for activating a collective memory.

What is it then, that Aki Kaurismäki is conveying? One probable reading is that the film presents a tale of male and nationalistic loss. In Kaurismäki's version, it is new technology that liberates the woman. The Shemeikka of the mythological 1950s is a wealthy international businessman from the city and he arrives in a sports car to the remote cottage. In one of the central turning points of the story, when Marja becomes aware of her attractiveness and therefore of herself as an individual with needs and desires of her own, she starts to heat food for Juha in a microwave oven. It is, of course, the male gaze that triggers the awareness of Marja; Shemeikka sees her coming out of a barn and his gaze establishes Marja, in a shot/reverse-shot pattern as the one to be looked at. There is no dialogical relation between both faces; Shemeikka is the one who is looking, while Marja is not actually looking back. Instead, we can see on her face that she discovers that she is being observed. After this crucial moment Marja begins to look at herself and becomes aware of herself in terms of how she is looked at.

The scene with the microwave oven is consciously anachronistic, bringing in props from the wrong time-setting. By such a distancing device Kaurismäki shows how the liberating technology also is destroying the nation and the hegemonic male culture. Kaurismäki is very precise on this point. For example, the mythological Shemeikka of the 1990s is not only a wealthy businessman from the city, he is also older than Juha. As his appearance is not iconic, as in the earlier versions of the story, he becomes a figure who also opens a space for Marja to be and act in. But his part as someone who also takes advantage of the situation and makes use of his female protagonist is retained in Kaurismäki's version

It is the merit of the film that it tells the story with such an awareness of technique and practice that it is not directly winding time back to a stage before modernity. However, the film is also a suitable space for projecting the mourning of a time lost, a time when national identity was less problematic and had a more obvious, Manichean cultural landscape. When it comes to the function of the film for collective memory, it performs the function of mediating and handing over a story of a nation's relation to a superpower, be it Sweden, Russia or the European Union. The story is so difficult to realise in the Finland of the late 1990s, because of the unbounded nationalism, chauvinism and conservatism that it has to be transferred and condensed into a complex constellation, where the techniques of telling and the practice of remembering are moulded into a disparate unity.

Kaurismäki's strategy can be seen to be successful. It enables the handing over of an out-of-fashion nationalistic story to contemporary Finland. When the film had its premiere, the critics and reviewers focused mainly on the film as another piece in the oeuvre of Kaurismäki the *auteur*, criticising and/or praising the form of the film and questioning the moments of nostalgia. A more careful scrutiny would have brought into attention also the intertwining of both poetics and politics in the chosen mythological narrative, a fact which in itself proves Kaurismäki's abilities to hand down a classical national tragedy as memory for future generations. The story retold refers to something that does not exist anymore and can only be remembered. Thus it becomes a space configured for the projection of a collective memory and for the persistence of content already archived as history.

In a Finnish national context, Kaurismäki's decision to make *Juha* was both difficult and demanding. The film had to be in resonance with a social and historical situation and context that yields the cultural act and intervention a meaning. Hence, there had to be a situation to trigger the story, render the condensation possible and put pressure on the collective memory. That is a strong parallel, I think, with the new situation: the supposed multinational (or transnational) pressure from the European Union on Finland, a nation with a very young history and an unstable identity.

As a result, new ways of writing the history of Finland have emerged, along with a call to remember that which no longer exists. That memory, both painful and out of time, is embodied by the silent film and the condensed images, a perfect poetic device to depict a necessary but outdated story. Aki Kaurismäki's *Juha* is thus a part of a nation's ongoing memory-work and its effort to construct a new identity.

John Sundholm

THE WAKE

MICHAEL KVIUM/CHRISTIAN LEMMERZ, DENMARK, 2000

This story starts in 1962 at The Nikolaj Church (The Church of St Nicholas) in Copenhagen. During five days in November the very first Scandinavian festival with artists from the newly-born Fluxus art movement was held in the church. It was a controversial event that underlined the leading role Denmark has had in Scandinavian Fluxus history. This will not be another story about Fluxus or about the origins of intermedia, interactive art and happenings, but about some visual elements important to Fluxus and a discussion of how they relate to the Danish film and multimedia installation *The Wake* (2000), by artists Michael Kvium and Christian Lemmerz. It is often said that new digital media has become an incentive to reinvestigate earlier media platforms and to some extent that is what shall be undertaken here, using the perhaps less known visual and experiential strategies of Fluxus as a point of comparison. In so doing this chapter will situate both Fluxus and *The Wake* in a theoretical and historical framework that is here called *post-medium visuality*. On the way it will also provide some comments on the significance of this discussion for Scandinavian and Danish visual experimental art.

To go back to the church, it is fair to say that the Nikolaj Church has played an important role in Danish art life, and still is playing. In a Nordic context Denmark, and Copenhagen in particular, has been a Fluxus stronghold and Eric Andersen is probably the best known Nordic artist connected to Fluxus. Today the church is an established art venue and holds, for example, a permanent installation by Andersen.

But when Fluxus first came to the church there was, not surprisingly, institutional friction. Originally the festival was planned to take place at the Society for Young Composers, but protests among 'serious' musicians stopped them, and the initiator Addi Køpcke went to work with Knud Pedersen, then the librarian at the Nikolaj Church, to give the festival there. It was both a success and a scandal. Pedersen lost his job in the uproar, and went on to establish the Kunsthbiblioteket which he still directs today and where he has been building up a Fluxus archive.

Even though this is not about defining some Danish avant-garde or experimental art scene, it might be interesting to know that, for example, Fluxus historian Hannah Higgins uses national characteristics to explain the importance of Fluxus in Denmark. Higgins puts Denmark in a liberal tradition, writing that 'in Denmark Fluxus festivals have served as testimonials to variety and individualism, both hallmarks of that country's liberal tradition'. Indeed, one of the most common arenas to discuss aspects of national or regional issues in relation to art are catalogues from regionally selected exhibitions.

The 1990s was an expanding decade for Scandinavian art, and if one looks at some of these catalogues one gets a significant share of stereotypes about 'the North', but recently also several texts stressing that the geographical peripheries of Europe can no longer be understood as cultural margins. Nordic art has become increasingly international both in regard to distribution (*The Wake* is no exception and has been touring, for example, to the USA and Brazil) and on a thematic level. Curator Åsa Nacking believes this makes it impossible 'to speak of anything like a specific Nordic expression in connection with contemporary artistic activity'.

Perhaps she is right and a key issue is of course that there no longer are any clear national frontiers to stem the information exchange. Denmark is very much part of an internationalisation of art, and perhaps even a Nordic forerunner. Among many interesting Danish contemporary artists are video artist Peter Land, video and sound artist Eva Koch, documentary video artist Bette Villhelmsen, the more situationist art of the group N55, the collective Superflex with their web-based art, just to name a few.

In relation to Fluxus and experimental Danish art, one important step was the foundation in 1961 of The Experimental School of Fine Arts. The Eks School, as it became known, was a rebellion against the technical and figuratively determined teaching in other art schools. Without any fixed programme, the new school disseminated ideas from conceptual art, process art, American pop art, and so on. Today the situation is more varied and experimental media art is produced, for example, at The Royal Danish Academy of Art (where Kvium and Lemmerz studied in the 1980s).

When Hannah Higgins writes about Fluxus she is not really interested in regional or national versions of Fluxus, but more generally in what she sees as some neglected aspects of Fluxus art as *experience*. Fluxus is perhaps best described as an international group of artists who have been challenging and disrupting ideas of what art can be since the early 1960s. There has been many discussions (often quite uninteresting) on what Fluxus actually is, who should count as a real Fluxus artist, is George Maciunas really the main character, and so on. Rather than trying to define the movement in any way, we can use Higgins phenomenologically-inspired understanding of what she calls 'Fluxus experience'. Higgins, of course, quotes the well-known 'intermedia chart' of Fluxus pioneer Dick Higgins and argues that one aspect of Fluxus is precisely the use of a space between media, not primarily of a mix of media but of the dynamic and tension that she finds between media. It is true that Fluxus is often multisensory, but in this context a delimitation to vision and the aspect of visual experience is the primary link with *The Wake*.

With a three-year retrospect one could dare to say that *The Wake* is quite typical for the turn of the century. It can be placed in a theoretical framework based on a combination of two well-known ideas or concepts from the late twentieth century: one is 'the visual turn', the other is 'the post-medium condition' and together they constitute a rough outline of what is here called a post-medium visuality.

The basic components of the concept are quite simple. In a differentiated media landscape there are different visual arts like painting and photography. For cinema this 'condition' is dominated by the link to photography and the importance of the indexical image (that is, the photographic image as an index, a trace of light from the real world). But in the post-medium condition you no longer have the separation of different visual media or arts, but on the other hand an expanding visual culture where indexicality comes into question.

In new media it is clear that experimentation and manipulation becomes easier; it becomes easier to model the image – fact that has influenced the status of an indexical image of reality (for example, due to the digital manipulation that makes realistic images possible without the indexical link). The idea of photographic indexicality has actually lost a great deal of its importance and in post-medium visuality aspects of plasticity and filmic materiality due to image manipulation (that is typical for *The Wake*) take over some of this importance.

The Wake is an eight-hour free adaptation of James Joyce's novel *Finnegans Wake* and like Joyce's work exhausts almost every possibility of the language; it is trying to exhaust the possibilities of cinematic language. *The Wake* is not primarily conceived for the cinema. It is meant to circulate in a number of different forms and contexts from the event-like occasion via an exclusive publication with stills and 2 x 4 hours DVD to a possible Internet version. As the Danish writer and curator Lars Movin puts it: 'All in all a presentation that, like Joyce, challenges our preconceptions of what comprises a work and our notions about the medium.'

Even though it is not really an adaptation for the screen of *Finnegans Wake*, one obvious analysis of the film would be a comparison with Joyce's work, but that is not a path to be followed here; with these two works a comparative reading holds many possible interpretive problems. Instead it is helpful to briefly contextualise the film, both historically and theoretically, in relation to the concept of a post-medium visuality. In this respect *The Wake* is perhaps more typical than seminal, but nevertheless very interesting as an example of Danish film – the film is partly sponsored by the Danish Film Institute – and a way that visual art and film come together.

Michael Kvium (born 1955 in Denmark) and Christian Lemmerz (born 1959 in Germany) are not originally filmmakers (but a painter and a sculptor, respectively), but since the early 1980s they have also explored other ways of expression, such as film, video, performance and theatre. For example they were both involved in the performance group *Værst* (*Worst*). They made their first film in 1986; a short film called *Grød* (*Porridge*), and in 1994 followed this with their first long film, *Voodoo Europa*, a low-budget feature film recorded on video. Lemmerz was also represented at the recent Fluxus exhibition at Aarhus kunstmuseum with his piece *Christbaum* from 1984.

In regard to the 'visual texture' of *The Wake*, Kvium and Lemmerz have said in notes accompanying the film that 'The film medium is so bound by tradition that its limits are astonishingly narrow. For example, if you want to use blurred images, there has to be some kind of symbolic reason for doing so, such as a character from the film going blind or moving around in a dream. Or soft porn.' This is often true in commercial cinema, but the kind of painterly experimentation with film images they are referring to also have a history, and in the domain of the avant-garde or experimental film the use of blurred images is quite common; for example, in some of the visual strategies important to the Fluxus movement.

When Hannah Higgins discusses Fluxus films like John Cavanaugh's *Flicker* (1966) and Yoko Ono's *Eyeblink* (1966) she puts focus on the visible as experience. Experientially, she correctly argues, *Flicker* 'initiates a visual impression – the colourless blob registered by the optic nerve – that is radically distinct from what is shown, namely, alternating frames of black and clear celluloid'. *Eyeblink* is the opposite, a film in extreme slow-motion of a blinking eye, and Higgins' point is that both films replace the illusion of a unified film space with primary experience (as opposed to secondary, more interpretive and associative experience).

The alternative to scopic unity (posited by perspectival art and photography) is what Higgins calls an 'experiential disunity'. For her the Fluxus films affirm a broader physiological basis of vision. There are many points of convergence with these films (and other Fluxus films) and *The Wake*. This is perhaps most obvious in the visual strategy of Fluxus that Higgins identifies as the use of 'haptic images'. For Higgins these are images that suggest touch by emphasising the 'surface textures or outline of things'. Here is a familiar component of looking closely, of wanting to touch, but also to imagine the object as actually presented instead of represented.

The Wake is a silent film (but with an experimental soundtrack) and the purpose of Kvium and Lemmerz is quite clear: 'We are living in the most visual century of history; images have taken over reality, but mostly as clichés for manipulating opinions and capital. By denying ourselves the spoken language with its restrictive names and meanings we are liberating a figurative language that has deleted all well-known cultural subtitles'.

Being a silent film The Wake heavily draws upon a tradition of visual acoustics. One sees a lot of sounds that one does not hear. Screams, laughs, crashes, splashes, things breaking and falling, and so on. With their work they are 'seeking to transgress the limits defining contemporary film', and with their multiple platforms they also write themselves right into the post-medium condition.

When Rosalind Krauss tries to define this post-medium condition she does it through an analysis of the work of artist Marcel Broodthaers from the 1960s and 1970s. She concentrates on Broodthaers' hybrid and intermedial strategies as an announcement of 'the termination of the individual arts as medium-specific'. One of her basic arguments is that this period (and the work of Broodthaers) is a decisive moment in the history of medium-specificity. As with Fluxus we have an intermedia loss of specificity for the individual arts that is typical for Broodthaers, for example in his fictitious Museum of Modern Art, Eagles Department.

At about the same time when Broodthaers, Fluxus artists and others were mixing media, the first reasonably cheap video cameras and monitors made possible the entry of video in art practice. For Krauss, the advent of the portapak and the heterogeneity of activities that characterised video art occupied 'a kind of discursive chaos'. Like the work of Broodthaers, video 'proclaimed the end of medium-specificity', she writes. Krauss highlights the subversive strategies of Fluxus and Situationists as essential to these tendencies. And twenty-five years later, as Krauss remarks, 'the international spread of the mixed-media installation has become ubiquitous'.

If we accept that we live a post-medium condition, there is still the fact of a visual dominance in late twentieth-century art and mass culture. The visual may not be medium-specific, but it is still sense-specific. When there are no media, there are still senses, not at all separated, but nevertheless often perceived as such. The separation of sense experiences is perhaps also a conventional one, and the use of a visual emphasis here should primarily be seen as a delimitation and a way of focusing the discussion, not an ontological statement of any kind. One can also see *The Wake* as an example of visual shift from indexicality to materiality that is one distinguising mark for the visual turn. When Kvium and Lemmerz talk about blurred or unfocused images without any apparent motivation in the story, they chose instead to underline plastic and material aspects of moving images.

Krauss argues that 'in the 1960s, "opticality" was also serving as more than just a feature of art; it had become a *medium* of art'. But these aspects do exist also in earlier films and film theory. Just to give an idea of the early discussion, at least two classical texts from the 1920s deserves to be mentioned. In his *De la cinéplastique Élie*, Élie Faure writes about the 'cineplastic' as something that can give us the impression that most mediocre films do 'take place in a musical space'. Film is to Faure the tension between movement and rest that changes continually 'in the depth and surface of the screen', That same year (that is, 1922) Fernand Léger published a short text on Abel Gance's film *La Roue*: 'The coming of this film is so much more interesting because it gives a place in the plastic community to an art form that so far, with a few exceptions, is descriptive, sentimental and documentary'. Léger argues further that the film is not about imitating the movements of nature, but 'to make images *visible*'.

If Dziga Vertov's *The Man with a Movie Camera* is often referred to as a catalogue of cinematic devices, *The Wake* perhaps comes closer to an orgy in cinematic effects. One important aspect is precisely to *make images visible* and with a formulation that echoes clearly of Vertov Kvium and Lemmerz talk about 'a film wanting to invent its own images, its own grammar and its own world'. Speed variations are omnipresent in the film and they continually use anamorphic images, grainy images, multiple exposures and different versions of stratified images as a middle way between abstraction and representation. Images are shown, for example, through reflections in dirty water, in a roughly treated mirror and the vision is continually disturbed and constrained and therefore, in a way, *felt*. One instance of this occurs in chapter 5 (of the DVD edition) when people are filmed as if they are inside an aquarium; the surface of the screen becomes like softly rolling waves.

Overall, one could say that there are three recurring themes in the film which all integrate with the visual strategies: nature, body and sex. As a viewer one is often left with unidentifiable body fluids and body parts in extreme close-ups. Sometimes it resembles the opening sequence of Alain Resnais' *Hiroshima, mon amour*, and sometimes it is more like badly-filmed hardcore pornography. In both cases the camera becomes a penetrating Benjaminian surgeon. Their use of kaleido*scopic* sex offers a strange kind of voyeuristic feeling where one is never really sure of what one sees. The artists themselves have an explicit visual idea regarding this strategy: 'We wanted to make abstract pornography, a kind of stream of consciousness porno that was visually stimulating, and create a sensation in pictures corresponding to the experience of having sex with your lover.'

Water and nature (and sex and bodies) are often used as abstraction in this and many other films, for example through extreme close-ups or extreme slow-motion. 'Between water and ice, between the liquid and the solid, a new matter is created, an ocean of viscous movements', as filmmaker and film theorist Jean Epstein would have it about one of his films where the sea outside Bretagne is continually filmed in slow-motion.

In its visual experiments it can be said that *The Wake* draws upon a video art tradition, and the work of Bill Viola is one evident point of reference. Both thematically and stylistically the film resembles many of Viola's works. For example, the underwater scenes in *The Passing* (1991) is very reminiscent of the underwater sequences from the first chapter of *The Wake*. Like for Viola the images in *The Wake* also evoke passages between different states, between water and air, between sleep and wakefulness, between life and death. On the opposite side of the speed-scale, the fast-motion sequences of a cloudy sky in *The Wake* are reminiscent of the video *Sunrise 5am* (2001) by Swedish artist Petra Lindholm, or the fast-motion clouds in Jean Epstein's *Le Tempestaire* (1947). Nature and its moving parts are perhaps one of the most frequent venues for filmic media experiments.

The Wake is full of contrasts, but it is also quite an uneven piece of varying quality. At its best moments the film resembles the suggestive images of Bill Viola at his best, and at its worst it is nothing more than a provocation, failing to provoke, with crazy people doing crazy things. There is also a repetitive element in the film; images come back form earlier sequences, sometimes with a rewinding and repetitive soundtrack. The last chapter (chapter 8 on the DVD edition) actually repeats the whole film (or at least most of it) in reversed fast-motion. The films own memory flashes by and creates what appears as a false sense of unity that one would probably never get it in any normal viewing situation.

But when it comes to viewing practices Kvium and Lemmerz also have a clear and quite sympathetic strategy. They describe it thus: 'It is an event film, a visual art film, which people can relate to in the same way as you relate to visual art. When you look at paintings you look for two minutes, perhaps, and then your attention is captured by something else. Then you look back. Just like most of the things in life. When people are talking to each other they also have the odd break, look out of the window, thumb through the pages of a book, and then resume their conversation.' A statement that, in my opinion, involves both a Fluxus mentality and a Fluxus experientiality. As Hannah Higgins puts it: 'Fluxus transforms the avant-garde (as institutional critique, as iconoclasm) to become, in part, its opposite: aesthetic experience.'

The Wake is, in a way, like a visual mapping of different sense experiences and this is also the most obvious connection between Rosalind Krauss and 'the visual turn' as described by Angela Dalle Vacche. There is a tension between the mapping of the senses and the system of the arts. Important for Dalle Vacche's version of the visual turn are the terms discussed by the art historian Alois Riegl: the haptic and the optic. As a rough simplification, optic art is more distant and addresses primarily the viewer's eye, and haptic art is closer and appeals more to the sense of touch, but it is nevertheless, for Riegl, a tactile way of seeing.

And it is this kind of haptic opticality that is very present in *The Wake*, for example in the abstract sex scenes. The film is a good example of a tendency where 'the filmic image abandons its photographic origin', as Dalle Vacche puts it. Also, Ricciotto Canudo is often quoted in this context with his description of cinema as 'plastic art in motion' and this simple statement positions the filmic screen as scenery for modelling the image. In *The Wake* this becomes an obvious strategy. When people talk about Nordic art this has, until not too long ago, often been about themes connected to nature, light, melancholy and insanity. Today the international information flow makes national characteristics less important, but in a very strange, post-mediated and visualised way these themes re-emerge in *The Wake*. It is probably pure coincidence, but, then again, tradition is also a flow.

Karl Hansson

REFERENCES

Dalle Vacche, A. (ed.) (2003) *The Visual Turn*, New Brunswick, NJ: Rutgers University Press.

Epstein, J. (1975 [1947]) 'La Férie réelle', in *Ècrits sur le cinema 2*. Paris: Seghers.

Faure, E. (1963 [1922]) 'De la cinéplastique', in *Fonctions du cinéma*. Paris: Gonthier.

Higgins, H. (2002) *Fluxus Experience*. Berkeley: University of California Press.

Krauss, R. (2000) *'A Voyage on the North Sea' – Art in the Age of the Post-Medium Condition*. New York: Thames & Hudson.

Léger, F. (1970 [1922]) 'Essai critique sur la valeur plastique du film d'Abel Gance, *La Roue*', in

Fonctions de la peinture. Paris: Gonthier.

Movin. L (2000) Interview with Kvium and Lemmerz from the film's website www.wake.dk

Nacking, Å. (2000) 'Notes on Contemporary Art and Nordicness', from the catalogue for *Norden
– Zeitgenössische Kunst aus Nordeuropa*. Wien: Kunsthalle Wien.

HEFTIG OG BEGEISTRET COOL AND CRAZY

KNUT ERIK JENSEN, NORWAY, 2001

In the year 2000 the veteran Norwegian filmmaker Knut Erik Jensen released his documentary *Heftig og begeistret* (a literal English translation might be 'Wild and Enthusiastic') for theatrical distribution in Norway with its premiere at the Tromsø International Film Festival. The film was an immediate success with the critics and audiences. This came as a great surprise for the production company, Norsk Film, as well as the distributor, witnessed by the fact that a meagre number of prints had been ordered for distribution. Within a very short time *Heftig og begeistret* became the must-see film for Norwegian audiences and by the summer of 2002 an impressive number of Norwegians – 550,000, out of a total population of 4.5 million – had found their way to movie theatres showing the activities of the Berlevåg Male Choir who lived in a tiny fishing village near the North Cape. In terms of attendance, Jensen's film was only bested by another Norwegian film, Academy Award-nominee *Elling*, directed by Petter Næss (2001).

Furthermore, the documentary also became a modest success on the international film festival circuit, winning the main prize at Gothenburg Film Festival and at festivals in the UK and the US, with the more catchy title, *Cool and Crazy*. In a review for *The Observer* (10 February 2001) Philp French stated that 'I felt my life being enhanced as I watched *Cool and Crazy*.' Other international reviewers compared the movie favourably to Wim Weders' *Buena Vista Social Club* (1999). The film also did surprisingly well in commercial distribution in Denmark and Sweden, earning the Berlevåg Choir something of a cult status. In the summer of 2001 the choir, white singers' hats and all, were invited to the Roskilde Rock Music Festival in Denmark for several appearances, opening the final concert with the British rock group Travis to an enthusiastic audience of more than 40,000.

The stardom conferred on the group led to a dramatic change in the life of the choir that up until the release of the movie had led the same anonymous life as similar choirs all over Norway: rehearsals on Tuesdays, concerts for friends, neighbors and relatives three to four times a year – the high point usually being the annual gathering and concert of regional choirs, maybe even attendance at the National Choir Festival. Suddenly the concept of not being able to fill all requests for concerts arrived, together with the necessity of hiring a booking manager.

Where the audience had once been mostly local, the new CD of the choir sold better than most Norwegian pop music CDs. Groupies appeared: the bachelors of the choir (and some of the married men as well) received offers of marriage. The tabloid press was suddenly at the heels of the choir members, and their appearances at social events were duly noted, not to mention several 'confession' stories appearing in the tabloid press.

The success of *Cool and Crazy* inevitably raised the idea of a sequel, with Jensen and the choir more than eager to follow up with a 'road trip movie' following the Choir's subsequent tour of Norwegian-American audiences in New York and the Midwest in 2001. There was no lack of warning voices to this project, voices that were more or less proven right by a lukewarm critical reception and dismal audience figures in Norway and little or nothing of the international acclaim of the first movie.

The aim of this chapter is to give some background to the astounding success of Jensen's film, the main thesis being that *Cool and Crazy* in many ways is a typical Jensen film. It contains and refines a set of themes and techniques developed over his years as a regional and modernist documentarist based in northern Norway. The gist of the argument is that consistency pays off.

In the case of *Cool and Crazy*, then, a biographical and historical overview is necessary. Knut Erik Jensen was born in Finmark in northern Norway in 1942. During childhood he experienced the trauma of the evacuation of Finmark, the nothernmost, largest (approximately the size of Denmark) and most sparsely populated county of Norway, sharing a border with arctic Russia in the northeast. In 1944, the occupying German army, fearing a Russian invasion, decided on using 'scorched earth' tactics. All the inhabitants of Finmark were ordered to be evacuated and the county put to the torch. Apart from the town of Kirkenes near the Russian border, every house – private, business or official – in the county was set fire to, villages and townships were razed. The larger part of the population were evacuated under appalling conditions to southern Norway, while a considerable number hid from the Germans in makeshift camps and in abandoned mines, enduring considerable hardship during the winter of 1944–45. During these winter months Finmark became the first part of Norway to be liberated from the Germans by the rapidly advancing Soviet Red Army, whose soldiers were naturally greeted as saviors by the remaining population.

After finishing his elementary education in Finmark, Jensen went on to study languages at the University of Oslo, before deciding on attending the London International Film School in 1973. Back in Norway, he became involved in local filmmaking, setting a pattern he has followed ever since. From the late 1970s onwards, he has worked as a cinematographer, editor and director for the regional branch of the Norwegian public service company NRK, producing a prolific oeuvre over three decades. This includes documentaries, a documentary series for television and three fiction films.

His most important work as a television director and producer is undoubtedly the documentary series *Finmark mellom øst og vest* (*Finmark Between East and West*, 1985–86), consisting of six installments varying in length from 55 minutes to 1 hour 33 minutes. In this series he attempted to present an audio-visual history of Finmark based on archival material and interviews with a polemical undertone: in the task of rebuilding their wasted Finmark, the people had to rely on their own strength and their loyalty to their land, often in the face of adverse intervention from the 'southerners' of the Norwegian administration.

Gunnar Iversen points out Jensen's documentary series as an eminent example of 'writing history from below', stating, 'The many small participants in history, each with a story to tell, are documented by Jensen's camera and saved for posterity. These stories are simultaneously a corrective from below and a complement to other sources and historical discourses. The experience of the people is placed in the centre.' With this series, then, as with all of his work, Jensen has stayed with his subject: the people of Finmark, their past and their present, over three decades.

Jensen has made three feature-length fiction films, *Stella Polaris* (1993) *Brent av frost* (*Burnt by Frost*, 1997) and *Når mørket er forbi* (*Passing Darkness*, 2000). All films are representative of Jensen's documentary work in several ways, the most immediate trait being that they share a specific historical and geographical background. In *Stella Polaris* the central conflict develops from events connected to the wartime evacuation and burning of Finmark as experienced by a child. Formally it is strongly impressionistic-modernist, relying totally on the images to relate a story, without the use of dialogue. At times this technique of Jensen's is reminiscent of French modernist filmmakers of the 1960s like Resnais, leaving the viewer to sift through visually coded memories, without being too generous in terms of assisting the viewer.

The faint echo of the problematic relationship with the Soviet Union present in *Stella Polaris* becomes the central theme in *Burnt by Frost*. Employing much of the same fragmented narrative as its predecessor, *Burnt by Frost* recounts the story of the Norwegian partisans from Finmark working with and from the Soviet Union and their problematic divided loyalties after the outbreak of the Cold War. The central narrative has as its background several cases where former partisans in the 1950s were tried and convicted as Soviet spies.

In *Passing Darkness*, Jensen brought his narrative into the realm of the present. Based on a crime novel by Alf R. Jacobsen, Norwegian film critics were unanimously negative in their reception of what was considered a 'contrived "artistic" stew based on soap opera material' and Jensen was advised to stay in the field of documentary.

However, in terms of the relevance for *Cool and Crazy*, Jensen's forays into the realm of fiction film underline an aspect relevant to his work, whether in documentary or fiction: that of playful formal experimentation. In addition, three consistent themes may be seen in Jensen's work, coming together in *Cool and Crazy*. The first theme is the *iconoclastic*, with specific reference to Jensen's choice of formal expression. As noted above, Norwegian critics were less than happy with his highly fragmented narrative in *Passing Darkness*, and although the reception of the two previous films was a lot more benign, critics also noted what many felt was a contrived modernism as a blemish. Several of his documentaries share this tendency to depart from the beaten road, as he did in three documentaries made about nature and human life in the Svalbard Archipelago in the extreme north.

In a documentary he made for Norwegian children's authorities about the need to secure children's playgrounds against harsh climatic conditions, he turned the tables on his mandate. In *Natur-Barn-Natur* (*Nature-Children-Nature*, 1987) he maintains that children in Norway are, and have always been, able to adapt to the climate. The problem, as Jensen sees it, is desk-bound bureaucrats trying to justify their existence by launching mindless campaigns like the one he has been asked to make a film about. Thus, both formally and in terms of content, the film may be viewed as an attack on the Griersonian utilitarian documentary approach.

Jensen himself has, on several occasions found reason to defend his iconoclastic approach to filmmaking, both fiction and documentary. In connection with the criticism his Svalbard film *Kald verden* (*Cold World*, 1986) was met with, he comments, in the volume on Scandinavian documentary by Sören Birkvad and Jan Anders Diesen: 'It is my belief that when people have been watching the same [documentaries] for 20–30 years, they tend to react when shown something different. But they will not necessarily react because of the quality of that film. They may react because in 20–30 years they have been subjected to bad and boring programmes.'

Another thread in Jensen's production is his frequent return to strongly individualistic persons. In the third film in his Svalbard trilogy *Min verden* (*My World*, 1987) he presents a fur trapper who has chosen a lonely life in the arctic wildness as a conscious alternative to modern 'civilised' life. The portrait is by no means a flattering one – at times one may think the loner has done society a favour by choosing to stay in the wilderness – but what emanates from this and similar documentary portraits by Jensen, is a great respect for the individual and his or her choices.

According to Jensen, he is inspired by the Norwegian author Knut Hamsun in his treatment and presentation, and relates this to his own choice to remain true to his northern background: '[Hamsun also] was preoccupied with the small villages in northern Norway. He is mainly writing about events and personalities he knew. His marvellous prose is about simple people and intimate relationships in a small place. The big cities are temples of loneliness, where people write about their own frustrations.'

According to this view, the strength of the northern individualists in Jensen's portrayal is that, however individualistic and egregious they may appear, they always have the strength of the collective with them. Nowhere in Jensen's prolific documentary production is this stated more clearly than in his very first film *Farvel da, gamle Kjelvikfjell* (*Goodbye, Old Kjelvik Mountain*, 1974). In this film, three bachelors are the only remaining inhabitants of what was once a thriving fishing village. Jensen follows them through their daily chores, allowing the viewer to become acquainted with them as individuals, as well as a functioning collective. Through their reminiscences and with the help of still photos, the image of the village as the lively society it had once been, emerges. Soon enough the neglected houses of the place take on new meaning as witnesses to a lifestyle that might have been harsh, but that was warm and inclusive as well. These qualities now become apparent in the three elderly men, as individuals and as a functioning collective based upon mutual respect, a strong common cultural and historical background and a close relationship to nature.

And this mixture of the individualistic collective is the exact quality to be found in Jensen's film about a group of singers of mediocre talent, but of great personal and collective character, nearly three decades later. In a review of *Cool and Crazy* for *The New York Times* (19 October 2001), Dave Kehr makes the following observation: 'The Berlevåg Male Choir is a casting agent's dream, a group of about thirty men who range in age from early thirties to late nineties, each with a spectacularly weather-beaten Nordic face and an endearingly shy demeanor.' Other reviewers have made similar observations and here we may consider some of features of Jensen's documentary that have contributed to the surprising – and, indeed, implausible – fact that a group of middle-aged and elderly men from northern Norway should attain the status of film stars.

A key concept here is – as Kehr pointed out – the question of casting. In choosing the Berlevåg Choir as his subject, Jensen has played to his main strength as a documentary filmmaker – the ability to coach from his subjects a presence that goes beyond the superficial. In many of his earlier documentaries, Jensen made a foray into the field of documentary portraits and his experience in this field has paid off in *Cool and Crazy*. The crucial point here is his background as a participant as well as an observer. The fishing villages of Finmark are part of his cultural and artistic background, and he is able to use this knowledge in a wider connection, using his experience and scholarly background from studies of French, Russian and Art History to put the local in a global perspective, a fact he himself is very clear about: 'When I am standing at the town square in Honningsvåg, I like to state that I am standing at the centre of the world. Wherever I turn, there is a Frenchman or a Japanese passing, all on their way to the North Cape. You may be in the centre even if you are living in the periphery.'

A returning theme in Jensen's work is the construction of a unique northern Norwegian cultural expression, where the individual and the collective does not operate as opposites, but as a composite. In his portrayal of the singing Berlevågians, he operates with a thin line separating a stereotype from character. Jensen's use of stereotypes is apparent from the way he is playing up to some of the expectations and prejudices that Norwegian 'southerners' have about their Northern countrymen. The northern Norwegian is perceived as outgoing and slightly promiscuous, given to a vocabulary of swear words both admired and feared.

These stereotypes are played with in Jensen's film, as for instance in the portrayal of the amorous communist, conveniently placed in a bath tub: 'In my youth I was a satyr...' or the deadpan presentation of one of the elderly members of his house: 'This is the bedroom. I used to call it The Activity Room, but I guess it is more of a museum now...' The stereotyping of the northern Norwegian as a physically robust person, able to survive harsh climatic conditions, is also duly played with by Jensen in his shots of the choir singing outdoors in a blizzard, icicles forming from the nose of 97-year-old Olaf Strand.

In all these examples Jensen apparently operates with a playful attitude towards stereotypes. There is, nevertheless, an underlying tone of seriousness in his treatment of the men from Berlevåg based on Jensen's idea of the unique individual and collective qualities the harsh landscape of Finmark lends to its inhabitants.

Cool and Crazy is constantly vacillating between the individual and the collective. The individual is primarily taken care of in the presentation of the members in their daily lives and their conversations with the invisible director and photographer. The collective is portrayed in the appearances of the Choir, who offer themselves up as prey to Jensen's whims, whether they have to endure a blizzard or bask in the midnight sun, climb a lighthouse or sing among the cod on the way to being filleted. Common to both expressions, individual and collective, are the references to a perceived common culture grounded in special and geographical historical conditions. Thus, the collective also appears as an individual – the typical North Norwegian.

This is reinforced by dramaturgical means. *Cool and Crazy* is constructed so as to build up to a narrative climax around the tour to Murmansk in Russia. At this point several personalities have been carefully constructed through the individual presentations. Jensen then lets the drama of post-war Finmark play out with the Choir's communist as a kind of protagonist, weeping at the monument to the Red Army soldiers, liberators of Finmark, enduring the shame of the ecological disaster left by his ideological heroes, but finally reconciled with his choirmates in a Russian folk song, being enthusiastically received by the Russian audience.

Thus, the unique and unusual attraction of *Cool and Crazy* is not as much an example of the mysterious ways of popular success, but of a careful and skilled treatment and presentation of a culture – the culture of northern Norway – by the insider Knut Erik Jensen, who has carefully taken advantage of the common stereotypes about this culture by giving background and insight into individual characters forming a unique collective.

Bjørn Sørenssen

REFERENCES

Birkvad, S. and J. A. Diesen (1994) *Autentiske inntrykk. Møte med ni skandinaviske dokumentarfilmskaparar.* Oslo: Det norske samlaget.

Brinch, S. and G. Iversen (2001) *Virkelighetsbilder. Norsk dokumentarfilm gjennom hundre år,* Oslo: Universitetsforlaget.

TAXI

IVAR VEREIDE, NORWAY, 2001

Under the slogan '*Lotto* Millionaires are Unlike Ordinary Millionaires', Norwegians have been exposed to 24 different commercials promoting the *Lotto* game between 1993 to 2001. The commercials have been screened on television as well as in cinema theatres. Almost every Norwegian knows what a *Lotto* millionaire is and everyone is familiar with the films' main message. Several of the *Lotto* commercials have won prizes for their quality, both in Norway and abroad. One of them, *Taxi*, was awarded with the title of the best lottery commercial world-wide in 2002, at the World Lottery Association.

Moviegoers and television viewers appear to be entertained by these films. The commercials have succeeded in installing a new concept in Norwegian language. The concept of *Lotto million-aire* has taken on its own, specific meaning. The commercials seem to live on in oral culture, inspiring jokes and puns, particularly amongst younger people. When one *Lotto* commercial joked about the community of Værdal, the area experienced a boost in tourism. Even though the Værdal *Lotto* commercial was screened in 1999, in 2002 people still arrive by bus at Værdal to play *Lotto*.

This chapter looks at the reasons for the commercials' success. However, to do this it is necessary to take a closer look at how the *Lotto millionaire* is presented in the *Lotto* commer-cials. In the older films, the *Lotto* millionaire is depicted in contrast to the privileged class in society. This latter group are shown indulging in activities like riding (1993) and salmon fishing (1994), or being escorted in expensive limousines (1994). They are immaculately, if staidly, dressed. They also have servants. And yet, they appear to be bored. They do not enjoy life. The *Lotto* commercials picture the ordinary millionaires as dull and unexciting. The *Lotto* millionaires are seen to be very different. As members of the *noveau riches*, they enjoy the new possibilities the money has offered them. They are individualists, staging their own specific dreams, such as in the film where the old, traditionally dressed farmers' wife enters the luxury dog styling saloon (1996). Here, white poodles wearing pink ribbons are the norm, but the farmer's wife steps inside with her sheep to have it styled in the poodle way. The well groomed ladies, present with their poodles, look on in astonishment. The farmer's wife, as well as the styling salon and its clients are parodies, wildly beyond any real life people.

In another *Lotto* commercial a blind man enters a motorcycle shop (2001). To the shop owner's surprise, the man wants to buy the most extravagant Harley Davidson. The film's last shot shows him riding it atop a trailer pulled by a car driven by the man's female companion. The *Lotto* millionaires are ordinary people. The way they dress and act in no way relates to those already wealthy. But these people have highly original ideas. They find ways to express their individualism. They are able to enjoy life and express their feelings.

The effect of humour in advertising has been widely discussed. Jib Fowles finds that one of the advantages of humour is that it somehow disguises the advertising message. To viewers, humourous commercials seem more like ordinary entertainment. A funny story, like a joke, diminishes the resistance that viewers may have against being told what to buy or what to do. It is less easy to reject a message when you laugh. You may even experience feelings of gratitude for being allowed to enjoy yourself.

New Deal, the advertising agency that has produced the *Lotto* commercials discussed here, also state as their explicit strategy that they want their commercials to be appreciated by the audience. They are aware that there are many unpopular commercials on TV, films that the viewers experience as nagging, pushy, noisy or just stupid. This strategy of wanting to be liked by the audience is an important factor in explaining the choice of funny stories in commercials. Such a strategy also covers repetition. How many times should a commercial be screened, within how long a period of time? If screened continuously, the viewers could start to hate even a funny commercial, no matter how entertaining they found it to begin with.

For winning an audience over with the *Lotto* commercials, the films' producers worked very carefully on the *sujet* of the films. To follow David Bordwell, the *sujet* refers to the film as a chain of events presented to the audience. The *Lotto* sujets generally withhold information. The action does not make sense. The viewers are not able to construct the *fabula* (the real story conceived or constructed by the audience) until the last shot of the films. Of course, as we are discussing commercials here, of a short duration. The commercials last for 60 seconds at most, but employ techniques for keeping audience interest high until the pay off at the end, when the stories present a humourous twist.

Taxi, screened in 2001, presents a strange taxi driver who refuses to let passengers into his car. He is driving slowly along people in line for a taxi, but locks his door from the inside when an elegant young businessman tries to enter the cab. He also refuses to take as a passenger a woman heading for the airport. Sweet's 1970's hit *Ballroom Blitz*, playing on the car stereo, increases in volume. The driver leaves his car. His hair is long and untidy. He is a large man, but moves about, playing air guitar and pretending to sing *Ballroom Blitz*, in front of those waiting for a taxi. The camera angle is looks up from ground level, as if the spectator was in front of a scene, watching a performance on the stage.

A short businessman in the back of the line is watching carefully. In a testing manner he enters the singing and dancing and moves towards the driver. The look on the driver's face tells him he has grasped the whole meaning, and they indulge one hundred percent in Sweet's hit, rocking, dancing, moving their bodies, mimicking to the lyrics before they run together to the cab and drive off, still singing *Ballroom Blitz*. A concluding text is imposed on the shot, stating that *Lotto* millionaires are unlike ordinary millionaires. This is followed by the *Lotto* logo as well of the Norsk Gambling logo, and this ends the film.

The viewer, or at least the one familiar with *Lotto* commercials, is able to construct a fable about a Taxi driver who won a fortune at the game of *Lotto*. This made it possible for him to relate more playfully to his work. As a fan of rock music and particularly Sweet, he only bothers to drive rockers like himself. The *Taxi* commercial conveys the general *Lotto* commercial format. The films are stories, humourous ones with surprising endings. They lack dialogue and commentary, or, as in *Taxi*, dialogue is scarce, as the stories unfold to a popular song or piece of music.

Globally, lottery businesses are regulated by national authorities. The Norwegian example differs significantly. Norsk Gambling, the company responsible for the *Lotto* game, is wholly owned by the state. *Lotto* is the main game of Norsk Gambling. The company holds almost 40 percent of the Norwegian gambling market, according to their annual report for 2001. Each week, 2,1 million of Norway's population of 4.5 million participate in one of Norsk Gambling's games. 1,1 million play *Lotto*, which translates into 41 percent of the total turnover at Norsk Gambling. The average *Lotto* player invested 42 Norwegian kroner per week in 2001, some £3.50. *Lotto* tops the list of Norwegian money games, with the second most popular game some way off.

Games in which money can be won were introduced relatively late on the official Norwegian market. Winning money in games implied criminal activity. The state's Money Lottery had existed since 1913, but tickets were cheap and only small prizes were paid out to winners. Horse gambling was introduced in 1927, initiated by the farmer's organization and supported by the then powerful political party of the farmers, as a way to contribute to economic growth in the countryside. Football gambling was rejected when a move was made to introduce it, in the 1930s. A leader within the national organization of sports had proposed gambling as a way to earn money for building indoor swimming pools. But the majority of the sports organization's members felt that money should be earned through work. Playing with money in games was unacceptable, and although recognizing that swimming pools were needed, the sports movement wanted to have nothing to do with money derived from gambling.

However, the issue of football gambling was raised again after World War II. The proposal included splitting of the earnings between sports and research. At that time the objections were less. The country needed to be rebuilt, and sports and recreation offered a mostly harmless way to make money. Again, prizes were modest to prevent an unhealthy indulgence in gambling. Football gambling was finally permitted in 1948, overseen by Norsk Gambling. The Norwegian gambling market remained relatively stable until the 1980s.

The game of *Lotto* has attracted more players almost every year since it was started in 1986, but the profits from money games has generally increased since the late 1980s. Norwegians are very willing to spend larger amounts of money on gambling. Dreams of becoming rich quickly are infectious and these dreams are central to Norsk Gambling's advertising. As the company's annual report of 2001 put it: '*Lotto* is conceived of just as pure and innocent fun. The dream of taking home the big pot is what makes the players participate.'

The success of *Lotto* in Norway is often explained by referring to the way *Lotto* is advertised. In the USA for example, lotteries spend little more than one percent of their budgets on marketing. This is certainly not the case for Norsk Gambling. It has a marketing budget of considerable size. Lottery games, like *Lotto*, must be detached from the concept of *gambling*, instead being presented as a fun and exciting diversion for the ordinary person. Norsk Gambling's advertising agency, New Deal, found a way to do this. The *Lotto* advertising has not focused so much on the beneficiaries of the game. Advertising tells little about the outcome for sports and research, at least in the commercials. Norsk Gambling has other channels for such information, such as their website or annual report.

Norsk Gambling worked with New Deal from the early 90's until late 2002. Ivar Vereide was the main creative force behind the advertising strategy that is used in all the *Lotto* film. He has won many prizes for his commercial films, both in Norway and abroad. Colleagues describe him as a person who knows how to make popular stories, which speak to ordinary people. Some of the other Norwegian commercial directors work in other areas as well, making feature films, for instance, but Vereide concentrated solely on advertising till he left New Deal in 2000. He had held central positions as creative leader and director in New Deal, and was also an agency partner, but he went on to work with Dinamo, a company that presents itself as a 'House of Communication' on their website. Dinamo also works in advertising, but Vereide, now a Dinamo partner, participates in a unit called *Story*, a development department geared towards the creation of commercial and cultural programmes, across different media and arenas. In 2003, Dinamo scored a significant success with a TV reality series that looked at elderly people.

Vereide is one of the most prize winning advertising directors in Norway. New Deal presents itself as the country's most prize winning advertising agency. Norsk Gambling, left New Deal in the fall of 2002. By the end of 2003, only one commercial had been produced by the new agency, but the old slogan *Lotto* millionaires are unlike ordinary millionaires was still in use, and the structure of the commercial was quite similar to those produced by New Deal.

The success of these films, with audiences as well as on the competitive arena, has much to do with the quality of the productions, from the writing and direction through to the acting. English actors are frequently used. Those chosen are likely to be unknown to Norwegian audiences, in order to increase each character's credibility as ordinary people having been lucky at the lottery. Very often, some strange milieu or item is presented, such as when two young drivers in a convertible drive off the road (1996). They had annoyed the farmer and his cows, acting as if they had exclusive rights to use the road for themselves. But when the farmer follows after them on his cow-bike, they finally get their comeuppance. Or there is the commercial introducing the female *Lotto* millionaire (1998). She has staged a traditional national romantic scene for herself, in the Norwegian mountains. She is served milk as part of her breakfast in bed, fresh from one of her cows, by a professional butler. She also appears to require other services from him.

In commercials, the milieu presented must be recognized immediately. There is no time for elaborate set-ups. Staging and locations are always perfect in *Lotto* commercials. Editing is strict, as *timing* is important in films with a surprising ending. there has to be complete understanding of how long an audience needs to see a shot to gain all the information they need? The commercial must also ensure the audience's interest is maintained. A good idea, like the *Lotto* millionaires being unlike ordinary millionaires, could be ruined by a lack of 'craft', as stated by advertiser Bente Amundsen, when discussing quality in advertising films. In her opinion, however, the opposite could never be the case. No matter how beautiful, elegant, perfectly edited or well directed a commercial would be, it would still be a bad commercial if it was not successful in conveying its message to an audience.

Every Norwegian adult is a potential *Lotto* player, and the advertisers certainly have a challenge in reaching such a broad, diversified audience. It is known that the average age of the *Lotto* player is 49. There are slightly more males than females among them: 53 versus 47 percent. A way of appealing to such an audience is to monitor their values. Norwegian Montior, a continuing mapping of Norwegians' values produced by MMI, one of the largest market analyzers in the country, find that the values of Norwegians evolve around the axis of modern – traditional on the one hand, and materialist – idealist on the other.

When these two axes are combined, we come up with four different main value groups: modern materialists, traditional materialists, modern idealists and traditional idealists. Norwegian monitor also maps the values that seem to go together, within these four main groups. Modern idealists are likely to be non-autoritarian, tolerant and they appreciate feelings and spontaneity, while the traditional idealist supports religion, and are puritanical and modest. What splits the materialists, then, has to do with the modern ones being hedonists, with less respect for authority. They are urban and egocentric. The traditional materialists favor patriotism, security, conformity and have a more rural orientation.

The traditionalists, whether of the idealist or materialist sort, are old, according to Norwegian Monitor. The modern materialists are younger, and in this capacity an important target group. One can argue that convincing materialists about the joys of becoming a millionaire by winning at the *Lotto* game should be an easy task. But it must be done in such a way that the idealists do not take offence. So the *Lotto* commercials have to balance the message of the joy of money. As we have seen, the commercials' main message is that the million(s) achieved by winning the game makes it possible for personal dreams to come true.

The *Lotto* millionaires never indulge in ordinary, vulgar consumption. Rather, they use the money to express themselves in original and idealistic ways. There is the old lady, traditionally dressed, giving a hard rock performance on the streets (1995), the peace activist entering the military field in his decorated tank (1995), and the fishermen from the Northern parts of Norway (2000). They are presented inside their boat, listening to the weather forecast for their area, which promises storms. But the next shot presents them on deck. The northern fishermen have moved to southern seas. They are still performing their ordinary work, but in a different way, a way more appealing to them as individuals.

Two USA lottery commercials won prizes at the Cannes festival in 1997 on a concept that resembles the Norwegian one. One of them shows a lady sending flowers to herself, the other presents a man in a fishing boat. After taking in several fishes, he gets an old boot. He complains to a diver, who apparently has been delivering him the fishes from underwater. The diver apologizes for his mistake. These millionaires are, like the Norwegian ones, staging some personal dreams by means of *Lotto* game money. They are eccentric, but the idealistic dimension is weaker than in the Norwegian concept. US *Lotto* millionaires do not work, they do not deliver a social statement, and they express their individuality in more limited ways.

In the 1980s *Lotto* was offered to a population that used to have negative attitudes towards gambling. Money should be earned by work. The strategy of presenting *Lotto* as innocent excitement and pure fun has appealed to the Norwegian mass audience. The commercials' main message of making some personal dreams come true by means of *Lotto* millions, has been presented in ways that are acceptable in a culture where egalitarian and idealistic values still have some strength.

Still, *Lotto* playing and *Lotto* commercials exist within the framework of the consumer culture. Several authors have underlined how consumption gains importance in (post)modern societies. Consumption takes place not only to fill some special need but is also crucial for processes like creating meaning and construct identity. The social psychologist Helga Dittmar has even stated that *to have* equals *to be* in consumer culture. Consumer culture must also be conceived of as constructed, and commercials play a part in this respect, by underlining the joy of consumption time and again. At least in Norway, consumer culture seems to be strong and healthy. Norwegian consumption as well as advertising costs have increased steadily throughout the 90s. The later part of the twentieth century was certainly a good time for advertising a game that may turn any ordinary people into millionaires.

The *Lotto* commercials are examples of a film culture of considerable size that is rarely discussed as film culture, although it may be successful measured by its intentions. When the strategy of entertainment and humour is applied for advertising *Lotto*, the films address their viewers as equals. 'Let's have a good time together', they seem to say, wanting to share a funny story and letting it unfold without any comments. The *Ballroom Blitz* taxi driver has found a soul-mate for a customer, and while the (potentially dull) trip to his destination goes on, the *Lotto*-millions give an opportunity of having a good time. 'The having good-time' ethic is even extended to the audiences as they – sharing the musical experience, too – get the point of the story.

Communication like this gives the receiver an opportunity to interpret the story for themselves. The viewers are addressed as people and not as mere objects to be imposed by another party's will. This takes place in spite of the *Lotto* commercials being strategic communication. The films want something from their audience. They are designed to make people play *Lotto*, but the paradox is that they seem to succeed with their task exactly because this task is underplayed. Instead, the *Lotto* commercials concentrate on entertaining their audience and seek to be perceived as ordinary popular culture entertainment.

Researchers, when trying to give a precise definition of the concept of popular culture, understand it in connection with the cultural industry. Popular culture can also be seen to be about making money. TV programs, magazines, films and music, no matter how loud their creators may talk about expressing their personal artistic vision, are designed to make money. As commercials, the *Lotto* films are openly and explicitly about money. They are there on the TV screen to persuade their viewers to spend money on the game of *Lotto*. Still, these films seem to try to deny this fact and present themselves as any other popular culture entertainment. In many ways, the *Lotto* commercials are examples on how the borders between advertising and popular culture in general are blurred.

Kathrine Skretting

REFERENCES

Bordwell, D. (1985) *Narration in the Fiction Film*. Madison: University of Wisconsin Press.

Dittmar, H. (1992) *The Social Psychology of Material Possessions: To Have Is To Be*. Hemel Hempstead: Harvester Wheatsheaf.

Fowles, J. (1996) *Advertising and Popular Culture*. Thousand Oaks, CA: Sage.

MELANCHOLIAN 3 HUONETTA THE 3 ROOMS OF MELANCHOLIA 24

PIRJO HONKASALO, FINLAND/SWEDEN/DENMARK/GERMANY, 2004

What began as a cinematic reflection upon the Eighth Commandment, 'Thou shalt not bear false witness against thy neighbour', was transformed into a study of how images of the enemy are constructed and how they are experienced by children in Russia and Chechnya. In September 2004, when *Melancholian 3 huonetta* (*The 3 Rooms of Melancholia*) premiered at the Venice Film Festival, it was received as testimony of the Russo-Chechnyan war. The Festival took place just a few days after the school hostage crisis and massacre in Beslan, North Ossetia, in Russia, where almost 200 children lost their lives. The event haunted the reception of the film, providing Europeans with a painful reminder of their tacit compliance in the ongoing crisis in that region. After 11 September 2001, Russians – and the rest of the world – redefined the Chechen war as one against terrorism. The borders were closed and all footage became a matter of life and death.

Although the film does not feature any scenes of dramatic action, director Pirjo Honkasalo and her long-time producer, Kristiina Pervilä, risked their lives travelling in the Chechnyan and Ingushetian countryside with cameras. The film footage featured people living in a war zone, and the ethical issues involved were highly complex. Anything could happen to the people that Honkasalo filmed, even children, if somebody were to regard them as traitors. In the middle of the filming process at the Military Academy of Kronstadt in October 2002, the Chechen nationalists stormed the Dubrovka Theatre in Moscow. The hitherto benevolent Russian officials turned increasingly suspicious, and the producer had to fight daily for permission to continue their work. The filming carried on in Ingushetia the following year, but had to be suspended when Honkasalo and her bodyguard were suddenly told that they had twenty-four hours to leave the country.

While Honkasalo did not intend her film to be interpreted as a direct political commentary on the Russo-Chechnyan war – but rather a more general study of the legacies of hatred – history overran her intentions. In Venice, the film was given The Human Rights Film Network Award and The Lina Mangiacapre Award for female directors. Since then, *The 3 Rooms of Melancholia* has been awarded prizes at documentrary film festivals in Copenhagen,

Amsterdam, Tel Aviv, Chicago, North Carolina, Thessaloniki and Zagreb. Although it has been theatrically distributed in Sweden, Denmark, Italy, France, Germany, the UK, the US and the Benelux countries and invited to participate at the Sundance Film Festival, *The 3 Rooms of Melancholia* is in many ways a distinctively anachronistic film: an *auteur* film that deals with war, trauma and hatred by focusing on intimacy, silence and spirituality.

At a time when the power of producers, in line with the Hollywood model, is taking over in European cinema productions, Honkasalo represents the old European *auteur* tradition. The first idea for *The 3 Rooms of Melancholia*, however, came from an American producer who planned a series of European and American documentaries on the Ten Commandments – a documentary version of the Decalogue. The negotiations were, nevertheless, unsuccessful, as Honkasalo stubbornly claimed her right over the final cut.

Born in 1947 and trained in Finland's Film School, naming Andrzej Wajda, Robert Bresson, Federico Fellini and Andrei Tarkovsky as her inspirations, Honkasalo declared herself a staunch believer in the European *auteur* tradition. For her, the words of the disappointed US producer were unforgettable: 'I opened you Heaven's gate and you were too stupid to walk in.' The conflict was yet another expression of the discrepancy between two filmmaking traditions: the notion of films as works of art (European) and the notion of cinema as industry (Hollywood). Within a year, Honkasalo and Pervilä managed to raise new financing from Finland, Sweden, Denmark and other Nordic and European sources. This kind of multinational funding lies behind all of Honkasalo's films from the 1990s, making her profile, together with her choice of subjects, anything but nation-bound.

In Finland, Honkasalo was, for two decades, one of the few women visible in the film community. Contrary to what one might think, her oeuvre as a filmmaker has not been restricted to matters usually regarded as feminine or feminist. In the 1970s, she worked as a camerawoman or a scriptwriter with the Finnish male directors Rauni Mollberg, Mikko Niskanen and Jörn Donner. For Mollberg, she worked as an assistant director in *Maa on syntinen laulu* (*The Earth is a Sinful Song*, 1973). As director, Honkasalo started her career working with Pekka Lehto. By the mid-1980s, they had co-directed two biopics, *Tulipää* (*Flame Top*, 1980) and *Da Capo* (1985), a fictional account featuring Nikita Mihalkov in a leading role; *250 grammaa* (*250 Grammes: A Radioactive Testament*, 1983); and a number of documentaries dealing with issues in Finnish history and politics: *Ikäluokka* (*Their Age*, 1976), *Vaaran merkki* (*The Sign of Danger*, 1978) and *Kainuu 39* (*Two Forces*, 1979). In 1998, Honkasalo directed her most recent fiction film, *Tulennielijä* (*Fire-Eater*), which investigated burdens that earlier generations pass on to their children through a portrayal of two sisters. As such, the film was thematically associated with the *Trilogy of the Sacred and the Evil*, a series of three documentaries: *Mysterion* (1991), *Tanjuska ja 7 perkelettä* (*Tanjuska and the Seven Devils*, 1993) and *Atman* (1996). *Atman* was awarded the prestigious Joris Ivens Award in Amsterdam the year it was released. *Fire-Eater* won the AFI Grand Prix in Los Angeles in 1998.

In Honkasalo's work, the notion of *auteur* is not merely about visions and the power to decide, but also about practices and skills. She is also the scriptwriter, cinematographer and editor of her documentaries. Honkasalo says that she requires very few actual takes when she is behind the camera, which is not simply a question of saving film stock, but also reflects her view of film as way of approaching that which cannot be spoken about. Explaining her working methods, Honkasalo recounts how she spends long periods just standing by the side with her camera, looking through the lens as if in waiting, not always knowing what she is waiting for. She maintains that the task of a film director is to create an atmosphere where a person – whether an actor playing a role or a 'real' person – chooses to show something of their inner self, something that the director perhaps has not understood or been able to request: 'The part of a human being that in my documentaries expresses itself as spirituality is quite remarkable. One cannot expose it when asked, and you cannot ask for it. It goes beyond the director's ability, too,' she says. In her approach, as with many other contemporary filmmakers, the boundary between fiction and documentary is highly porous: 'If we want to show the truth, we need fictitious means, we need poetry – not in its capacity of literary genre but as a way of thinking – in order to be able to strive for the unknown, the existence of which we do not know.'

As a continuation of her *Trilogy of the Sacred and the Evil*, all parts of which focus on spirituality and religious practices, *The 3 Rooms of Melancholia* has the structure of a triptych. This was a common model for altar-pieces from the Middle Ages to the Renaissance and a form that is commonly seen today, for instance, in brochures. The two outer parts fold over the middle one, and in the tradition of painting, the different parts often reflect and comment on each other in an interplay of resemblances and inversions. Here, the three parts of the triptych also represent three different spaces: the isle of Kronstadt near St Petersburg, the centre of Grozny and a refugee area in Ingushetia. The three rooms also have thematic inter-titles that call for interpretations. The first 'room' of the film, Room no. 1, is titled 'Longing', Room no. 2, 'Breathing', and Room no. 3, 'Remembering'. One reading of these might be that in the first room, the Russian boys seem to miss their parents, long for their mothers and, perhaps, yearn to become adults. The middle part, where three small children are separated from their mother, who is too ill and too poor to take care of them, is so painful that the only means of enduring the situation – both for the children and the viewers – seems to be to breathe in and out. The third room depicts a camp for Chechen children refugees who might be looking back to their homeland, trying to keep up and remember its customs and social structures.

In this film, the first and the third rooms are shot in colour and the middle one in black-and-white. In each part, the camera moves sideways repeatedly, panning over a dim landscape with horizontal lines and few deviations: by the Finnish Bay outside St Petersburg it is grey, full of snow and ice; in Grozny barren, black-and-white, raped and naked; in Ingushetia the foggy mountains are covered in pale greenness and the shades of a setting sun. As a contrast to such landscapes, the intimate close-ups of the children's faces echo the long tradition of religious icon painting.

Thematically, the first and third rooms (Kronstadt and Ingushetia) deal with the education and socialisation of children: first, Russian boys participating in basic military training at the Academy and then Chechen boys participating in religious rites in a refugee camp. While the parts of the triptych remain distinct, they are blurred at the narrative level. For example, we meet Aslan, who is probably Russian but wants to be Chechen and Muslim, as well as Sergei, who is Russian but comes from Grozny and is therefore bullied by his fellow cadets who call him Chechen. Some parallels are grizzlier than others. In Kronstadt, we learn that Popov's alcoholic mother was killed falling from a balcony. In Ingushetia we meet Adam, who survived an attack by his mentally ill mother, who tried to push him off a ninth-floor balcony.

The second room – the middle one – depicts Grozny, the ruined capital of Chechnya. This is the stripped heart of the film, registering the loss of mother, the painful parting – but also the signs of remaining solace and intimacy. In this room, a surrogate mother, Xhadizhat Gataeva, is introduced as she searches for abandoned children and those in the ruins in need of immediate care. Despite the fact that the enveloping parts of the triptych depict action – the boys at the Kronstadt Academy subjected to drill and learning, and those in the Ingushetian camp training for orderliness and tradition – the comfort and closeness emerging so palpably in the middle part is mirrored, too, at the level of imagery and sound.

This intimacy is built up through the images of sleeping children, which recur in all three rooms. There is no difference between a dozing Russian or Chechen boy; one cannot identify them by their toes. The tender voices of the mother-substitutes trying to wake a sleeping child, softly, questioning, correspond in a gentle manner to the counter-tenor singing on the sound-track. Both soften and veil the boundaries between reality and dream. The close-ups of feet, the sparse lighting on the hands, ears, faces and feet of the sleepers make them glow as if the light came from within. While Honkasalo maintains in an interview that she is not religious, here, her image-language again evokes the tradition of Christian Orthodox icon painting where feet, ears and hands stand for significant elements.

At one point, in the room of Kronstadt, the cadets participate in an Orthodox service. The camera depicts the faces of the young boys, their attentive eyes wandering from place to place, from religious images to the other participants. The camera seems to follow their gazes, remaining at the eye level of most children, coming to a halt – with the attentive eyes of Popov – on a Russian icon called *Umilenie* – The God's Mother of Tenderness. It is one of four main types of God's Mother icons, most likely a variation of God's Mother of Kazan, sometimes called The Mother of the Russian Damp Earth. It is an icon with especially close ties to Russian history and spirituality. The original icon, painted in the twelfth century, played an important part as the Russians defended themselves against the Tatars in fourteenth-century Moscow. However, the icon itself has its origins in Constantinople – in Asia Minor, that is – in the areas that today belong to Islam.

In this particular icon, the Holy Child, held in his Mother's arms, presses his cheek against hers, thus expressing the intimacy between the two and the sense of belonging. In *The 3 Rooms of Melancholia*, the mothers are absent, or being lost. The boys in Kronstadt who still have a mother write letters telling how they have sewn yet another teddy bear for her at camp: 'like the previous one, but bigger!' The boys in Ingushetia live with Gataeva, who has vowed to act as a surrogate mother to 63 children saved from the ruins of Grozny. In the Grozny part of the film, the young widow Louisa has to give up her three small children. The good-byes are pro-longed and agonising. The home has mouldy walls and lacks furniture except for the mother's bed. Over and over, the small children press their faces against their mother's cheeks, kissing her, and the little boy tries to wipe away her tears – as well as his own – with the sleeves of his sweater. The movement resembles that of the Holy Child in the icon.

The intimacy depicted in the religious icons, and which is characteristic of the cinematic texture of Honkasalo's film, is inverted in the enfolding rooms of the triptych. It is striking how the media images displaying the Moscow theatre siege, in which we see boys both in Kronstadt and in Ingushetia watching television, differ qualitatively from the rhetoric of the film. In them, there is nothing of the 'warmth' of the icons. While Honkasalo's camerawork addresses the viewer by *showing*, media images are explanatory, always already over-determined by causes and effects. Intentionally or not, however, the faces of the dead terrorist women in the television footage are framed by dark scarves similar to that of a God's Mother in the icon.

While the image track evokes Russian Orthodox traditions, the original music, composed by Sanna Salmenkallio, links the film with Catholic music traditions. Having experimented with female voices (too maternal!) and young male voices (too angelic!), Salmenkallio and Honkasalo chose the androgynous voice of a countertenor, the Estonian Risto Joost. Even though Salmenkallio decided to echo the three-part structure of the image track in the manner of a symphony or a sonata, and not include elements of ethnic music in her composition, the singer does represent cultural differences. In the film, he sings poems by a young Russian boy in Kronstadt, performed here both in Russian and in Chechnyan. The voice of the counter-tenor connects the film with the Western music of passion plays and, explicitly, the role of the Evangelist. Honkasalo's first idea was to make the film music function like the role of Archangel Gabriel who is said to have both dictated the Koran and appeared before Virgin Mary, thus linking the traditions of Christianity and Islam. The voice, then, is The One Who Sees, who follows the characters and intervenes at times.

In the vein of Tarkovskyan aesthetics, Honkasalo – in *The 3 Rooms of Melancholia*, but also in her *Trilogy of the Sacred and the Evil* – underlines what is not in the frame, what cannot be spoken about, be it called the soul, a spirituality or truth. In *The 3 Rooms of Melancholia*, references to Tarkovsky's films are indeed many: the theme of lost childhood echoes *Ivan's Childhood* (1962); the juxtaposition of colour and black-and-white film stock evokes *Andrei Rublev* (1966); and the film title focusing on Melancholia obviously suggests Tarkovsky's late study of homesickness – *Nostalghia* (1983). Whereas Tarkovsky's *Nostalghia* depicted on old man's longing for home, the young Russian and Chechen boys in Honkasalo's film are mel-ancholics who have lost their objects of love (mothers, fathers, siblings, relatives) and who embrace these losses in 'tenacious self-absorption', to quote Walter Benjamin's characterisation of melancholia. Having survived parental suicides, abandonment, war, street life and sexual abuse, the young boys seem alarmingly calm. According to psychoanalytical accounts, mel-ancholia results in a lessening of one's life force, as the ego denies the loss by attaching itself to the lost love object and thus remains incapable of attaching itself to new love objects. Another symptom of melancholia, according to Freud, writing in the aftermath of the First World War and the immensity of grief, is an internalisation of aggression: hatred towards others is directed at oneself, resulting in violence and self-harm.

The question of the psychological effects of war is one framework evoked by the notion of melancholia, and the theme of adolescence is undeniably recurrent in Honkasalo's films, yet the film refuses to be reduced to that. Melancholia can also be understood as a mode of viewing – a space that audiences enter, perhaps reflecting the director's gaze, but most certainly that of the *fin-de-siècle* Western viewer, who is paralysed by their own inability to act. In this respect, *The 3 Rooms of Melancholia* suggests films by Luc and Jean-Pierre Dardennes, *La Promesse* (1996) and *Rosetta* (1999), which in the reading of the cultural theorist Lauren Berlant pose a troubling question concerning the notion of the 'good life' as social belonging: for whom is this dream available and under what conditions?

At a time when public mourning is loud and visible, *The 3 Rooms of Melancholia* approaches its emotionally upsetting and shocking subject by looking for silence (waiting, observing, dozing off, waking and sleeping) instead of action. Silence, in this case, also means reservedness in affective rhetoric. Salmenkallio's original music does not express the assumed emotional content of the images, but instead works independently. By not imitating Russian or Chechnyan folk music but instead working within the register of Western classical music, it situates the viewer at a distance from the photographed world – even when we watch intimate close-ups. In Honkasalo's words, 'For me, it is about the art of showing the silence in an individual, signalling about the ineffable.' By showing the silence in the Russian and Chechen boys, the film restores to them what the news coverage of war victims tends to obliterate: the spirituality or soulfulness beyond action. The toes that cannot be categorised, the dreams that remain riddles, dreams and hopes about the future.

The 3 Rooms of Melancholia ends with close-ups of silent Chechen boys, absorbed in their thoughts, preceded by a scene in which we follow Milana, now 19, reliving the trauma she carries after having been raped at the age of twelve by Russian soldiers and having gone through abortion when she was seven months pregnant. Speaking for many of the children staying at Gataeva's home, Milana sits in prayer, also drawing our attention to the gender specificity of war traumas. While the young boys, in cross-cut scenes, participate in an all-male religious rite moving rhythmically in a circle, Milana serenely addresses 'Dear Allah, Almighty God. Keep us away from evil, save me from shame, save Xhadizhat from shame also.' The men – deprived of everything – still act as a group; the woman faces her desperation alone, in a silent prayer.

While, for many audiences, the film reads as a political statement given current events in Chechnya, for Honkasalo it is also a project that illustrates the proximity of politics and poetics in documentary filmmaking. Above all, however, it is a project driven by guilt and shame, a shame different from that experienced by victims of war. She has acknowledged how she grew up in Finland with full knowledge of Soviet prison camps and the state's ongoing harassment of dissidents. She accepted all this – along with most of her leftist generation – as an internal Soviet matter. With this film, silence is made impossible. At the same time, in this film, silence is all that matters.

Anu Koivunen and Tytti Soila

REFERENCE

Honkasalo, P. (2002) 'Auteuren, jagets bärare', in G. Gunéer and R. Hamberg, *Auteuren, återkommst eller farväl*. Göteborg: Filmkonst nr 77.

FILMOGRAPHY

KONG HAAKON VII ANKOMMER CHRISTIANIA THE ARRIVAL OF KING HAAKON VII IN CHRISTIANIA 1905
Director: Hugo Hermansen
Photography: Charles Magnusson
Cast: King Haakon, Crown Prince Olav, Prime Minister Michelsen
Running time: c.120 seconds

SYLVI 1911–13
Director: Teuvo Puro
Producer: Frans Engström, Teuvo Puro and Teppo Raikas
Screenplay: Teuvo Puro, based on Minna Canth's play.
Photography: Frans Engström
Editing: Frans Engström
Art Direction: Carl Fager
Cast: Aili Rosvall (Sylvi), Teuvo Puro (Aksel Vahl), Teppo Raikas (Viktor Hoving), Olga Salo (Alma Hoving), Ester Forsman (Karin Löfberg), Olga Leino (Elin Grönkvist), Eero Kilpi (Harlin), Jussi Snellman (Idestam), Paavo Jännes (judge)
Running time: c.48 minutes

DUNUNGEN DOWNIE 1919
Director: Ivar Hedqvist
Screenplay: Selma Lagerlöf
Photography: J. Julius aka Julius Janzon
Cast: Ivar Hedqvist, Reneé Björling, Jenny Tschernichin-laarsson, Ernst Öberg, Mia Gründer, Ragnar Widestedt, Carl Brovallius, Anna Whabom, Bell hedqvist, Carl-Gunnar Wingård, Bror Öbergson, Bertil Wallroth, Mia Backman
Running time: 131 minutes

KUN ISÄLLÄ ON HAMMASSÄRKY WHEN FATHER HAS TOOTHACHE 1923
Director: Erkki Karu
Screenplay: Artturi Järviluoma
Photography: Kurt Jäger
Editing: Erkki Karu
Cast: Armas Fredman, Eino Jurkka, Emmi Jurkka, Naimi Kari, Aku Käyhkö, Toivo Louko, Martti Tuukka
Art Direction: Karl Fager
Running time: 24 minutes

MED FULD MUSIKK WITH PIPES AND DRUMS 1933
Director: Lau Lauritzen, Sr.
Screenplay: Lau Lauritzen, Sr., Lau Lauritzen, Jr., Alice O'Fredericks
Photography: Carlo Bentsen
Sound: Poul Bang, Erik Rasmussen
Music: Victor Cornelius, (lyrics Carl Viggo Meincke, Conductor: Kaj Julian)

Cast: Carl Schenstrøm, Hans W. Petersen, Aase Clausen, Erling Schroeder, Olga Svensen, Christian Arhoff, Christian Schrøder, Victor Cornelius, Gerd Gjedved, Finn Olsen, Eigil Reimers, Jørgen Lund.
Running time: 95 minutes

EN KVINNAS ANSIKTE A WOMAN'S FACE 1938
Director: Gustaf Molander
Screenplay: Gösta Stevens, Stina Bergman, Ragnhild Prim
Photography: Åke Dahlqvist
Editing: Oscar Rosander
Sound: Lennart Unnerstad
Music: Eric Bengtson
Cast: Ingrid bergman, Tore Svennberg, Anders Henrikson, Georg Rydeberg, Gunnar Sjöberg, Hilda Borgström, Karin Kavli, Erik Bullen Berglund, Sigurd Wallén, Gösta Cederlund, Magnus Kesster, Göran Berrnhard
Running time: 104 minutes

TVÅ MÄNNISKOR TWO PEOPLE 1945
Director: Carl Theodor Dreyer
Screenplay: Carl Theodor Dreyer
Photography: Gunanr Fischer
Editing: Carl Th Dreyer, Edvin Hammarberg
Sound: Lennart Svensson
Music: Lars-Erik larsson, Geni Sadero. Ludwig van Beethoven
Cast: Georg Rydeberg, Wanda Rothgardt, Gabriel Alw, Stig Olin
Running time: 74 minutes

8 KAMPEN OM TUNGTVANNET LA BATAILLE DE L'EAU LOURDE OPERATION SWALLOW 1948
Director: Titus Wibe-Müller
Screenplay: Jean Martin
Photography: Hilding Bladh, Marcel Weiss
Editing: Jean Feyte
Music: Gunnar Sønstevold
Cast: Jens A. Poulsson, Johannes Eckhoff, Arne Kjelstrup, Claus Helberg, Henki Kolstad, Claus Wiese, Knut Haukelid, Andreas Aabel, Fredrik Kayser, Hans Storhaug, Odd Rodhe
Running time: 98 minutes (French release version, 80 minutes)

TVÅLEN BRIS BRIS THE SOAP 1951
Director: Ingmar Bergman
Screenplay: Ingmar Bergman
Photography: Gunnar Fischer
Editing: Ingmar Bergman
Cast: John Botvid, Erna Groth
Running time: 1 minute 10 seconds

ELDFÅGELN THE FIRE-BIRD 1952
Director: Hasse Ekman
Screenplay: Hasse Ekman
Photography: Göran Strindberg
Editing: Lennart Wallén
Sound: Olle Jacobsson

Music: Stig Rybrant. Maurice Jaubert, Igor Stravinsky, Margiúrite Monnot, Paolo Tosti, Petr Chaikowsky, Nino Valente, Gioacchino Rossini, Guy Lefarge, Phillipe Bloch
Cast: Tito Gobbi, Ellen Rasch, Eva Henning, Georg Rydeberg, Åke Falck, Märta Arbin, Alana Blair, Margherita Nicosia, Märta Dorff, Gull Natorp, Björn Holmgren, Gun Skoogberg, Maurice Béjart, Leon Björker, Sven-Erik Jacobsen
Running time: 99 min

NISKAVUOREN HETA HETA NISKAVUORI 1952
Director: Edvin Laine
Production: Oy Suomen Filmiteollisuus/T. J. Särkkä
Screenplay: Hella Wuolijoki and Paula Talaskivi, Photography: Pentti Unho
Editing: Armas Vallasvuo
Music: Heikki Aaltoila
Art direction: Karl Fager
Cast: Rauni Luoma, Kaarlo Halttunen, Mirjam Novero (Hilja Elsa Maanoja, Siiprikko, the Broken-Winged), Leo Lähteenmäki (Santeri Lammentausta), Martti Katajisto (Jaakko), Hillevi Lagerstam (Aliina), Marjatta Kallio (Kerttu)
Running time: 95 minutes

DET STORA ÄVENTYRET THE GREAT ADVENTURE 1953
Director: Arne Sucksdorff
Screenplay: Arne Sucksdorff
Photography: Arne Sucksdorff
Editing: Arne Sucksdorff
Sound: Nils Gustaf Örn
Production management: Nils Gustaf Örn
Music: Lars-Erik Larsson
Cast: Anders Nohrborg, Kjell Sucksdorff, Sigvard Kihlgren, Holger Stockman, Arne Sucksdorff

TUNTEMATON SOTILAS THE UNKNOWN SOLDIER 1955
Director: Edvin Laine
Screenplay: Väinö Linna, Juha Nevalainen
Photography: Osmo Harkimo, Kalle Peronkoski, Antero Ruuhonon, Olavi Tuomi, Pentti Unho
Editing: Osmo Harkimo, Armas Vallasvuo
Sound: Taisto Lindegren, Kaarlo Nissilä, Yrjö Saari, Kurt Vilja
Music: Ahti Sonninen, Jean Sibelius
Cast: Kosti Klemelä, Heikki Savolainen, Reino Tolvanen, Veikko Sinisalo, Åke Lndman, Pentti Siimes, Leo Riuttu, Kaarlo Halttunen, Matti Ranin, Jussi Jurkka, Tauno Palo, Pentti Irjala, Vilho Siivola, Martti Romppanen, Tapio Hämäläinen, Olavi Ahonen, Tarmo Manni, Veli-Matti Kaitala, Kale Teuronen, Vili Auvinen, Saulo Haarla
Art Direction: Aarre Koivisto
Running time: 181 minutes (Finnish release version, 170 minutes)

EVA - DEN UTSTÖTTA DIARY OF HALF-VIRGIN SWEDISH AND UNDERAGE 1969
Director: Torgny Wickman
Screenplay: Torgny Wickman
Photography: Max Wllén
Editing: Jerry Gränsman
Sound: Gösta Björck
Music: Mats Olsson, Bengt Arne Wallin
Cast: Solveig Andersson, Barbro Hiort af Ornäs, Einar Axelsson, Jan-Erik Lindqvist, Segol Mann, Göthe Gerfbo, Maud Hyttenberg, Börje Nyberg, Caroline Christensen, Siw Mattson, Arne Ragneborn, Dennis Dahlsten, Inger

Sundh, Karin Miller, Chris Wahlström, Leif Liljeroth, Conny Ling
Running time: 95 min.

MAZURKA PÅ SENGEKANTEN BEDROOM MAZURKA BEDSIDE MAZURKA 1970
Director: John Hilbard
Screenplay: Bob Ramsing, Soya
Photography: Eirik Wittrup Willumsen
Sound: Henrik B. Bøving Hansen, Preben Mortensen
Music: Ole Høyer
Cast: Ole Søltoft, Axel Strøbye, Annie Birgit Garde, Paul Hagen, Karl Stegger, Birte Tove, Anne Grete Nissen, Christoffer Bro, Joen Bille, Carsten brandt, freddie Andersen
Art Direction: Lars Kolvig
Running time: 92 minutes

ELVIS! ELVIS! 1977
Director: Kay Pollack
Screenplay: Maria Gripe, Kay Pollack
Photography: Mikael Salomon
Editing: Lasse Lundberg
Sound: Ulf Reinhard
Music: Ralph Lundsten
Cast: Lele Dorazio, Lena-Pia Bernhardsson, Fred Gunnarsson, Elisaveta, Allan Edwall, Kent Andersson, Victoria Grant, Kim Anderzon, Kjerstin Dellert, Svea Holst Ingrid Boström, Lars Edström, Marian Gräns, Ove Kant, Anna-Lena Ebenståhl,Gunnar Fredriksson, Ted Åström Camilla Lundberg
Running time: 100 minutes

EBBA THE MOVIE 1982
Director: Johan Donner
Producer: Lisbet Gabrielsson
Screenplay: Johan Donner
Cinematography: Per Källberg
Editing: Antonia Carnerud, Thomas Holewa and Johan Donner
Sound: Jan Pehrsson
Music: Ebba Grön, Dag Vag and Blå Tåget
Running time: 52 minutes

KAN VI BRY OSS OM VARANDRA? CAN WE BOTHER ABOUT EACH OTHER? 1988
Director: Roy Andersson
Script: Roy Andersson
Photography: Istvan Borbas
Editing: Roy Andersson
Sound: Stig-Åke Nilsson
Music: Lars Demian
Art Director: Roy Andersson
Cast: Lucio Vucina among others
Running time: 70 seconds

IDIOTERNE THE IDIOTS 1998
Director: Lars von Trier

Screenplay: Lars von Trier
Photography: Casper Holm, Jesper Jargil, Kristoffer Nyholm, Lars von Trier
Editing: Molly Marlene Stensgård
Sound: Per Streit, Johan Winblandh
Cast: Bodil Jörgensen, Jens Albinus, Anne Louise Hassing, Troels Lyby, Nikolaj Lie Kaas Louise Mieritz, Henrik Prip, Luis Mesonero, Knud Romer Jörgensen Trine Michelsen Anne-Grethe Bjarup Riis
Running time: 117 minutes

JUHA 1999
Director: Aki Kaurismäki
Screenplay: Juhani Aho, Aki Kaurismäki
Photography: Timo Salminen
Editing: Aki Kaurismäki
Sound: Tom Forsström, Jouko Lumme
Music: Anssi Tikanmäki
Cast: Sakari Kuosmanen, Kati Outinen, André Vilms, Markku Peltola, Elina Salo, Esko Nikkari, Jaakko Talaskivi
Art Direction: Markku Pätilä, Jukka Salmi
Running time: 78 minutes

THE WAKE 2000
Idea/Concept/Direction: Michael Kvium and Christian Lemmerz
Producer: Dino Raymond Hansen
Director of Cinematography and On-line Editor: Lars Beyer
Editor: Anja Farsig
Supervising Editor: Jacob Thuesen
Composer and Conductor: Dror Feiler
Composer and DJ: DJ Wunderbaum/Anders-Peter Andreasen and August Engkilde
Cast: Claus Christensen, Niels Olaf Gudme, Sarah Boberg, Elina Løwensohn, Rikke Louise Andersson, Hildigunn Eydfinsdottir, Thomas Bo Larsen, Sonny Tronborg, John Frey, Philippe Richard, Merete Nørgaard
Running time: 462 minutes

HEFTIG OG BEGEISTRET COOL AND CRAZY 2001
Director: Knut Erik Jensen
Screenplay: Knut Erik Jensen
Photography: Aslaug Holm, Svein Krøvel
Editing: Aslaug Holm
Sound: Sturla Einarson, Arne Hansen, Alf Christian Hvidsteen
Cast: Odd Marino Frantzen, Einar F. L. Strand, Arne Wensel, Kare Wensel, Arne Blomsø, Leif Roger Ananiassen, Eirik Daldroff, Odd-Arne Olsen, Eirik Nilsen, Nils Gronberg, Reidar Strand, Ragnar Rotnes, Randulf Antonsen, Ole Jenny Larsen, Einar Kristian Straumsne, Alf Hakon Pedersen, Harald Wensel, Kolbjørn Svendsen, Karl Ananiassen, Bjarne Mathisen, Tommy Bergsen, Oddvar Hansen, Einar Saetervoll, Therje Hakon Blickfeldt, Arne Nygard, Ken Hugo Jensen, Trygg Lund, Kai Olav Jacobsen, Hilmar Wensel, Brynjar Langas
Running time: 104 minutes

TAXI 2001
Director: Ivar Vereide
Music: "Sweet"
Running time: 60 seconds

MELANCHOLIAN 3 HUONETTA THE 3 ROOMS OF MELANCHOLIA 2004

Director: Pirjo Honkasalo
Screenplay: Pirjo Honkasalo
Photography: Pirjo Honkasalo
Editing: Niels Pagh Andersen and Pirjo Honkasalo
Sound: Mart Otsa Martti Turunen
Music: Sanna Salmenkallio
Cast: Russian, Chechnyan people
Art Direction: Pirjo Honkasalo Kristiina Pervilä
Running time: 106 minutes

BIBLIOGRAPHY

GENERAL WORKS

Birkvad, S. and J. A. Diesen (1994) *Autentiske inntrykk. Møte med ni skandinaviske dokumentarfilmskaparar*. Oslo: Det norske samlaget.

Cowie, P. (1997) *Cinema in Scandinavia*. Hanoi: Vietnam Film Insititute.

Fullerton, J. and J. Olsson (eds) *Nordic Explorations: Film Before 1930*. Sydney. John Libbey & Aura.

Nestingen, A. and T. G. Elkington (eds) *National Cinemas in Global North: Nordic Cinema at the Milennium*. Detroit: Wayne State University Press.

Soila, T., A. Söderbergh Widding and G. Iversen (1998) *Nordic National Cinemas*. London and New York: Routledge.

Weibull, J. and P. J. Nordhagen (eds) *Natur och nationalitet*. Höganäs: Förlags AB Wiken.

Waldekranz, R. (1986) *Filmens Historia, Parts 1–3*. Stockholm: Norstedts.

DENMARK

Björkman, C. (1945) 'Masterpiece or Pompous Trash', *Veckojournalen*, 24.

Björkman, S. (1996) 'Naked Miracles', *Sight and Sound*, 6, 10, 14.

Bondebjerg, I. (1996) *Film Comedy, Modernization, and Gender Roles*. Copenhagen: Sekvens.

Bordwell, D. (1981) *The Films of Carl-Theodor Dreyer*. Berkeley: University of California Press.

Brøgger, C. (1979) *30'ernes danske spillefilm*. Copenhagen: Det Danske Filmmuseum.

Brusendorff, O. and P. Henningsen (1957) *Erotik for millioner: kaerligheden i filmen*. Copenhagen: Thaning & Appel.

Dinnesen, N. J. and E. Kau (1983) *Filmen i Danmark*. Copenhagen: Akademisk Forlag.

Engberg, H. (1939) *Filmen*. Copenhagen: Gyldendal.

Engberg, M. (1980) *Fyrtårnet og Bivognen*. Copenhagen: Gyldendal.

Floyd, N. (1996) '*Sea breeze*. For actors, working with Lars von Trier is far from a chore.' *Time Out*, 9–16, October, 28–9.

Hjort, M. and I. Bondebjerg (2001) *The Danish Directors: Dialogues on a Contemporary National Cinema*. Bristol: Intellect.

Kau, E. (1989) *Dreyers Filmkunst*. Copenhagen: Akademisk Forlag.

Kelly, R. (2000) *The Name of This Book is Dogme95*. London: Faber and Faber.

Lange-Fucks, H. (1979) *Pat und Patachon, Dokumentation*. Ammersee: Programm Roloff and Seesslen.

Matthews, P. (1999) 'Review of *Festen*', *Sight and Sound*, 9, 3, 39–40.

Neergaard, E. (1960) *Historien om Dansk Film*. Copenhagen: Gyldendal.

Oppenheimer, J. and D. E. Williams (1996) 'Von Trier and Müller's Ascetic Aesthetic on *Breaking the Waves*', *American Cinematographer*, 77, 12, 18–22.

Piil, M. (1998) *Gyldendals Filmguide – Danske Film fra A til Z*. Copenhagen: Nordisk Forlag.

Roman, S. (2000) '*I Confess*', RES: *The Future of Filmmaking*, 3, 3, 46–52.

Skoller, D. (ed.) *Dreyer in Double Reflection: Translation of Carl Th.Dreyer's Writings About the Film*. New York: E. P. Dutton.

Ulrichsen, E. (ed.) (1963) *Dreyer, C. Th Om filmen*. Copenhagen: Gyldendal.

FINLAND

Anon. (1945) 'Suomen elokuvatuotannon ensiaskeleet. Teuvo Puro raottaa muistinsa esirippua', *Elokuvateatteri*, 9.

Cowie, P. (1990) *Finnish Cinema*. Helsinki: VAPK & SEA.

Hirn, S. (1991) *Kuvat elävät. Elokuvatoimintaa Suomessa 1908–1918*. Helsinki: VAPK-Kustannus.

Hällström, R. af (1936) *Filmi – aikamme kuva. Filmin historiaa, olemusta ja tehtäviä.* Jyväskylä and Helsinki: Gummerus.

Haarla, L (1923–24) 'Näyttelijäkunta ja Kansallisteatteri', *Näyttämö*, 16.

Hietala, V., A. Honka-Hallila, H. Kangasniemi, M. Lahti, K. Laine and J. Sihvonen (1992) 'Uuno Turhapuro – The Lying Finn', in R. Dyer and G. Vincendeau (eds) *Popular European Cinema*. London: Routledge.

Honkasalo, P. (2002) 'Auteuren, jagets bärare', in G. Gunéer and R. Hamberg (eds) *Auteuren, återkommst eller farväl*, Göteborg: Filmkonst nr 77.

Jäderin, A. (1891) *Brottsjöar. Verklighetsteckning*, Stockholm: Svanbäck.

Koivunen, A. (1995) *Isänmaan moninaiset äidinkasvot. Sotavuosien suomalainen naisten elokuva sukupuoliteknologiana.* Turku: SETS.

____ (2003) *Performative Histories, Foundational Framings.Gender and Sexuality in Niskavuori Films.* Helsinki: SKS.

Koivunen, A. and K. Laine (1993) 'Metsästä pellon kautta kaupunkiin (ja takaisin) – jätkyys suomalaisessa elokuvassa', in P. Ahokas, M. Lahti and J. Sihvonen (eds) *Mie-heyden tiellä*. Jyväskylä: Nykykulttuurin tutkimusyksikkö, Jyväskylän yliopisto, 136–54.

Koski, P. (1996) 'Hella Wuolijoki, 1886–1954. Hulda Juurakko, Finland', in K. E. Kelly (ed.) *Modern Drama by Women 1880s–1930s: An International Anthology.* London: Routledge, 214–17.

____ (2000) *Kaikessa mukana. Hella Wuolijoki ja hänen näytelmänsä.* Helsinki: Otava.

Laine, E. (1983) *Tuntematon sotilas ja pylvässänky. Elämäni esirippuja ja valkokankaita.* Helsinki: Tammi.

Laine, K. (1994) *Murheenkryyneistä miehiä. Suomalainen sotilasfarssi 1930-luvulta 1950-luvulle.* Turku: SETS.

____ (1999) 'Pääosassa Suomen kansa', in *Suomi-filmi ja Suomen Filmiteollisuus kansallisen elokuvan rakentajina 1933–1939.* Helsinki: SKS.

Lindman, Å. (1992) *Åke ja hänen maailmansa.* Helsinki: Tammi.

Pöysti, L. (1992) *Lainatakki.* Helsinki: Otava.

Peltonen, M. (ed.) (1996) *Rillumarei ja valistus. Kulttuurikahakoita 1950-luvun Suomessa.* Helsinki: Finnish Historical Society.

Puro, T. (1942) 'Muistelmia kotimaisen elokuvan alkutaipaleelta', *Uusi Suomi*, Sunnuntailiite, 24 May.

Salmi, H. (2002) *Kadonnut perintö. Näytelmäelokuvan synty Suomessa 1907–1916.* Helsinki: Suomen elokuva-arkisto, SKS.

Suomen kansallisfilmografia (1996) K. Uusitalo, S. Toiviainen, J. Junttila, R. Kautto, M. Kejonen, L. Tykyläinen, K. Vase, M. Marttila. Helsinki: Edita and SEA.

Uusitalo, K. (1972) *Eläviksi syntyneet kuvat. Suomalaisen elokuvan mykät vuodet 1896–1930.* Helsinki: Otava.

____ (1975) *T. J. Särkkä. Legenda jo eläessään.* Helsinki: WSOY.

Varpio, Y. (1979) *Pentinkulma ja maailma. Tutkimus Väinö Linnan teosten kääntämisestä, julkaisemisesta ja vastaanotosta ulkomailla.* Helsinki: WSOY.

NORWAY

Brinch, S. and G. Iversen (2001) *Virkelighetsbilder. Norsk dokumentarfilm gjennom hundre år.* Oslo: Universitetsforlaget.

Dahl, H. F., J. Gripsrud, G. Iversen, K. Skretting, B. Sørenssen (1996) *Kinoens mørke, fjernsynets lys; Levende bilder I Norge gjennom hundre år.* Oslo: Gyldendal.

Evensmo, S. (1955) *Trollspeilet – Streiftokt i film.* Oslo: Gyldendal.

____ (1967) *Det Store Tivoli.* Oslo: Gyldendal.

Film og Kino Årbok 1949 (1949) Oslo: Kommunale Kinematografers Landsforbund.

Iversen, G. and T. O. Svendsen (1995) *Okkupasjonsdramaene – fem år slik vi har sett dem på film*, Oslo: Norsk Filminstitutt.

Nordhagen, P. J. (1995) 'From National icons to tourist photography – Grand themes in the depiction of Norwegian scenery', in R. Erlandsen and V. S. Halvorsen (eds) *Darkness and Light.* Oslo: National Institute for Historical Photography/Norwegian Society for the History of Photography.

Skretting, K. (1999) 'Kvalitet i reklame', *Norsk medietidsskrift*, 1.

Solberg, N. P. (2002) *Norske filmdivaer i Hollywood.* Oslo: Samlaget.

SWEDEN

Bjökman, S., T. Manns and J. Sima (1986 [1970]) *Bergman on Bergman: Interviews with Ingmar Bergman*. New York: Simon & Schuster (Touchstone Edition).

Donner, J. (1962) *The Films of Ingmar Bergman: From Torment To All These Women*. New York: Dover Publications.

Dymling, C. A. (1950) *Krönikor 1949-1950*. Stockholm: Zetterlund & Thelanders Boktryckeri AB.

Ekman, H. (1955) *Den vackra Ankungen*. Stockholm: Wahlström & Widstrand.

Florin, B. (1997) *Den nationella stilen, Studier i den svenska filmens guldålder*. Stockholm: Aura förlag.

Forslund, B. (2003) *Molander, Molander, Molander, En släktkrönika med tonvikt på Gustaf och Olof*. Stockholm: Carlsson Förlag.

Furhammar, L. (1991) *Filmen i Sverige*. Höganäs: Förlags AB Wiken.

Frykman, J and O. Löfgren (1979) *Den kultiverade människan*. Lund: Gleerups.

Gado, F. (1986) *The Passion of Ingmar Bergman*. Durham: Duke University Press.

Gunér, G and R. Hemberg (2002) *Auteuren: Återkomst eller farväl*. Göteborg: Filmkonst.

Habel, Y. (2003) *Modern media, Modern Audiences*. Stockholm: Aura Förlag.

Höök, M. (1962) *Ingmar Bergman*. Stockholm: Wahlström & Widstrand.

Jerselius, K. (1987) *Hotade reservat, spelfilmerna med Edward Persson*. Uppsala: Filmhäftets förlag.

Koskinen, M. (1988) 'Tvålopera à la Bergman', *Chaplin*, 30, 2–3.

Lange-Fuchs, H. (1979) *Der Frühe Ingmar Bergman*. Lübeck: Amt für Kultur.

Quist, P. O. (1986) *Jorden är vår arvedel*. Uppsala: Filmhäftets Förlag.

_____ (1995) *Folkhemmets bilder; Modernisering, motstånd och mentalitet i den svenska 30-talsfilmen*. Lund: Arkiv Förlag.

Soila T. (1991) *Kvinnors ansikte, stereotyper och kvinnlig identitet i trettiotalets svenska filmmelodram*, Stockholm: Institutionen för teater och filmvetenskap, Stockholms universitet.

Svensk filmografi, Parts 1–10 (1986) L. Åhlander (ed.). Uppsala: Almqvist & Wiksell.

INDEX